"What a winsomely fresh book! There is the freshness of John Goldingay's translation of the text and the way he lets the Old Testament speak for itself by getting us to actually read so much of it for ourselves (fancy that for a fresh idea!). And then there is that vintage Goldingay style—straightforward and simple yet often quizzical and unexpected, humorous at times yet serious in intent, making us think afresh (whether or not we agree). We are invited into the world of Old Testament Israel as curious guests from the twenty-first century and end up asking more challenging questions about our own cultural and ethical assumptions than about theirs (which is the way it should be with the Bible). We see familiar old stories and characters in ways that perhaps we never thought of before and read unfamiliar texts that perhaps we never even noticed (or wincingly avoided). This book is what it says—a guided tour, designed to stimulate a desire to go back and enjoy exploring the terrain more fully."

Christopher J. H. Wright, Langham Partnership, author of *Old Testament Ethics for the People of God*

"There are many books on Old Testament ethics that are thoughtful and reflective. This book is such, but it is also very practical and one that recognizes the complexities of daily life, relationships, and challenges in our less-than-ideal world. Goldingay's disarming style and unconventional categories help to juggle the mind into fresh insights and perspectives. This book does not just talk about ethics in the Old Testament, but it actually helps readers discover what the Old Testament says through an encounter with the biblical text."

Athena E. Gorospe, biblical studies faculty, Asian Theological Seminary, Manila, Philippines

"Like a great tour guide, Goldingay skillfully leads his readers through the ethically problematic pages of the Old Testament, covering the usual topics (compassion, justice, nations) as well as the less typical yet perhaps more timely topics (contentment, animals, migrants). This book is infused not only with massive quantities of Goldingay's fresh translation of Scripture but also with his brilliant (and sometimes quirky) textual and theological insights. Readers are sure to find the book illuminating, challenging, and inspiring."

David T. Lamb, Allan A. MacRae Professor of Old Testament at Missio Seminary, author of *God Behaving Badly*

"Textually comprehensive, wonderfully conversational, immensely practical, and sensibly direct—all the qualities we expect from Goldingay are on display in *Old Testament Ethics: A Guided Tour*. The Old Testament matters for life, and Goldingay engages the breadth of that canonical resource to encourage readers to embody God's will today. Each chapter ends with questions for continued reflection and conversation. An immensely helpful guide in a time when many disparage the ethical value of the Old Testament."

M. Daniel Carroll R. (Rodas), Blanchard Professor of Old Testament, Wheaton College

"Goldingay opens a window to the Old Testament that has the potential to shape not only ethics but our understanding of the ancient Hebrews' culture and experience of God. Like a good rabbi, at times Goldingay seems to raise more questions than he answers, which makes the book both challenging and stimulating. *Old Testament Ethics: A Guided Tour* offers a new lens through which to encounter the Old Testament."

Shannon Lamb, assistant regional director, InterVarsity Christian Fellowship USA

OLD TESTAMENT ETHICS

A Guided Tour

JOHN GOLDINGAY

IVP Academic

An imprint of InterVarsity Press
Downers Grove, Illinois

InterVarsity Press
P.O. Box 1400, Downers Grove, IL 60515-1426
ivpress.com
email@ivpress.com

©2019 by John E. Goldingay

All rights reserved. No part of this book may be reproduced in any form without written permission from
InterVarsity Press.

InterVarsity Press® is the book-publishing division of InterVarsity Christian Fellowship/USA®, a
movement of students and faculty active on campus at hundreds of universities, colleges, and schools
of nursing in the United States of America, and a member movement of the International Fellowship
of Evangelical Students. For information about local and regional activities, visit intervarsity.org.

All Scripture quotations, unless otherwise indicated, are the author's translation.

A full translation of the Old Testament is available in John Goldingay, The First Testament (Downers Grove, IL:
InterVarsity Press, 2018).

Much of chapter 11, "Violence," first appeared in John Goldingay, "Another Day, Another Shooting: The Bible
and Terrorist Violence," Saint Barnabas Episcopal Church, Pasadena, May 2014, http://stbarnabaspasadena.org
/wp-content/uploads/2014/05/Another-Shooting.docx.
Much of chapter 27, "Cities," first appeared in John Goldingay, "The Bible in the City," Theology 92 (1989): 5-15.
Much of chapter 37, "Abraham," first appeared in John Goldingay, "The Bible in the City," Theology 92 (1989): 5-15.

Cover design and image composite: David Fassett
Interior design: Daniel van Loon
Images: crumpled paper texture: © narloch-liberra / iStock / Getty Images Plus

ISBN 978-0-8308-5224-6 (print)
ISBN 978-0-8308-7362-3 (digital)

Printed in the United States of America ∞

InterVarsity Press is committed to ecological stewardship and to the conservation of natural resources
in all our operations. This book was printed using sustainably sourced paper.

Library of Congress Cataloging-in-Publication Data
A catalog record for this book is available from the Library of Congress.

P   25   24   23   22   21   20   19   18   17   16   15   14   13   12   11   10   9   8   7   6   5   4   3   2   1

Y   37   36   35   34   33   32   31   30   29   28   27   26   25   24   23   22   21   20   19

CONTENTS

PREFACE
AND ACKNOWLEDGMENTS

This book is a spin-off from a series of short commentaries called "The Old Testament for Everyone" published by SPCK and Westminster John Knox. When I was coming to the end of writing these commentaries, Philip Law (whose brainchild they had been) suggested the possibility of one or two companion volumes covering topics within the Old Testament. Ethics is a hot topic; hence this book. Like those commentaries, it comprises a collection of short chapters and incorporates my translation of part of the biblical text. Each chapter is self-contained and you can read the chapters in any order; there's not much logic about the order, and there's no cumulative argument. Often the comment part starts from some experience of mine or some contemporary reflection, and the chapters end with some discussion questions that a group could use. If at any point you get confused about whether I live in the United States or in the United Kingdom, that's because I'm completing it as we prepare to move back from California to England. I'm grateful to my colleague Erin Dufault-Hunter and (as always) to Kathleen Scott Goldingay for commenting on a draft of the book.

The Old Testament translations are based on drafts of the versions in *The Bible for Everyone* (SPCK, 2018) and *The First Testament: A New Translation* (IVP Academic, 2018). Translations from the New Testament are also my own. Chapters 27 and 37 adapt material first published as "The Bible in the City," *Theology* 92 (1989): 5-15. There are one or two overlaps with my comments on Old Testament ethics in *Reading Jesus's Bible* (Eerdmans, 2017).

If you want to know more about Old Testament ethics from the angle that I take in this book, you could look at

John Goldingay, *Old Testament Theology Volume 3: Israel's Life* (IVP Academic)

Christopher J. H. Wright, *Old Testament Ethics for the People of God* (IVP Academic).

If you think this book looks a bit conservative, you could look at

John Barton, *Ethics in Ancient Israel* (Oxford University Press)

Cyril S. Rodd, *Glimpses of a Strange Land* (T&T Clark).

If you think it looks a bit liberal, you could look at

Roy E. Gane, *Old Testament Law for Christians* (Baker Academic)

Walter C. Kaiser Jr., *Toward Old Testament Ethics* (Zondervan).

If you want to think more about principles of interpretation in connection with Old Testament ethics, you could look at

John Barton, *Ethics and the Old Testament* (SCM Press)

John Barton, *Understanding Old Testament Ethics* (Westminster John Knox).

I'm putting the final touches to this book on New Year's Day, as the Rose Parade passes our house in Pasadena. It will be the last time I see the parade, given that we're expecting to move back to the United Kingdom. In our morning prayers today my wife and I prayed as we do each day that the God who has brought us safely to a new day (except that today we said "new year") may direct us to the fulfilling of his purpose. It's a monumental prayer, to whose achievement the Old Testament is important. Now I'll go and watch the parade for a bit.

INTRODUCTION

What is ethics? Ethics asks

- what sort of people we are (e.g., faithful, honest, compassionate, forthright, loyal, confrontational);
- how we think (e.g., about the world, about other people, about life and death, about wealth);
- what sort of thing we do (e.g., show hospitality, exercise generosity, enable people to keep Sabbath); and
- what sort of thing we don't do (e.g., murder someone, have sex with someone's spouse, steal someone's property).

It's easy to assume that the main focus of ethics is how we should approach certain tricky issues (e.g., what to do when a girl gets raped and made pregnant or whether to use nuclear weapons or whether torture is legitimate or what to do when someone is in such pain that they want to commit suicide). But one reason for the importance of the four broader sorts of question I just listed is that they have a big effect on how we approach the more specific tricky issues. They also have more impact on how we live our day-to-day lives. So I treat Old Testament ethics, in particular, as about the Old Testament's take on those four broad topics, though it may sometimes help us directly with the tricky questions.

We will look at Old Testament ethics from various angles:

- In the Old Testament, what are the qualities of a community and a person who live an ethical life? We will consider qualities such as faithfulness, compassion, pride, anger, and contentment.
- What does the Old Testament say about key aspects or areas of life? We will consider topics such as work, the environment, animals, wealth, violence, the Sabbath, and the administration of justice.

- How does the Old Testament look at relationships? We will consider friends, neighbors, parents, husbands and wives, nations, and other relationships.
- We will look at some key chapters that focus on ethical matters or are particularly significant for thinking about ethics: Genesis 1 and 2, Leviticus 19 and 25, Deuteronomy 15 and 20, Ruth, Psalm 72, and the Song of Songs.
- We will look at the lives of some people that open up ethical questions: Abraham, Sarah and Hagar, Joseph. Shiphrah and Puah, Samson, David, Nehemiah, and Vashti, Esther, and Mordecai.
- And in a postscript we will look at the question, "What about the Canaanites?"

In thinking about the Old Testament and ethics, two questions may be uppermost in our minds. One is the way the Old Testament may support us in connection with issues that are important to us—questions such as justice or the conservation of creation or same-sex marriage or caring for migrants. The other is the way the Old Testament raises problems for us—questions such as polygamy or the annihilation of the Canaanites. With the first sort of question, we have set the agenda and we are seeking to let the Old Testament say something about what is important to us. With the second sort of question we think we know what is right and we are seeking to let the Old Testament off the hook when it doesn't fit with our understanding. In this book I will pay some attention to both those interests of ours, but I want my readers to get more interested in a different sort of question. I focus more on what is the Old Testament's own agenda and how it raises questions that we have to respond to.

A friend of mine has suggested to me that Christian ethics has become primarily about principles ("We stand with Jesus on the side of love, justice, and liberation"). It's assumed to be obvious what love, justice, and liberation imply. But the risk is that the outworking of those principles comes mainly in accepting and encouraging the commitments of other progressive people. And the danger is that our thinking and lives are thus substantially shaped by the culture we live in, by our social context. We are inclined to assume that our way of thinking must be broadly right. But we need to have our way of thinking confronted. Jesus implies that what we call the Old Testament is an important resource in this connection.

Some Pharisees once asked Jesus what he thought about divorce. "What does it say in the Torah?" Jesus replied. On another occasion he declared, "I came to fulfil the Torah and the Prophets." Paul said something similar: "the proper requirement of the Torah is fulfilled in us as we live according to the Spirit." On yet another occasion Jesus told some people, "You need to work out what the Prophets mean when they say 'God wants mercy not sacrifice.'" (Those are paraphrases of sayings in Mk 10:3; Mt 5:17; 9:13; Rom 8:4.) Jesus and Paul imply: if you want to know what's right and if you want then to walk according to the Spirit, you need to know what the Torah and the Prophets say. Or if you want to test whether you are actually walking according to the Spirit, you need to use the Torah and the Prophets to check the way you walk.

One consideration that makes it tricky to discern the implications of the Torah and the Prophets as a whole is that the Old Testament wasn't all written in one go. It issued from the work of many different people over the best part of a thousand years, two or three thousand years ago. It comes from cultures different from those in which modern Westerners live. It can thus seem remote. It can seem to accept things that we wouldn't expect God to accept. The situations the Torah and the Prophets were addressing were different, and God needed them to say different things in different contexts. In giving us guidance about what's right, the Old Testament isn't systematic, and it isn't organized by topics. Part of the challenge and the richness of the Old Testament is its colorful variety. Yet in due course these writings became one book. So how can it become a resource to us?

In observations such as the ones I have already noted, Jesus himself offers several suggestions. One arises out of that comment at the beginning of the Sermon on the Mount, that he didn't come to annul the Torah and the Prophets but to fulfill them (Mt 5:17). In other words, he came to fill them out. How did he do so? When he goes on to say, "You've heard it said . . . but I say to you," he gives a number of examples. For instance, he implies it's possible to latch onto the commandment that prohibits murder and ignore the warnings the Old Testament gives about anger. He fulfills the Torah and the Prophets by pointing out things the Old Testament says and also things it implies that people might be inclined to avoid. To give another example, the Torah says, "Love your neighbor," and the context in Leviticus makes clear that it has in mind the neighbor who you don't get on with, but maybe Jesus knew of people who thought that as long as you loved your nice neighbor you could hate your enemy. Jesus fulfills the Torah by bringing out its implications.

A further guideline arises from another question he was once asked. What's the most important of all the commands in the Torah? It was a question that Jewish theologians liked to debate, though there was really little doubt about the answer. It's the command to love God with heart and soul and mind and strength (Deut 6:5). Like some other Jewish teachers, Jesus wanted to augment it with another command from the Torah: loving one's neighbor deserves to be set alongside loving God (Lev 19:18). Jesus then adds that the entirety of the Torah and the Prophets depends on these two commands. It's a significant comment in connection with thinking about Old Testament ethics. When you wonder about the point of an individual rule in the Torah, for instance, or when you're thinking that a particular command by God seems an odd thing for God to require, it's always worth asking, How is this command a working out of either love for God or love for neighbor?

A third insight emerges from that discussion of divorce (Mk 10:1-12). The Pharisees noted that the Torah allows divorce. Ah, says Jesus, the Torah allows divorce because you're hard-hearted. If you look back to the way things were at creation when God made the first man and woman and they got together, you can't imagine that divorce was intended to be part of the picture. But (he implies) God recognizes that some men do throw out their wives, so he provides a rule that regulates the way this grim event happens, and he offers the wife some protection. So paradoxically, there is another way in which the Torah expresses love for one's neighbor. It both lays out God's creation ideal and vision, and it makes allowance for the fact that we don't live up to it.

These three guidelines from Jesus will be important as we look at Old Testament ethics: ask how the implications of the Old Testament's teaching need to be spelled out, ask how its teaching expresses love for God or love for neighbor, and ask how far it is laying down creation ideals and how far it is making allowance for our hard-heartedness.

There's another piece of Old Testament background to these three guidelines. The Old Testament contains lots of "thou shalts" and "thou shalt nots," especially in the first five books. The title "the Law" for these five books is a misleading translation of the word *Torah*, which means "instruction" or "teaching." And it's generally misleading to think of its individual sections of teaching as "laws," as if they were like Western state law or canon law. A concrete indication of that fact within the Old Testament itself is that one can find little match between the prescriptions the Torah lays down and the way Israel actually handles offenses such as murder, idolatry, and adultery. It seems that it's not the case that Israel knows it's supposed (say) to execute murderers, idolaters, and adulterers, and fails to do so. Even faithful, Torah-keeping leaders don't treat the Torah as a statute book. They know they are not supposed to be literalistic in interpreting these "laws."

This phenomenon would be more puzzling were it not for the fact it features among other Middle Eastern peoples. When a king lays down a set of statutes, it doesn't mean they become the basis of legal practice. They are rather a collection of indications of the kind of moral and social norms that the king claims to be committed to. The Old Testament operates on a parallel basis. "Laws" that prescribe execution for murder, adultery, idolatry, and a long list of other acts are markers of the kind of religious, moral, and social commitments that God expects his people to accept. They are indications of how serious these offenses are. They comprise teaching on theological ethics in the form of laws. Understood this way, the Torah becomes more obviously useful for an understanding of Old Testament ethics. It turns out that asking about the ethical significance of the rules in the Torah is a form of study that corresponds to the Torah's own nature.

PART ONE

QUALITIES

We have noted that ethics asks about what sort of people we are, and the Old Testament's rules and sayings and stories are often concerned to give concrete expression to what sort of people we are and what sort of people we might long to be. In part one of this book we will look at some of the personal qualities the Old Testament wants to inculcate: godlikeness (especially in the combination of love and toughness), compassion, honor, anger (expressing the good kind and renouncing the bad kind), trust in God (a key to ethical behavior, the Old Testament implies), truthfulness, forthrightness, and contentment.

1

GODLIKENESS

"Be holy as I am holy" (Lev 19:2). So what is God like? A little earlier in the story of Israel at Sinai, he makes a proclamation about his own nature:

> Yahweh, God compassionate and gracious, long-tempered, big in commitment and truthfulness, preserving commitment toward the thousands, carrying waywardness, rebellion, and wrongdoing; he certainly doesn't treat people as free of guilt, attending to parents' waywardness in connection with children and with grandchildren, with thirds and with fourths. (Ex 34:6-7)

While this proclamation is designed to shape our thinking about the God we serve, the terms God uses are also ones that recur explicitly or implicitly when the Old Testament discusses the qualities that ideally describe human beings. So this proclamation also makes us think further about the God we are to resemble. He is

- *Compassionate.* The word is the plural of the Hebrew word for a woman's womb. It's a feeling you have that's like the feelings of a mother (see chap. 2 on compassion).
- *Gracious.* It's the attitude you show to someone when you treat them with favor even if they have done nothing to deserve it.
- *Long-tempered.* It's the attitude you take when you have good reason to get angry and to act accordingly, but you don't.
- *Big in commitment.* It's the generous loyalty you show to someone when you are under no obligation to them, or that you keep showing when they have let you down.

- *Big in truthfulness.* It's the reliability and steadfastness you show when you are consistently faithful to people.
- *Preserving commitment toward the thousands.* It's the generous loyalty that you keep manifesting year in year out, decade in decade out.
- *Carrying waywardness, rebellion, and wrongdoing.* It's the forgiveness you offer when you live with the consequences of people's actions rather than making them carry the consequences.
- *Not treating people as free of guilt.* It's the firmness you manifest when you refuse to let mercy triumph over justice in a way that treats right and wrong as things that don't matter.
- *Attending to waywardness in connection with children and grand-children, thirds and fourths.* It's the toughness you show even though it's costly through the fact that we live in one web of life.

One feature of God's self-description that may seem strange is that the word *love* doesn't come in it (though it does in some translations of Exodus, as a rendering of the word *hesed*, which I translate as "commitment": see chap. 34). For that matter, the ordinary word for "love" comes only twice in the entire first half of Genesis (for instance). Both times when it does come, Isaac is involved. The nice one is when Isaac's father, Abraham, sends his chief of staff to find Isaac a wife, and he brings back Rebekah. Isaac loves her, and incidentally recovers from his loss of his mother two or three years previously (Gen 24:67).

But earlier, God has referred to the fact that Isaac's father, Abraham, loves Isaac (Gen 22:2), yet that affirmation is preliminary to God's telling Abraham to offer up Isaac as a sacrifice. Subsequent references to love in Genesis are also quirky. Isaac loves one of the twin sons whom Rebekah bears, and Rebekah loves the other (Gen 25:28), which causes problems. Jacob loves Rachel more than Leah (Gen 29:18-32), which also causes problems (Deut 21:10-17 seeks to deal with some of them). Shechem loves Dinah and rapes or seduces her, which is not the last problem in that story (Gen 34). Jacob loves Joseph more than his other sons, which issues in complications of one kind or another (Gen 37). Whereas love can seem so simple and straightforward, in reality it isn't.

Love is (among other things) an emotion, and like any emotion it can be fruitful, but it can also be problematic. Maybe it's no wonder that Genesis doesn't explicitly talk about it much, even though one could properly say that creation was an act of love and that God's promises to Abraham were an act of love. And maybe its's no wonder that Exodus 34:6-7 doesn't use the word *love* even though love is what it's talking about.

When we do think of creation or of God's summons of Abraham as acts of love, we are presupposing that love isn't just an emotion. Indeed, it may not be an emotion at all. Only in Deuteronomy 4:37 does it become explicit that God loved Israel and its ancestors, and there the expression of love was that God chose Israel and got Israel out of Egypt. Love was an action. It fits that this declaration about love soon leads into a famous command about love: "Listen, Israel: Yahweh our God Yahweh one. You're to love Yahweh your God with your entire mind, with your entire being, with your entire might" (Deut 6:4-5).

Why does the word *love* suddenly appear in Deuteronomy, and what does it mean? In the background of this innovation is the fact that *love* was a political word in the Middle East. A superpower expected its subordinate powers to "love" it. The superpower didn't care much whether it was loved in the emotional sense. It did care whether its underling peoples were loyal to it. Deuteronomy picks up that way of speaking about love to urge Israel to give Yahweh its exclusive loyalty. Israel is to give nothing away to other gods. It's to place no reliance on them. It's never to ask them for anything. Israel's entire mind, being, might is to belong to Yahweh. So in this passage, one could translate the Hebrew word for "love" as "be loyal to."

That other great commandment, as Jesus calls it (Mt 22:35-40), requires love for one's neighbor (Lev 19:18; see chap. 19). While exclusiveness is not the point here, love as action and as loyalty is again the point.

If we look back over the Old Testament story from that point where God says "Be holy as I am holy" (Lev 19:2), what do we discover God is like, and therefore what we should perhaps be like?

- At the beginning God created the heavens and the earth (Gen 1:1).
    So be creative.
- There is to be light! (Gen 1:3).
    So bring light.
- God blessed (Gen 1:28).
    So bless.
- It pained his heart (Gen 6:6).
    So be open to pain.
- The inclination of the human mind is bad from its youth (Gen 8:21).
    So be realistic.

- I myself am going to implement my pact with you (Gen 9:9).

  So don't give up.
- All the kin-groups on the earth will bless themselves by you (Gen 12:3).

  So give people hope.
- To your offspring I shall give this country (Gen 12:7).

  So give people land.
- God tested Abraham (Gen 22:1).

  So test people.
- Their cry for help because of their servitude went up to God (Ex 2:23).

  So hear people's cry for help.
- I will be with you (Ex 3:12).

  So be there.
- The God of Abraham, Isaac, and Jacob has appeared to me (Ex 3:16).

  So be open, self-revealing.
- Send my people Israel off so they may hold a festival for me in the wilderness (Ex 5:1).

  So confront the imposition of servitude.
- You will not . . . (Ex 20:4, 7, 13, 14, 15, 16, 17).

  So be categorical.
- When people get into an argument . . . (Ex 21:18).

  So be concrete and practical.
- If you could carry their wrongdoing . . . (Ex 32:32).

  So be more merciful than judgmental.
- Congregate the entire assembly at the entrance of the appointment tent (Lev 8:3).

  So be available.
- In the people who draw near me I will show myself sacred (Lev 10:3).

  So be formidable.

That last reference takes us back to another feature of God's self-description in Exodus 34:6-7, which may seem strange. If there is one thing that people think they know about the God of the Old Testament, it is that he is full of wrath, especially when compared with Jesus. So why does he play down that aspect of his nature in Exodus 34:6-7? Maybe part of the answer is that the moment when he is here speaking to the Israelites is when they have just been on the receiving end of his wrath (as is the case in Lev 10:3, that last reference in the list above). And maybe this link is significant for Christian readers who think he is a God of wrath—he is saying to us, "Don't get this wrath motif out of hand."

On one occasion when God threatens to act in judgment on Judah, Isaiah says he will indeed do so:

> To do his deed—strange is his deed,
> to perform his service—foreign is his service. (Is 28:21)

Isaiah is saying that there is something alien to God about acting in judgment. He can do it, but it doesn't come naturally. Those words in Isaiah have further implications. One is that his bark is commonly worse than his bite. There are occasions in the Old Testament when he does act in wrath, but there are actually not so many of them. Your chances of living in a place and time when he did so are very small. You can read page after page in the Old Testament story and never read about it happening. He is always drawing lines in the sand and then doing nothing when people cross them.

The chapter in Isaiah describing the alien thing that God is about to do would make one think that he is about to surrender Jerusalem to the Assyrians. But he didn't do it. He arranged for the city to be relieved at the last minute. The wrath of God in the Old Testament is much more often something he threatens than something he acts out. He does sometimes act it out; he did eventually surrender Jerusalem to the Babylonians. But we miss what is going on if we take his warnings as descriptions of things that actually happened. The point applies just as forcefully to the prophets' declarations about wrath falling on other peoples. There is usually no record of its doing so, though the great empires such as Assyria and Babylon are the exception; they do fall, and Yahweh claims the credit, which is pretty worrying for those of us who belong to great empires.

Jesus follows his Father's example. He talks in chapter after chapter about weeping and gnashing of teeth and about hell and about judgment on his own people and about the destruction of Jerusalem, and he talks in chapter after chapter in Revelation about the fall of the great empire, but none of that prospect becomes reality in history within his lifetime or for decades afterward.

Oddly, therefore, being Godlike means speaking in fiery terms about judgment in order to seek to draw people back to God, in the manner of Jonah, and not worrying about God failing to implement the judgment he threatens. Because it's foreign to him, even though from time to time he will screw himself up to do it.

FOR REFLECTION AND DISCUSSION

1. What aspects of the character of God seem most important in connection with ethics?

2. What aspect of God is easiest to imitate?

3. What aspect of God is hardest to imitate?

4. In what way is it hard to love God?

5. In what way is it hard to love one's neighbor?

2

COMPASSION

A friend of mine who is divorced and has two children likes to comment that the image of God as husband and the image of his people as wife doesn't work very well for her because the marriage relationship is one that either side can terminate (and in this case did). The image of God as father or mother and of his people as God's children works better because she knows that her relationship as mother to her children is one that she could never terminate, and in a sense neither can they. They will always be her son and daughter, whether they like it or not. No matter what they do, they will still be her children. She gave birth to them. She nursed them.

We noted in chapter one that the Hebrew word for compassion (*rahamim*) is the plural of its word for the womb (*rehem*), which suggests that compassion is an aspect of that feeling a mother has for her children. And the Old Testament talks a lot about Yahweh's compassion, which can help us see what compassion means.

So, can a mother put her baby out of mind? The desperate circumstances of the siege of Jerusalem drove some women into cannibalism with their babies after they had died:

The hands of compassionate women
>   cooked their children.
They became food for them
>   through the breaking of my dear people. (Lam 4:10)

If a mother could put her baby out of mind so as not to have compassion on it, Yahweh will not do so with Jerusalem.

Can a woman put her baby out of mind,
> so as not to have compassion on the child of her womb?

Yes, these may put out of mind,
> but I—I cannot put you out of mind. (Is 49:15)

Not that the Old Testament is sexist about the matter: it also affirms that God's compassion for his people is like a father's compassion.

In accordance with a father's compassion for his children,
> Yahweh has had compassion for people who hold him in awe.
> (Ps 103:13)

Before making it the first quality he claims when he gives that systematic self-description in Exodus 34:6, Yahweh had already declared that his compassion was promiscuous: he has compassion on anyone he cares to, without having to provide a rationale or setting limits:

I grace whomever I grace and have compassion on whomever I have compassion. (Ex 33:19)

Indeed, he has compassion for everything he created:

Yahweh is good to all;
> his compassion is over all the things he made. (Ps 145:9)

It's just as well, because Israel tests those limits to breaking point. But when Yahweh speaks against his "son" Ephraim (that is, the northern Israelite nation) and determines to throw him out of the house, he can't quite do it, because Ephraim is the son he loves. He can't help having compassion for him.

Ephraim is a dear son to me,
> or a child in whom I took pleasure, isn't he.

Because every time I speak against him,
> I'm so mindful of him again.

That's why my insides moan for him,
> I have deep compassion for him. (Jer 31:20)

Actually Yahweh does from time say, "That's it!" and throw his people out for a while. But he can't finally let go of them or forget the commitment he made to them:

All these things will befall you in a later time but you will turn back to Yahweh your God and listen to his voice. Because Yahweh your God is a compassionate

God. He won't let go of you. He won't devastate you. He won't put out of mind the pact with your ancestors, which he swore to them. (Deut 4:30-31)

When he puts them down, his heart isn't in it, because his heart is compassion:

Because the Lord
      doesn't reject permanently.
Rather he brings suffering, but he has compassion,
      in the greatness of his acts of commitment.
Because it's not from his heart that he humbles
      and brings suffering to human beings. (Lam 3:31-33)

David knows that falling into Yahweh's hands is therefore safer than falling into human hands (2 Sam 24:14). But a theme running through the Old Testament suggests a side comment on David's observation. The Old Testament refers more often to the compassion of people outside Israel than to compassion within Israel. I don't think it's implying that Gentiles are more compassionate than Jews. It's implying that compassion is intrinsic to our created human nature. In this sense, we don't have to feel totally hopeless about falling into human hands. God can inspire compassion in Gentiles. Jacob prays for God to act in that way, Solomon prays that way, Nehemiah prays that way:

May God Shadday himself give you compassion before the man so he may release your other brother to you, and Benjamin. (Gen 43:14)

May you listen in the heavens, in the established place where you live, to their plea, their prayer for grace, and decide for them, and pardon your people who've done wrong in relation to you, for all their acts of rebellion that they have committed against you, and give them compassion before their captors so they may have compassion on them. (1 Kings 8:49-50)

Lord, please may your ear become heeding to your servant's plea and to the plea of your servants who want to live in awe of your name. Please enable your servant to succeed today and give him compassion before this man. (Neh 1:11)

And Yahweh promises it in respect of Judah's captors:

Don't be afraid of the king of Babel, of whom you are afraid; don't be afraid of him (Yahweh's declaration) because I am with you to deliver you and to rescue you from his hand. I shall give you compassion, and he will have compassion toward you and take you back to your land. (Jer 42:11-12)

When you turn back to Yahweh, your brothers and your children will find compassion before their captors and they will come back to this country, because Yahweh your God is gracious and compassionate, and he will not turn aside his face from you if you turn back to him. (2 Chron 30:9)

Yahweh keeps the promise. Admittedly, like other aspects of the way we were created in God's image, we can resist our natural gifts and lose them. It can even be the death of brotherly relations:

> For three rebellions by Edom,
> > for four I shall not turn it back,
> Because he pursued his brother with a sword,
> > destroyed his compassion. (Amos 1:11)

The Old Testament especially characterizes the superpowers that way. Realistically speaking, maybe you don't get to be a superpower if compassion is one of your main characteristics. And God can make use of a superpower's lack of compassion. He can use Babylon to put Judah down:

> There, a people is going to come from a northern country,
> > a big nation will arise from earth's remotest parts.
> They take firm hold of bow and javelin;
> > it's violent—they don't have compassion. (Jer 6:22-23)

I shall give Zedekiah king of Judah and his servants and the people, those who remain in this town from epidemic, sword, and famine, into the hand of Nebuchadrezzar, king of Babylon, and into the hand of their enemies, into the hand of the people seeking their life. He'll strike them down with the mouth of the sword. He won't have pity for them. He won't have mercy. He won't have compassion. (Jer 21:7)

And then, in turn, he can use Media to put Babylon down:

> Here am I, stirring up the Medes against them,
> > who don't think about silver.
> Gold—they don't want it,
> > but their bows will smash the young.
> They won't have compassion on the fruit of the womb,
> > their eye won't spare children. (Is 13:17-18)

It doesn't mean the empires get a pass from the guilt that attaches to lack of compassion, especially the lack of compassion that doesn't care about people like the aged:

> I was angry with my people, I treated my domain as ordinary,
>> I gave them into your hand.
> You didn't show compassion to them;
>> upon the aged you made your yoke very heavy. (Is 47:6)

The prophet is talking here to Ms. Babylon, the empire personified as a woman, and his indictment is that she lacks this basic womanly trait.

While compassion is to be expected of humanity in general, it is expected especially of people who live in awe of Yahweh. They are supposed to be like God in their character: in them compassion lives in the company of graciousness and faithfulness (a neat trinity). It means they act as light for the upright when things are dark for them—that is, they stand by people who are in the dark, protect them and bring them relief:

> The blessings of the person who lives in awe of Yahweh,
>> who delights much in his orders. . . .
> He rises in the darkness as light for the upright,
>> gracious, compassionate, and faithful. (Ps 112:1, 4)

Compassion is friends with truthfulness and commitment; it opposes the oppression of people such as widows, orphans, aliens, and the lowly:

> Exercise truthful authority, exercise commitment and compassion each person with his brother. Don't oppress widow and orphan, alien and humble. (Zech 7:9-10)

It even implies an attitude to animals:

> A faithful person knows his animal's appetite,
>> but the compassion of the faithless is cruel. (Prov 12:10)

So compassion is a natural feeling that we can encourage or discourage, one that we can urge on other people and on communities, cities, and nations as part of what they really know is involved in being human. It is quite indiscriminate in who it applies to. It may chastise, but it comes back to heal and restore. It implies that we treat other people and nations as brothers and sisters. It recognizes an obligation to the old as well as the young, and to other vulnerable people.

FOR REFLECTION AND DISCUSSION

1. Where is more compassion needed in your church?

2. Where is compassion needed in your local community (your village, suburb, city)?

3. Where is compassion needed in your country?

4. Where do you wish you experienced more compassion?

5. Where could you go and show compassion?

3

HONOR

It's said that traditional cultures are shame cultures in a way that Western cultures are not, but it's a myth that Western cultures are not shame cultures. In the West, too, honor is vital to a sense of well-being, and shame is horrifying. If people reviewing this book should say it's stupid or wrong or that I stole much of its contents from somewhere, I wouldn't be able to lift my head high. Likewise, achievement can be something to be properly proud of. If people reviewing this book say it's good, I shall be proud, pleased with myself.

So there's good and bad pride. The Old Testament makes that assumption. It talks a lot about majesty and impressiveness, and translations often use words implying arrogance in translating words that suggest majesty, which is both misleading and realistic. It's misleading because being impressive isn't wrong. A monarch is "her majesty" or "his majesty." A president is an important person. The problem comes when you get arrogant or egotistical about your reasons to be proud. The fact that Hebrew and English use the same words for good pride and bad pride reminds us of the temptation for good pride to turn into bad pride. It's hard to be majestic and not be arrogant. It makes you a bit God-like. It tempts people to think you are God. It tempts you to think you are God . . .

Many sayings from Proverbs take up this theme:

If [Yahweh] himself behaves arrogantly to the arrogant,
> to the lowly he gives grace. (Prov 3:34)

These six Yahweh repudiates,
> seven are abhorrent to him:

Haughty eyes, a lying tongue,
>   and hands that shed innocent blood. (Prov 6:16-17)

Superiority and self-importance and the way of evil,
>   and a crooked mouth, I repudiate. (Prov 8:13)

Arrogance comes, then humiliation comes;
>   with modest people there is wisdom. (Prov 11:2)

Only by means of arrogance does someone produce strife;
>   wisdom is with people who take advice. (Prov 13:10)

Poverty and humiliation—one who rejects discipline;
>   but one who heeds correction is honored. (Prov 13:18)

In the mouth of the stupid person is a shoot of arrogance,
>   but the lips of the wise guard them. (Prov 14:3)

Yahweh tears down the house of the arrogant,
>   but he establishes the territory of the widow. (Prov 15:25)

Anyone who is arrogant of mind is an abomination to Yahweh;
>   hand to hand he won't go innocent. (Prov 16:5)

Ceasing from contention is an honor for a person,
>   but every stupid person breaks out. (Prov 20:3)

Exaltedness of eyes and wide of mind:
>   the yoke of the faithless is an offense. (Prov 21:4)

I have seen a person wise in his own eyes;
>   there's more hope for a stupid person than for him. (Prov 26:12)

A rich person is wise in his own eyes,
>   but a poor person of understanding sees through him. (Prov 28:11)

So Yahweh hates haughty eyes, and when people get arrogant, he gets arrogant back—and of course he can do so appropriately and safely (Prov 3:34; 6:16-17; 8:13; 15:25; 16:5; 21:4). It's sensible not to behave as if you think you know everything (Prov 13:10; 14:3; 26:12). It's also sensible not to fight for your opinion as if it's a matter of honor (Prov 20:3). Don't let your wealth give you a false sense of your importance (Prov 28:11). Oddly, people who are stupid tend to arrogance; modesty is wiser (Prov 11:2; 13:18; 14:3).

> Awe for Yahweh is wisdom's discipline;
>> lowliness is before honor. (Prov 15:33)

> Arrogance goes before brokenness,
>> majesty of spirit before collapsing. (Prov 16:18)

> Humbleness of spirit with the lowly
>> is better than sharing plunder with the arrogant. (Prov 16:19)

> Gray hair is a splendid crown;
>> it's attained by way of faithfulness. (Prov 16:31)

> Before being broken a person's mind is arrogant,
>> but before honor comes lowliness. (Prov 18:12)

> One who pursues faithfulness and commitment
>> finds life, faithfulness, and honor. (Prov 21:21)

> The haughty, presumptuous person—arrogant his name—
>> acts in a frenzy of haughtiness. (Prov 21:24)

> The effect of lowliness is awe for Yahweh,
>> wealth, honor, and life. (Prov 22:4)

> A stranger should boast about you and not your mouth,
>> a foreigner and not your lips. (Prov 27:2)

> An individual's majesty will make him fall,
>> but one lowly of spirit will attain honor. (Prov 29:23)

> If you have been mindless in exalting yourself,
>> and if you have schemed—hand on your mouth! (Prov 30:32)

It you're arrogant, being put down may follow; whereas if you have no pretensions, you can only move upward; being lowly before God and being faithful helps you to be lowly in relation to people and thus to be wise (Prov 15:33; 16:18-19; 18:12; 29:23). Paradoxically, being lowly also helps you to be in awe of God (Prov 22:4; 30:32). Let other people advertise you, rather than advertising yourself (Prov 27:2; 30:32). If you've realized you've fallen into a trap in this connection, shut up! (Prov 30:32).

Proverbs has individuals in mind, though it has in mind individuals in the context of communities because that's where honor and pride, humility and arrogance operate. Isaiah has the community of Judah in mind:

Yahweh Armies has a day
    against all majesty and exaltedness,
Against all that is high—
    and it will fall down,
Against all the cedars of the Lebanon, exalted and high,
    against all the oaks of the Bashan,
Against all the exalted mountains,
    against all the high hills,
Against every lofty tower,
    against every fortified wall,
Against every Tarshish ship,
    against all the impressive vessels.
Human loftiness will bow down,
    people's exaltedness will fall down.
Yahweh alone will be on high
    on that day. (Is 2:12-17)

Nations can be affected by the same dynamic as individuals. Nations care about their honor (quite rightly). There's an often-repeated saying by Dean Acheson, when US Secretary of State (Foreign Secretary in UK-speak): "Britain has lost an Empire and has not yet found a role." I don't know if Britain feels it needs a role, but if it does, that's a way of saying it's dealing with questions about pride and shame and honor.

In different respects, things went up and down in Isaiah's day, but in the time to which Isaiah 2 relates, things were evidently going well, economically, politically, and militarily. And when it looks north to its usually more-powerful big brother Ephraim (which is maybe having a harder time under pressure from the Assyrians), Judah can also be proud of the fact that it has as its king the descendant of David, whom Yahweh chose, and as its capital the Jerusalem that Yahweh chose, and as its worship center the temple that Yahweh let David and Solomon build—not the fake monarch and capital and sanctuaries that Ephraim has. But Judah has come to put its confidence in itself and in its position, and therefore Yahweh is bound to put it down. Within Isaiah's lifetime, the whole country was ravaged by the Assyrians, and the king and the capital and the temple had narrow escapes. They were temporary escapes, too; another century later, their impressiveness gave way to shame:

From Ms. Zion

all her glory went away. . . .

All the people who had honored her treated her as wretched,

because they saw her exposure. . . .

Yahweh, look at my humbling,

because the enemy has got big. . . .

He threw down Israel's glory

from the heavens to the earth. (Lam 1:6, 8, 9; 2:1)

FOR REFLECTION AND DISCUSSION

1. When the publishers are trying to sell this book, they will want me to tell everyone about it. Can I do so and not fall foul of Proverbs?

2. Do you know anyone who has "made it" in life through being modest rather than through being pushy?

3. What about yourself are you proud of in a proper sense?

4. Is it true that God tears down the house of the arrogant?

5. Does your nation think it has a role? Does its self-understanding involve any arrogance?

4

ANGER

We are inclined to assume that anger is simply a sin, so there's not much else to say about the ethics of anger. Popular culture may see it otherwise. There was once a comic book hero called the Incredible Hulk. An ordinary, quite mild scientist gets affected by some gamma rays in such a way that when he's under stress he transforms into a creature of superhuman strength. In the television version his catchphrase was, "Don't make me angry. You wouldn't like me when I'm angry." But we do, in that the thing that transforms him often turns him into someone who can be of help in a situation. He can put down the bad guys.

The Old Testament includes a great story about King Saul's finest hour. Actually he's not really King Saul yet. He's been designated king, but nobody's quite sure what happens next as they've never had a king before. So Saul is carrying on being a farmer (setting an example for the disciples who go fishing after Jesus' resurrection because they don't know what else to do). He comes back from a day's plowing and hears a horrifying story.

The Israelites have some relatives called the Ammonites, who live next to Israel on the other side of the Jordan. They evidently have territorial ambitions and are seeking to fulfill them by taking over one of the key Israelite towns that side of the Jordan, Yabesh, in the region of Gilead, across from where Saul lives in Gibeah.

> Nahash the Ammonite went up and camped against Yabesh-in-Gilead. All the
> men of Yabesh said to Nahash, "Solemnize a pact to us and we'll serve you."
> Nahash the Ammonite said to them, "On this basis I'll solemnize one to you,

on the basis of gouging out the right eye of every one of you. I'll make it a reviling to all Israel." The elders of Yabesh said to him, "Let us go for seven days and we'll send envoys through all Israel's border. If there's no one who'll be a deliverer of us, we'll come out to you." The envoys came to Gibeah-of-Saul and spoke the words in the people's ears, and the entire people lifted up their voice and wailed. (1 Sam 11:1-4)

Evidently the Ammonites aren't content with the idea that the people of Yabesh might simply surrender to them. They want to mutilate them and humiliate them. Maybe it's just a way of getting them simply to leave. When their brothers and sisters in the main part of Israel hear about it, they wail, which doesn't do anyone any good.

But there, Saul was coming in behind the herd from the fields. Saul said, "What's happened to the people that they're wailing?" They told him the words of the men from Yabesh. And God's spirit thrust itself onto Saul when he heard these words, and his anger raged right up. He got a pair from the herd and cut them up and sent them off through the entire border of Israel by the hand of envoys, saying, "Anyone of you who doesn't go out after Saul and after Samuel: so it will be done to his herd." Dread of Yahweh fell on the people and they went out as one person. He numbered them at Bezeq; there were 300,000 Israelites and 30,000 Judahites. They said to the envoys who had come, "Say this to the people of Yabesh-in-Gilead: 'Tomorrow there will be deliverance for you, when the sun gets hot.'" The envoys came and told the people of Yabesh and they rejoiced. The people of Yabesh said [to the Ammonites], "Tomorrow we'll go out to you and you can act toward us in accordance with everything that's good in your eyes."

Next day Saul made the company into three units, and they came into the middle of the camp during the morning watch and struck down Ammon until the day got hot. Those who remained dispersed; among them there did not remain two together. The people said to Samuel, "Who was the person who said, 'Is Saul to reign over us?' Give the people over and we'll put them to death." But Saul said, "No one is to be put to death this day, because today Yahweh has brought about deliverance in Israel." (1 Sam 11:5-13)

It turns out that the Israelites' wailing did some good, after all. It got to Saul. It helps to arouse his anger. What's needed in Israel at this moment is someone with drive and energy—and anger. Because anger can motivate you to do the right thing. It turns out that anger is a fruit of the Spirit. It impels

Saul to impel the Israelites to take decisive action against the Ammonites. One of the things about the fruit of the Spirit and the gifts of the Spirit is that they can turn you into someone you wouldn't otherwise be or make you do things you wouldn't otherwise do. It needn't mean you do something alien to who you are deep inside. It more likely means that the Spirit enables potentials to find expression that you didn't even know you had. That's what happens with Saul. He's a mild kind of guy who didn't want to be king; he hid when they were organizing the election. But God found him out.

The people of Yabesh never forgot what he did for them. When Saul lost his life and his body was put on display in one of the Philistine cities in a much more grievous humiliation than the one the Ammonites had in mind, it was men from Yabesh who marched all night to take the body down, take it home, and give it decent burial.

Given that Old Testament and New Testament put a lot of emphasis on God's anger, it would be odd if they didn't also sometimes put a positive spin on the notion of human anger; Nehemiah is someone else who shows how anger can be a fruit of the Spirit (see chap. 42). On the other hand, there are many sayings in Proverbs that make the more familiar point about anger and indicate that the ethical implications of anger are negative.

> One who is short-tempered will do stupid things;
>> a person of schemes will be repudiated. (Prov 14:17)

> Long-temperedness is much understanding,
>> but shortness of spirit exalts stupidity. (Prov 14:29)

> Don't befriend a person characterized by anger,
>> don't go about with someone hot-tempered,
> Lest you learn his ways
>> and get a snare for your life. (Prov 22:24-25)

> A stone is weighty and sand is heavy,
>> but a stupid person's vexation is heavier than both of them. (Prov 27:3)

> There is the cruelty of fury and the flooding of anger,
>> and who can stand before passion? (Prov 27:4)

It's typical of Proverbs to focus on the pragmatic side to ethics—that is, Proverbs believes that doing the right thing and doing the sensible thing are the same. So getting angry makes you do wrong things and makes you do stupid things, and it doesn't achieve your aims (Prov 14:17, 29; 22:24-25; 27:3, 4).

Jealousy [arouses] a man's fury;
he won't pity on the day of redress. (Prov 6:34)

A stupid person—his vexation makes itself known at the time,
but a shrewd person conceals a humiliation. (Prov 12:16)

The favor of a king [will be] toward a servant of good sense,
but his rage will be [toward] a shameful one. (Prov 14:35)

The king's wrath is death's aide,
but the wise person will expiate it. (Prov 16:14)

The king's rage is a growl like a lion's,
but his favor is like dew on grass. (Prov 19:12)

One who is big in wrath carries a penalty;
if you rescue [him], you'll do it again. (Prov 19:19)

The dreadfulness of a king is a growl like a lion's;
one who infuriates him loses his life. (Prov 20:2)

A man gets angry if you give him reason to be jealous—presumably by chatting up his wife; so be careful (Prov 6:34). Showing that you're angry is inclined to make you look stupid (Prov 12:16). It's especially dangerous to arouse a leader's anger (Prov 14:35; 16:14; 19:12; 20:2). It's unwise to get too involved with angry people in general (Prov 19:19; 22:24-25).

The longing of the faithful is only good;
the expectation of the faithless is wrath. (Prov 11:23)

A gentle response turns back wrath,
but a hurtful word arouses anger. (Prov 15:1)

A heated man stirs up arguments,
but one who is long-tempered quietens contention. (Prov 15:18)

Better to be long-tempered than a warrior,
and ruling over one's spirit than taking a city. (Prov 16:32)

A person's good sense lengthens his anger,
and his glory is passing over an act of rebellion. (Prov 19:11)

A gift in secret calms anger,
>   a present in the pocket [calms] fierce wrath. (Prov 21:14)

A north wind may stir up rain,
>   and a secretive tongue an indignant face. (Prov 25:23)

People who mock stir up a town,
>   but the wise turn away anger. (Prov 29:8)

Pressing milk produces butter,
>   pressing the nose produces blood,
>   and pressing anger produces contention. (Prov 30:33)

The hopes and schemes of the faithless tend to end up making their victims angry (Prov 11:23). So it's a good idea to cultivate ways of speaking and acting that discourage rather than encourage anger (Prov 15:1, 18; 19:11; 21:14; 25:23; 29:8; 30:33), and to cultivate control of your own anger (Prov 16:32).

FOR REFLECTION AND DISCUSSION

1. Can you think of an example of someone doing something really good because they were angry?

2. Can you think of someone failing to do something really good because they weren't angry enough?

3. What makes you angry?

4. Can you think of an occasion when you made someone angry? What were the dynamics of what happened?

5. Do you know any ways to control anger?

5

TRUST

Exactly fifty years ago my first wife got pregnant with our first son. The problem was that she had multiple sclerosis and her neurologist believed it was dangerous for her to proceed with the pregnancy; she should have an abortion. We thought hard about it and decided we had to trust God about it. Things worked out okay, and our son will celebrate his fiftieth birthday next year.

When you're making an ethical decision, trust in God can be a factor in the public realm as well as in the private realm. In Western thinking nonviolence has become an important ethical category. The Old Testament from time to time urges people not to take violent action or presupposes that they won't take violent action, but it works with a different framework. In its framework, the key category is not nonviolence but trust in God, which issues in refraining from violent action because violent action presupposes that we are not trusting in God. When you're tempted to take violent action because people are attacking you, you trust God for your deliverance instead.

> It had been told David's household, "Aram has set down on Ephraim," and his mind and his people's mind shook like the trees in a forest shaking before wind. Yahweh said to Isaiah, "Go out, please, to meet Ahaz, you and 'A-remainder-will-go-back' your son, at the end of the Upper Pool channel, at the Washer's Field causeway. You're to say to him, 'Keep watch over yourself, be calm. Don't be afraid, your mind is not to go soft on account of these two stumps of smoking firewood, because of the angry burning of Rezin and Aram and ben Remalyahu. Since Aram has counseled something bad against you (Ephraim and ben Remalyahu),

saying, "We'll go up against Judah and dismay it and break it open for ourselves
and enthrone as king within it ben Tabeel," the Lord Yahweh has said this:

> It won't arise,
>> it won't happen.
> Because the head of Aram is Damascus,
>> and the head of Aram is Rezin.
> Within yet sixty-five years
>> Ephraim will shatter from being a people.
> The head of Ephraim is Samaria,
>> and the head of Samaria is ben Remalyahu.
> If you don't stand firm in trust,
>> indeed you won't stand firm at all." (Is 7:2-9)

The Arameans (we would called them the Syrians) have made an alliance
with Ephraim, the northern kingdom of Israel, in order to be able jointly to
rebel against the Assyrian superpower, and they want to get Judah, the
southern kingdom (among other little powers in the area), to join them. But
Judah isn't convinced it's a good idea, and Aram and Ephraim are determined
to put a little pressure on Judah in this connection. If necessary they will
remove the Judahite king and put in his place someone who is more sympathetic to their plans. The Arameans have maybe marched into Ephraim in
order to mount a joint invasion with Ephraim. So the Judahite king and his
people are understandably all aflutter, and King Ahaz is out checking on
his defenses. Jerusalem may need to withstand a siege, and in that connection
the town's water supply is a key consideration.

So Isaiah is out to offer Ahaz some unsolicited advice. Isaiah takes with
him his ambiguously named son. (Does his name promise that the Assyrians
are going to be defeated and decimated, or that Aram and Ephraim are, or
does it warn that Judah will be?) Ahaz is to get a grip on himself, to calm
down, not to panic. The kings of Aram and Ephraim (Rezin and Remalyahu)
look like something fiery, but they are really just firebrands that are going out.
The reason Isaiah is able to make that statement is not that he has better
military intelligence than Ahaz. It's because he's taking another consideration
into account. It's because he knows Yahweh is involved. And therefore "if you
don't stand firm in trust, you won't stand firm at all." Isaiah uses the same verb
in two different forms. The first time he uses the verb, he is challenging Ahaz
to stand firm, but more or less every time the Old Testament uses the word it

means standing firm in the sense of trusting firmly. The verb is *aman*, from which we get the word *amen*. Trusting means saying *amen*, yes, I believe that!

Later on, Isaiah will bring the same message to Ahaz's son Hezekiah, who faces a similar political challenge except that now it's the Assyrians who are invading Judah, and Yahweh declares,

> Here am I founding in Zion a stone,
>> a testing stone, a valuable corner stone,
> A well-founded foundation;
>> the one who stands firm in faith will not be hasty. (Is 28:16)

In both contexts Isaiah declares the importance of trust in God in connection with making political decisions. If you stand firm in the sense of trusting, then you will find that God makes it possible for you to stand firm when the crisis comes.

In between messages to Ahaz that come in Isaiah 1–12 and messages to Hezekiah that come in Isaiah 28–39, the book of Isaiah includes a sequence of prophecies that are formally addressed to many of the nations around, in Isaiah 13–23 (chaps. 24–27 are about the nations in general). Although they are formally addressed to people such as the Moabites and the Egyptians, I don't imagine these peoples ever knew about them. The messages were actually given to Judah, because they were designed to shape Judahite foreign policy. They talk a lot about calamity coming on these different peoples, though also about the prospect of them experiencing blessing. The prospect of their being put down has two implications for Judah. One is that Judah shouldn't be in awe of these peoples (Ahaz's temptation): Yahweh is the one to be in awe of (Is 8:13). The other is that they shouldn't trust them as resources and allies (Hezekiah's temptation). Yahweh is the one to trust (Is 36).

The Psalms embody the stance of people who know Isaiah is right.

> Instruct me in your way, Yahweh,
>> lead me on a level path.
> In view of the people watching for me,
>> don't give me over to the will of my adversaries.
> Because there have arisen against me false witnesses,
>> a person who testifies violence.
> Unless I trusted to see good things from Yahweh
>> in the country of the living. . . .

Hope in Yahweh, be strong,
>   may your mind stand firm, hope in Yahweh! (Ps 27:11-14)

It's the kind of psalm that could be prayed by a king like Ahaz if he took Isaiah's message seriously, but it could as easily be prayed by someone like Nehemiah or some ordinary person who was under pressure. The psalmist prays to be kept walking in the right way and to be protected from adversaries who are accusing him of stances or intentions or acts of which he is not guilty and who are threatening him with violence in the way that the Syrians and Ephraimites were threating Ahaz, or in the way that leaders in the surrounding provinces were threatening Nehemiah. So, does he go in for a preemptive strike? Whether he has the capacity to do so or not, his intention is to trust Yahweh instead. His testimony reflects the link between trust and hope. Trust in God's promises is another way of talking about hope. Trust in God and hope in God thus shape the way he relates to people who are against him.

The Psalms also provide the testimonies of people who have proved Isaiah was right.

Death's ropes encompassed me,
>   Sheol's restraints found me.
When I find pressure and sadness,
>   I call out in Yahweh's name:
"Oh now, Yahweh,
>   save my life!"
Yahweh is gracious and faithful;
>   our God is compassionate.
Yahweh keeps watch over simple people;
>   I sank low, and he delivered me.
Turn back, my entire being, to your rest,
>   because Yahweh—he has dealt to you.
Because you pulled out my life from death,
>   my eye from tears, my foot from being pushed down,
I can walk about before Yahweh
>   in the land of the living.
I trust, because I could say,
>   "I—I have become very low."
I—I said in my haste,
>   "Every human being lies."

What shall I give back to Yahweh,
>   for all his dealings with me?
I will lift the deliverance cup,
>   and call out in Yahweh's name. (Ps 116:3-13)

The contents of the psalm suggest it may be a king's testimony. The mortal danger and the overwhelming pressure of which it speaks came from people who were pushing him down and imperiling his place in the land of the living. He was helpless. He was tempted to think there was not a single human being who could be trusted, and maybe he was right. But he has known Yahweh reach out to him in that situation and he can therefore declare, "I trust." He did not need to do anything. Being able to trust makes a world of difference when people attack you.

Elsewhere the psalms use the other Hebrew word for trust, *batah*:

In you our ancestors trusted;
>   they trusted and you enabled them to survive.
To you they cried out and they escaped;
>   in you they trusted and they were not shamed. (Ps 22:4-5)

Because it's not in my bow that I trust;
>   my sword doesn't deliver me.
Because you've delivered us from our adversaries,
>   and shamed the people hostile to us. (Ps 44:6-7)

Psalm 22 begins "My God, my God, why have you abandoned me"; it's the psalm Jesus takes up while he is being lynched. It's a psalm for situations when you are under attack and there's nothing you can do. Psalm 44 incorporates reference to fighting that people did do; in this sense they were not helpless. But even then they knew that the key factor in deciding what happened would be God, so that action without trust would be pointless. Trust is key whether you can take action or whether you can't. One ethical implication is that the Old Testament places a question mark by a principle of just war thinking which says, only make war when there's a good chance you can win. Whether or not you think you can win is irrelevant, says the Old Testament.

In the wilderness, Satan tempted Jesus in several ways, and each time he responded by quoting Deuteronomy. Here's one of the passages.

You're to be mindful of the entire way that Yahweh your God had you go these forty years in the wilderness, in order that he might humble you by testing you so as to know what was in your mind, whether you would keep his orders or not. He humbled you and let you be hungry and fed you the *man* [manna] which you hadn't known and your ancestors hadn't known, in order that he might get you to acknowledge that human beings don't live on the basis of bread alone but on the basis of everything that comes out of Yahweh's mouth. Your clothing hasn't worn out from upon you and your foot hasn't swollen these forty years. (Deut 8:2-4)

In other words, the experience in the wilderness was designed to get Israel to live on the basis of trust in God, which takes training (Erin Dufault-Hunter points out to me). Here is one of the great Old Testament quotes for ethics, which links with that paragraph from Deuteronomy.

He has told you, people, what is good,
    what Yahweh requires from you:
Exercising authority and being loyal to commitment,
    and being diffident in how you walk with your God. (Mic 6:8)

Translations traditionally say that God "requires justice and mercy," and this translation of the verse has gained a life of its own. No harm is done: God does require justice and mercy. But in Hebrew the nouns that lie behind this translation have rather different meanings (chaps. 34–35, on Ruth and on Psalm 72, talk more about them), and it's always worthwhile paying attention to what the biblical text says as well as to other truths that have been built on it.

In this verse in Micah, "exercising authority" and "being loyal to commitment" comprise one idea formulated as a twofold expression (a hendiadys)—like a phrase such as "law and order" in English. The twofold expression refers to the kind of exercise of authority and making of decisions in the community (on one hand) that involves being serious about commitments to one another (on the other hand). That kind of thinking is common in the Old Testament. The expression that is unique to Micah comes in the last line. It suggests that you avoid thinking that you are in a position to make decisions about what to do, and that therefore you're willing to defer to God. It presupposes trust, in fact.

FOR REFLECTION AND DISCUSSION

1. In what ways is trust in God a factor in your nation's decision-making?

2. In what ways is trust in God a factor in your church's decision-making?

3. Have you had an experience of making a decision on the basis of trust in God, and it worked out okay?

4. Have you had an experience of making a decision on the basis of trust in God, and it didn't work out okay?

6

TRUTHFULNESS

Death and life are in the hand of the tongue (Prov 18:21). We can maybe do as much damage with our mouths as with any other part of our body, so the mouth definitely needs consideration in the context of ethics. Thus if we want to be ethical people, we need to watch our mouths.

I love the expression "being economical with the truth," and I'm sad that its specific implications get lost if it's used simply as a euphemism for lies. In origin it suggests the idea of not saying everything that could be said, which sometimes can be a wise and proper restraint—though on other occasions it may mean being so misleading that it is not so different from lying. Proverbs believes in being economical with the truth, and in this chapter we will focus on Proverbs. Much of its argument in this connection rests on the principle that such restraint is wise.

> Where there is a multitude of words, rebellion isn't lacking,
>> but one who restrains his lips in sensible. (Prov 10:19)

> One who guards his mouth preserves his life,
>> but one who opens his lips wide—ruin is his. (Prov 13:3)

> One who seeks a relationship covers over rebellion,
>> but one who repeats a matter separates a friend. (Prov 17:9)

> One who knows knowledge holds back his words;
>> a person of understanding is cool of spirit. (Prov 17:27)

> Even a stupid person, keeping silence, is thought wise;
>> keeping his lip closed, [is thought] understanding. (Prov 17:28)

The mouth of a stupid person is his ruin,
> and his lips are a trap for his life. (Prov 18:7)

One who returns word before he listens—
> it's his stupidity and shame. (Prov 18:13)

The first person in a dispute seems right,
> then his neighbor comes and examines him. (Prov 18:17)

Someone who reveals a confidence goes about as a slanderer;
> don't share with someone who has his lips open. (Prov 20:19)

One who guards his mouth and his tongue
> guards his life from troubles. (Prov 21:23)

He kisses with the lips,
> the one who replies with straight words. (Prov 24:26)

Don't answer someone stupid in accordance to his denseness,
> lest you become like him, you too. (Prov 26:4)

Answer someone stupid in accordance with his denseness,
> lest he become wise in his own eyes. (Prov 26:5)

In the absence of wood a fire goes out,
> and when there's no gossip, arguments go quiet. (Prov 26:20)

A stupid person expresses all his feelings;
> a wise person holds them back. (Prov 29:11)

If you see someone hasty with his words,
> there's more hope for a stupid person than for him. (Prov 29:20)

Guarding your lips guards your life from troubles (Prov 13:3; 21:23). Conversely, talking a lot may get you into trouble (Prov 10:19). Beware of someone who talks a lot about the good things they intend to do, because it may be a sign that they actually intend to act rebelliously (Prov 10:19)—and beware if you yourself are the person who talks a lot about the good things you intend to do. It's wise to be restrained in declaring what you plan on. Holding back and being cool of spirit can convey an impression of wisdom—and can be an expression of wisdom (Prov 17:27, 28; 29:11, 20). Talking about things that someone has told you in confidence is dangerous as well as pernicious, so be wary what you say to someone who is inclined to talk loosely (Prov 20:19). Being discrete about the

way you discuss other people's wrongdoing is also an expression of wisdom
(Prov 17:9) and a bringer of healing (Prov 26:20). Related to the idea of not
saying everything is the wisdom of listening, especially listening before speaking
(Prov 18:13, 17). It's wise to restrain yourself from responding until you've heard
the other person out: otherwise, your words can trap you (Prov 18:7). Admittedly there are limits to the wisdom of this economy. There are contexts in which
one needs to talk straight and in which it will be as welcome as a kiss (Prov 24:26).
The challenge is recognizing when to speak straight and when to be more ret-
icent, as one wonderful juxtaposition of sayings suggests (Prov 26:4-5).

To put it positively, truthfulness is a precious thing.

The mouth of a faithful person is a fountain of life,
>   but the mouth of faithless people conceals violence. (Prov 10:11)

The words of the faithless are a deadly ambush,
>   but the mouth of the upright rescues them. (Prov 12:6)

There is one who rants like sword thrusts,
>   but the tongue of the wise person is a healing. (Prov 12:18)

Anxiety in a person's mind weighs it down,
>   but a good word makes it rejoice. (Prov 12:25)

A gentle response turns back wrath,
>   but a hurtful word arouses anger. (Prov 15:1)

A healing tongue is a tree of life,
>   but deviousness in it is brokenness in spirit. (Prov 15:4)

In the response of his mouth there is joy to a person,
>   and a word at its time—how good! (Prov 15:23)

Nice words are a honeycomb,
>   sweet to the soul and healing for the body. (Prov 16:24)

Death and life are in the hand of the tongue;
>   those who give themselves to it eat its fruit. (Prov 18:21)

There is gold and abundance of jewels,
>   but lips with knowledge are a valuable object. (Prov 20:15)

Golden apricots in silver settings
>   is a word appropriately spoken. (Prov 25:11)

One can maybe bring as much blessing with the mouth as with any other part of the body. So lips with knowledge are as valuable as jewels (Prov 20:15; 25:11). There will be a natural link between faithfulness as one of your personal qualities and fruitfulness in the wisdom of the things you say, and your mouth can then bring life to a person (Prov 10:11). It can pasture them. It can bring healing. It can bring joy where there had been heaviness. Its words can thus be as sweet as honey to the palate (Prov 12:18, 25; 15:4, 23; 16:24). Gentleness in what you say can bring reconciliation and harmony in relationships (Prov 15:1). It can rebound on you in a good way (Prov 18:21).

One also needs to pay attention to the way one speaks the truth.

The mind of a faithful person talks in order to answer,
>   but the mouth of faithless people pours out evil things. (Prov 15:28)

The person who is wise in thinking is called understanding,
>   but sweetness of speech increases persuasiveness. (Prov 16:21)

The words from a person's mouth are deep waters;
>   a fountain of wisdom is a flowing wadi. (Prov 18:4)

One aspect of the "how to speak the truth" is whether you are speaking with relevance to the question in hand (Prov 15:28). One needs to pay attention to the persuasiveness of one's words as well as to their truth (Prov 16:21), or to pay attention to the seemliness of the way one speaks them (Prov 25:11).

On the other hand, speaking falsely can bring disaster to another person. The Old Testament is especially concerned about perjury in this connection.

False lips are an offense to Yahweh;
>   people who act truthfully are the ones he accepts. (Prov 12:22)

A faithless person takes a bribe out of his pocket,
>   to divert the processes of decision-making. (Prov 17:23)

A worthless witness is arrogant toward the taking of decisions,
>   and the mouth of the faithless swallows wickedness. (Prov 19:28)

Having regard for the person in making a decision
>   isn't good. (Prov 24:23)

Having regard for the person isn't good,
>   but a man will rebel for a piece of bread. (Prov 28:21)

Open your mouth for the dumb,
>   for the cause of all the people who are passing away. (Prov 31:8)

Open your mouth, exercise authority faithfully,
>   decide for the lowly and needy person. (Prov 31:9)

Naturally, then, Yahweh hates lying lips (Prov 12:22) and looks for people to resist the temptation to accept a bribe in this connection (Prov 17:23; 28:21). He looks for people in authority in particular to resist that temptation (Prov 24:23; 28:21). And he expects them positively to concern themselves with the taking of truthful decisions on behalf of powerless people (Prov 31:8, 9). His hatred also applies to falsehood more generally. Hosea critiques lying and deception as a key feature of Ephraim's life (Hos 10:13). People lie to Yahweh about their trust in him rather than in other gods and in military and political resources. They lie to a political overlord such as Assyria, professing loyalty while making secret overtures to the Egyptians. Priests and politicians lie to the administration in professing loyalty while conspiring to effect a coup.

Proverbs' point about lying is not just a moral one. It's that truthfulness is wiser, for a variety of reasons.

Someone who conceals hostility with false lips,
>   and the one who issues charges, he's a dimwit. (Prov 10:18)

The lips of a faithful person pasture many,
>   but stupid people die for lack of sense. (Prov 10:21)

The mouth of the faithful person is fruitful with wisdom,
>   but the crooked tongue will be cut off. (Prov 10:31)

A town rises up by the blessing of the upright,
>   but by the mouth of the faithless it breaks down. (Prov 11:11)

A faithful person walks about with integrity–
>   the blessings of his children after him! (Prov 20:7)

The violence of the faithless sweeps them away,
>   because they refuse to exercise [right] authority. (Prov 21:7)

One who stops his ears to the cry of the poor person–
>   he too will call and not be answered. (Prov 21:13)

Exercising authority is joy to the faithful
>   but ruin for the wrongdoer. (Prov 21:15)

Someone who says to the faithless person "You're in the right":
> peoples curse him, nations are indignant at him. (Prov 24:24)

A king who decides for the poor in truth:
> his throne will stand firm forever. (Prov 29:14)

Charging someone with wrongdoing when that person was guilty of no wrongdoing—it's stupid as well as wrong. It will rebound on you (Prov 10:18, 21, 31; 21:7, 13, 15; 24:24). The same applies to treachery (Prov 13:2). Conversely, the blessing that truthfulness brings is not confined to the person who speaks the truth (Prov 20:7). And this dynamic doesn't just apply to individual relationships: it applies to the flourishing of a community (Prov 11:11), and it applies to the administration (Prov 29:14).

FOR REFLECTION AND DISCUSSION

1. When have someone's words been life-giving to you?

2. When do you do wrong in the way you speak?

3. How can someone hurt you by the way they speak?

4. When do you do wrong by not speaking?

5. When have words caused pain in your congregation?

7

FORTHRIGHTNESS

Tumultuous changes in higher education and in theological education have caught two friends of mine in the midst of furious arguments about the future of their seminaries and their staffing. It's all very well to talk about being Christian communities, but . . . Then as I write, hospital doctors in England are about the go on strike because of a dispute with the government about pay and about working on the weekend. (It's said that people admitted to hospital on the weekend are more likely to die than people admitted on a Wednesday.) Our instinctive ethical thinking about contention, strife, and arguments is like our instinctive thinking about anger, hostility, and hatred. We assume that they are all simply wrong. In contrast, the Old Testament (and the New) assumes that there are things to argue about as well as things to get angry about. Yet contentiousness is indeed wearisome. It's been suggested that the United States is overly keen on claiming the moral high ground and critiquing other nations over some ethical and political issues. Is it our business to critique other nations? Amos, for instance, does so (see chap. 33), but as far as we know, he never presented these critiques to the nations themselves. They were for domestic consumption: they were designed to soften up Ephraim itself as Amos prepared to put the boot in (see Amos 2:6-16, following up Amos 1:3–2:5).

Proverbs is again eloquent on the subject:

The beginning of an argument releases waters,
before contention breaks out, abandon it. (Prov 17:14)

Better living on a corner of the roof
>than an argumentative woman and a shared house. (Prov 21:9)

A continuing drip on a rainy day
>and an argumentative woman are alike.
One who hides her hides the wind,
>and oil on his right hand announces her. (Prov 27:15-16)

A wise person may dispute with a stupid person,
>but he'll rage and joke and there will be no peace. (Prov 29:9)

Given that strife is tiring, we may be prepared to pay a price for peace and quiet, and the contention that can eventually arise from an argument may not be worth the overwhelming flood it brings. So it may be sensible to quit the argument early (Prov 17:14). Or it may be wisest to avoid the kind of circumstances that can generate strife—such as two families sharing the same house with the argumentativeness that such a situation may generate, especially among the women who have to try to do the cooking in such a situation (Prov 21:9; 27:15-16). Further, it's probably stupid to get into an argument with a stupid person—he'll just rage and joke and there'll be no peace (Prov 29:9).

The lot puts an end to arguments
>and separates powerful people. (Prov 18:18)

Who says "Oh," who says "Aagh,"
>who has arguments, who has complaints,
>who has wounds without reason, who has bleary eyes?
People who linger over wine,
>who come to investigate mixed wine. (Prov 23:29-30)

What your eyes have seen
>should not come out into contention quickly,
Lest—what will you do at the end of it,
>when your neighbor puts you to shame? (Prov 25:7-8)

One who seizes the ears of a passing dog
>is one who gets furious at a dispute that isn't his. (Prov 26:17)

Those considerations provide another reason for not drinking too much, because drink is a stimulus to arguments and fighting (Prov 23:29-30).

The same considerations provide a reason for not starting an argument too quickly with the risk that you will end up looking stupid (Prov 25:7-8). The principle applies to intervention in other people's arguments (Prov 26:17). It may be best to decide things by tossing a coin rather than insisting that you prove who is more powerful (Prov 18:18).

> Don't contend with someone for no reason,
>> when he hasn't done you any wrong. (Prov 3:30)

> A heated man stirs up arguments,
>> but one who is long-tempered quietens contention. (Prov 15:18)

> A crooked person stirs up arguments,
>> and a gossip separates a friend. (Prov 16:28)

> Charcoal for embers and wood for a fire,
>> and an argumentative person for heating up contention. (Prov 26:21)

> An angry person provokes arguments,
>> and a hot-tempered person rebels much. (Prov 29:22)

The important thing is that you should be arguing about the right thing. It's stupid to get into an argument for no reason with someone who hasn't done you any wrong (Prov 3:30). The need to offer such advice presupposes that there are people who do so. Maybe they are people who are just inclined that way, people who like being troublemakers, crooked people (Prov 16:28)— but the connotations of the word *crooked* in English make one think of people who stir up strife in order to achieve something for themselves. Maybe they are people of a certain temperament (Prov 26:21; 29:22): they then need to allow for the role of other people who find it easier to be long-tempered, who therefore can quieten contention (Prov 15:18).

But sometimes things need to be argued out, and that's when you need the other kind of person to channel their capacity for argument and express it over something worthwhile.

> Abraham had reproved Abimelek concerning a well of water that Abimelek's servants had seized. Abimelek said, "I don't know who did this thing. You yourself didn't tell me; I hadn't heard of it till today." So Abraham got flock and herd and gave them to Abimelek, and the two of them solemnized a pact . . . and Abimelek and Phikol, his army officer, set off and went back to the Philistines' country. (Gen 21:25-27, 32)

A well is a serious thing. If shepherds in the wilderness lose access to a well, the sheep die. Abraham speaks straight and things get sorted out.

Maybe arguing with someone with whom you have no reason to argue is a form of displacement; I can get frustrated and angry at a discussion in a meeting and then take it out on my wife or my next-door neighbor's cat. A government can pick a fight with the government of a neighbor in order to have an excuse to invade it, when its real motivation is to be able to take over some of its resources. To return to Proverbs:

> Animosity stirs up strife,
>> but love conceals all acts of rebellion. (Prov 10:12)

> Ceasing from contention is an honor for a person,
>> but every stupid person breaks out. (Prov 20:3)

It's in that connection that a nation and an individual are challenged by the observation that love conceals acts of rebellion (Prov 10:12). In the context, this love means the love of the person who has been offended concealing the wrongdoing from that person. Love means I don't see the wrong that's been done to me anymore. (Joseph in his relationship with his brothers is the great Old Testament example, but David sometimes operated that way, too.) Its effect is thus the opposite to the effect of animosity, which responds to wrong-doing with an understandable belligerence. In such circumstances, we're inclined to think that standing up for ourselves is important, but actually it may be stupid, and giving up and "losing an argument" may be honorable (Prov 20:3).

> Only by means of arrogance does someone produce strife;
>> wisdom is with people who take advice. (Prov 13:10)

> Drive out the arrogant person and arguments will depart;
>> lawsuit and humiliating will cease. (Prov 22:10)

> One broad of appetite provokes argument,
>> but one who trusts in Yahweh will be refreshed. (Prov 28:25)

So it can be greed or resentment that generates strife, whereas trust in Yahweh avoids it (Prov 28:25). Greed is often the real reason for making war. Arrogance, too, can generate strife (Prov 13:10; 22:10), in international relations as well as interpersonal ones. One of those seminaries got into a mess once because both the administration and the faculty thought they knew what needed to be done about a major issue, but they had different understandings of what was needed, and neither could look at the issues from a perspective other than their own. Characteristically, both sides in an argument see some things clearly because of the perspective from which they come, but it's not instinctive for them to see things from the other side.

FOR REFLECTION AND DISCUSSION

1. What was the last good argument you had? Why did it happen, and was it worth it?

2. Are you the kind of person who gets into an argument too easily or who lets things go too easily?

3. Is there some issue you think you should start an argument about?

4. Can you remember an occasion when someone acted in love by giving up an argument?

8

CONTENTMENT

The genius of Ecclesiastes is to look at all the concerns on which human beings focus and to point out that none of them ultimately gets us anywhere. So it's best to be content with something moderate, not to go for the moon. The things on which we focus are all of some value, but none are of ultimate value. All of them are *hebel*. It's the key word in Ecclesiastes. Some translations render the word by "worthlessness" or "vanity" or "meaninglessness," but those renderings give a gloomier impression than Ecclesiastes intends. The problem is more that the things on which we focus are evanescent, like a breath. They are hollow.

> Someone who loves silver doesn't have his fill of money, nor whoever loves riches of his yield. This too is hollow. With the increase of his goods, the people who consume them increase, so what's the profit of their owners except his eyes seeing them? The sleep of someone who serves is sweet whether he eats little or much. . . . Here's what I myself saw as good, that it's beautiful to eat and to drink and to see what's good in all his labor that he expends under the sun for the number of the days of his life that God gives him, because this is his share. Further, each person to whom God gives wealth and possessions and whom he empowers to consume some of them, to take up his share and to rejoice in his labor—this is God's gift. Because he won't be very mindful of the days of his life, because God busies him with his heart's rejoicing. (Eccles 5:10-12, 18-20)

That principle applies to money. The last of the ten commandments fits with it: You shall not covet (Deut 5:21).

It can seem that coveting has become the underlying principle of life in the West. It's easy to see the evidence in the persons of the executives who take away millions of dollars or pounds in salaries and bonuses. It adds insult to injury that they do so when they are also people who have got us into an economic mess, but even when they are not guilty in this connection, our hackles rise at the ever-increasing disparity between their incomes and those of ordinary people and poor people. And it's easy to be indignant at the swindlers whom Proverbs indicts:

> False scales are an abomination to Yahweh:
>> a true weight is what he favors. (Prov 11:1)

> Balance and scales for decision belong to Yahweh;
>> all the stones in the bag are his making. (Prov 16:11)

> Stone and stone, measure and measure,
>> both of them are an abomination to Yahweh. (Prov 20:10)

> All day someone may feel covetous,
>> but the faithful person gives and doesn't hold back. (Prov 21:26)

> Don't remove an age-old boundary mark,
>> one which your ancestors made. (Prov 22:28)

> Don't remove an age-old boundary mark,
>> and don't go into the fields of orphans,
> Because their restorer is strong;
>> he will contend their cause with you. (Prov 23:10-11)

But the rest of us can hardly afford to sit in judgment on those executives, because they are only doing more efficiently what the rest of us do in our small ways. Advertising presupposes the point. The executives wanted more money, and they found a legal way to get it. We want more money, and if we can find a legal way, we will get it. It was so in Israel.

> Hey, you people thinking up trouble,
>> doing something bad on their beds.
> At morning light they do it,
>> because it's in the power of their hand.
> They desire fields and steal them—
>> houses, and take them.

They defraud a man and his household,
an individual and his domain. (Mic 2:1-2)

A few years ago, when the house prices boom was at its height, every time one of the apartments in our block sold, people were asking keenly, "What did it sell for?" Every time the price went up it was good news for everyone else—it meant that their apartment was worth more. House prices weren't the only index of our covetousness. I've read that the average UK household has a consumer credit debt of £6,621 (more than $8,500). That's how far we are living beyond our means. Now many households are in that position because they hit a crisis—someone got ill or lost their job. But many are in that position because they kept seeing advertisements for plasma TVs and it seemed stupid not to get one. We give into covetousness. We are all living beyond our means.

The position we get into individually is the position we get into as nations. As nations we live beyond our means, and we keep going only because the rest of the world lends us its money, and because we are passing on our debts to the next generation. I write in US election season, and I've heard it said that a sequence of presidents have been elected on the combined commitment to lower taxes and reduce the national debt, despite the fact that these two commitments are mutually exclusive.

Our life is based on wanting and on borrowing in order to fulfill our wants. If you can live within your means and you are putting something aside for your retirement, then you probably don't keep it in dollar bills or pound coins under your bed. You put it in the bank or in some investment so that it increases in value. So you become not someone who borrows in order to get what you want but someone who lends in order to get what you want (and you may not even know who you are lending to and what they are investing in and whether it aligns with your ethics). Borrowers and lenders all function on the basis of coveting. We have needed a bailout of troubled financial institutions rather than letting them fail, because lending and borrowing would otherwise cease, which would be the death of the economy. It would mean recession. The survival of the country depends on people lending and borrowing money.

In itself the idea that the survival of the country and the state and the city and the family depends on lending and borrowing is not something to be concerned about. Lending and borrowing are key features of Israel's life, and

Jesus urges us to lend to anyone who wants to borrow from us (Lk 6:35). When situations were tough in Israel, when the harvest failed or enemies ruined the crops, people needed to borrow in order to survive, to get back on their feet. The way the community was then supposed to work was that people whose harvest hadn't failed or whose crops hadn't been ruined lent resources to people who were in a tough situation. The survival of the community depended on lending and borrowing, as ours does. The difference was that nobody was supposed to make money out of this arrangement in Israel because people weren't supposed to charge interest on loans. No doubt in practice people found ways around that ban, but that fact doesn't alter the significance of the principle. People borrowed money because they needed it, not because they needed a plasma TV but in order to have food to eat. And they lent money because this other person needed it and not because they wanted to make money.

That attitude would be possible only if people took the tenth commandment seriously. When credit cards first arrived in Britain, one of them devised a brilliant advertising slogan. Their credit card "takes the waiting out of wanting." We have now made the foundation of our economic life the assumption it encouraged, that wanting is to be affirmed and that borrowing is the way to fulfill it. The assumption in the Scriptures is that wanting is to be disaffirmed, and that lending is the way you show love.

What's so wrong with wanting? There's nothing wrong with wanting in itself. The first time this word comes in the Bible is when God makes all the trees in the Garden of Eden, with the lovely fruit that is the kind of thing that human beings will want, will fancy.

> Yahweh God planted a garden in Eden, in the east, and put there the human being he had shaped. Yahweh God made to grow up from the ground every tree that's desirable to look at and good for food. (Gen 2:8-9)

And God told the first human being that he could eat whatever he wished of this fruit, though there was one tree that he had to hold back from—otherwise there would be fatal consequences. There was nothing wrong with the desire to eat from all those fruit trees. But the wanting goes wrong in the next scene in the story, in connection with that other tree.

> The snake said to the woman, "You won't die at all. Rather, God knows that on the day you eat of it, your eyes will open and you'll become like gods, knowing

good and bad." The woman saw that the tree was good to eat and that it was an object of longing to the eyes, and the tree was desirable for giving insight. So she took of its fruit and ate, and also gave some to her man with her, and he ate. (Gen 3:4-6)

The commandment likewise refers to illegitimate wanting, to wanting something that belongs to someone else—someone else's house or spouse or servants or animals. There's nothing wrong with wanting an apricot off the tree in your garden. But wanting something that belongs to someone else is the first step to trying to defraud them of it. The coveting command comes after a series of commands about outward acts. What lies behind stealing, perjury, adultery, and never taking a day off? Coveting does. In different ways it can also lie behind serving other gods, murder, and so on. Jesus tells a parable about tenants committing murder in order to steal someone's inheritance. Coveting skews and screws up your attitude to everything and to everyone. Instead of wanting to live in generous love in relation to them, we want to get hold of their stuff.

And it skews and screws up your attitude to God. When Eve looked at the one tree that God had told them not to take the fruit of, she spotted that it was to be desired to make a person wise. One might have thought that there was nothing wrong with wanting to be wise. But God had said, "Don't take the fruit of that tree." And the man and the woman let their desire overrule that word from God.

There's something paradoxical here. There are two contexts in which you may be tempted to covet. One is when you haven't got much. The other is when you've got lots. One cannot blame people who haven't got much for wanting the wherewithal to live. But coveting becomes more of a problem the more you have. It's not so surprising because the things that we covet, that we borrow to buy, can never satisfy us (as Ecclesiastes says). It's lovely looking at that plasma TV for a week and then you take it for granted. I know. I've bought one. But it can't satisfy. Adam and Eve had got nearly everything, but they wanted the one thing they'd been told to keep away from. The result was that their wanting, their coveting, skewed and screwed up their relationship with God. Or rather, it indicated that their relationship with God was already screwed up. Otherwise they would just have been laughing at the snake. "You want us to take no notice of God when God has given us so much? You have to be joking."

Deuteronomy warns Israel about how that could happen, and a story in Joshua soon provides an illustration.

> Yahweh your God will clear away those nations from before you little by little. . . . The statues of their gods you're to burn in fire. You will not desire the silver and gold on them and take it for yourself, so you don't trap yourself by it, because it would be an offensive act to Yahweh your God. (Deut 7:22, 25)

> Akan answered Joshua, "Truly I'm the one who's done wrong against Yahweh, the God of Israel. This actual thing is what I did. I saw in the spoil a fine coat from Shinar, and 200 sheqels of silver, and a bar of gold fifty sheqels in weight. I desired them and took them. There, they're buried in the ground inside my tent, with the silver underneath." (Josh 7:20-21)

In Psalm 19, talk about coveting or desiring or wanting comes again. Here, it's God's words, God's rulings, that are to be "coveted." It's the same word as in the commandment.

> Yahweh's rulings are true;
> > they're faithful altogether.
> They're more desirable than gold,
> > than much pure gold,
> Sweeter than syrup,
> > than the juice of honeycombs.
> Yes, your servant takes warning through them,
> > and in keeping them there are great results. (Ps 19:9-11)

So here, too, there's nothing wrong with coveting, with desiring. The question is, what do we desire? Paul's testimony is, "Whatever gains I had, I have come to regard as loss . . . because of the surpassing value of knowing Christ Jesus my Lord" (Phil 3:8). It's all rubbish, he says, and he uses a really rude word to describe it. It's all crap. It's the only time this word comes in the Bible. Paul has seen through the uselessness, the emptiness, the worthlessness of all that stuff. I'm still coveting, he says, in effect, but I'm coveting Christ. I want to know Christ.

In the past, the church in much of the West has been able to assume that it lives in what are Christian countries, in some ways, and that the church could identify with the country and with the culture. Quite a while ago in Europe and in some other parts of the English-speaking world, and more recently in the United States, we reached a tipping point when that assumption was no longer possible. We are now well beyond it. The church has to stand over against the culture, not to affirm it. We have to model a different way of being. Declining to be a people defined by coveting is one of the ways in which we must do that. The last of the Torah's ten basic imperatives is a particularly important one in our culture.

FOR REFLECTION AND DISCUSSION

1. Think about the people you know: What do they most covet?

2. How does this coveting affect their lives?

3. What do you covet?

4. How does it affect your life?

5. How can you start coveting things it would be good to covet?

6. Does coveting affect your church's life and priorities? How?

PART TWO

ASPECTS OF LIFE

The study of ethics asks about how we think about things. How we think affects the way we act, and the way we act affects the way we think. But how we feel about things also affects the way we act, and the way we act affects the way we feel about things. So we need to reflect on what we feel and think about matters such as wealth and violence and justice and work and Sabbath. The Old Testament lays down rules about these matters, and sometimes it does so because it wants us to "just do it." But more often it is at least as concerned with how we think about it and feel about it, because reflecting on those questions helps to shape the approach we take to aspects of life about which it doesn't lay down the law.

9

MIND AND HEART

Ethics is a matter of both the inner person and the outer life. Sometimes people say that God is interested in the heart, not in outward actions. Put that way, it's wrong. Whether you do justice is what counts, not whether you care about justice. But that saying is onto something. While what you do affects the way you think, the way you think affects what you do. Some sayings from Proverbs:

> Don't disregard my teaching, son;
>> your mind is to safeguard my commands. (Prov 3:1)

> Commitment and truthfulness must not abandon you;
>> bind them on your neck, write them on the tablet of your mind.
>> (Prov 3:3)

> Trust in Yahweh with all your mind,
>> don't lean on your own understanding. (Prov 3:5)

> Above everything that you guard, protect your mind,
>> because from it things go out into life. (Prov 4:23)

> You'll groan at your end,
>> when your flesh and body are spent;
> You'll say, "How I repudiated discipline,
>> and my mind spurned rebuke." (Prov 5:11-12)

> The wise of mind accepts commands,
>> but the stupid of lips comes to ruin. (Prov 10:8)

The mind of a person of understanding seeks knowledge,
>   but the mouth of dense people feeds on stupidity. (Prov 15:14)

Anyone who is arrogant of mind is an abomination to Yahweh;
>   hand to hand he won't go innocent. (Prov 16:5)

The crucible for silver, the furnace for gold,
>   and Yahweh tests minds. (Prov 17:3)

Who can say, "I've kept my mind pure,
>   I'm clean from my offense?" (Prov 20:9)

All a person's way is upright in his own eyes,
>   but Yahweh weighs minds. (Prov 21:2)

He says to you, "Eat and drink,"
>   but his heart isn't with you. (Prov 23:7)

One who trusts in his own mind—he's stupid,
>   but one who walks in wisdom—he will escape. (Prov 28:26)

There's a key statement in Proverbs that is expressed in the King James Version as a need to guard your heart, because it's the wellspring of life (Prov 4:23). I've just discovered that in most Christian dating books (I didn't even know there were Christian dating books, but I'm not expecting ever to need one), one of the key pieces of counsel is to "guard your heart." Typically (a) this is true; (b) it hasn't got much to do with the text it's quoting; (c) we have to be wary of missing the important point that this Scripture does make through making it mean something else.

To start with, there's what we mean by the heart. In Western thinking the main thing about the heart is that it's the locus of feelings; we fall in love with our hearts. In the Scriptures, the heart is the inner person in a more general sense. The heart is where you do your thinking, form your attitudes, and evaluate what you have done. In other words, the heart covers the mind, the thinking, and the conscience. While the Scriptures can link the heart with emotions, in connection with emotions they are as likely to refer to the innards more generally. The place where we feel things is indeed lower in our insides than the heart. So guarding your heart implies being careful about the way you think, about the attitudes you cultivate and pick up. The more we live in a culture that lives by values and assumptions that differ from those of the Scriptures, the more we have to guard our hearts and minds.

The important thing then is not to assume you can work things out for yourself (Prov 3:3). In the West we're inclined to assume that we understand things better than previous generations did. We make that assumption because we do know more about matters such as the working of the physical world, and we forget that we probably know less about (say) personal relationships and wisdom.

The opposite of trusting Yahweh with our mind (Prov 3:5; 28:26), then, is to assume that we can work things out for ourselves. Our minds have to be open to learning, discipline, rebuke, and even orders (Prov 3:1; 5:11-12; 10:8; 15:14; 16:5). I'm often struck by the way people may solemnly assure us that they will tell us their presuppositions and assumptions. As if we knew what our presuppositions and assumptions are! We have to work on the hypothesis that only God does (Prov 17:3). Who can say that they've kept their mind pure? (Prov 20:9). You can convince yourself that you're an ethical person, but Yahweh knows you better than you know yourself (Prov 21:2). And you can think that someone else is glad to be with you, but you don't know what's going on inside them (Prov 23:7).

It may be the opposite of what you think.

The crooked in mind are an abomination to Yahweh;
> people of integrity in their way are the ones he favors. (Prov 11:20)

Anxiety in a person's mind weighs it down,
> but a good word makes it rejoice. (Prov 12:25)

Hope deferred sickens the heart,
> but desire that comes about is a tree of life. (Prov 13:12)

The heart knows its inner bitterness,
> and in its joy a stranger doesn't share. (Prov 14:10)

Even in laughter a heart may hurt,
> and celebration—its end may be grief. (Prov 14:13)

Someone who turns back in heart will be full from his ways,
> and the good person from his deeds. (Prov 14:14)

A healthy heart is life for the flesh,
> but passion is rot for the bones. (Prov 14:30)

Sheol and Abaddon are before Yahweh;
> how much more the minds of human beings. (Prov 15:11)

A joyful heart enhances the face,

  but by hurt in the heart the spirit is crushed. (Prov 15:13)

A joyful heart enhances healing,

  but a crushed spirit dries up the bones. (Prov 17:22)

Exaltedness of eyes and wide of mind:

  the yoke of the faithless is an offense. (Prov 21:4)

Your mind must not be envious of people who offend,

  but rather of [people who live in] awe for Yahweh all day. (Prov 23:17)

When we turn back in our hearts from the right way, it issues in the commensurate actions, and we'll pay the penalty for it (Prov 14:14). When our mind gets envious if someone without integrity does well, we're in trouble; that's when we have to push ourselves toward awe for God (Prov 23:17). When our ethics go wrong, it's because we are crooked of mind as opposed to being people of integrity (Prov 11:20). Proverbs assumes that unethical lives go against the structure of reality. Straightness is natural; crookedness is unnatural. Crookedness doesn't fit with the way things really are, and therefore it's bound eventually to come unstuck. To put it another way, there is a coherence between God's own straightness and integrity and the world's straightness and integrity, so when you go against the world's straightness and integrity, you go against God's. And that has to lead to trouble. In the West, we assume it's good to be broadminded and to reach high; maybe we are wrong (Prov 21:4).

What one might call the ethics of the heart are necessarily set in the context of the rest of the heart's order. Anxiety, disappointment, bitterness, hurt, and sadness threaten both the heart's integrity and the body's integrity (Prov 12:25; 13:12; 14:10; 17:22) and thus imperil its ethics.

Yet the culture out of which Proverbs comes evidently recognizes that it's easy to let go of matters such as commitment and truthfulness. We can see it is so from things the prophets and the psalms protest about. Their culture easily forgot them, like ours. So we have to put effort into keeping hold of them. There are rules in the Torah about binding the Torah on your arms and on your forehead, which many Jews take literally. Jesus could be rude about them because they can be mere outward show, like every religious observance. But the idea fits Proverbs 3:3.

The word *integrity* is the first word used to describe Job. He was a person of integrity and uprightness; he was in awe of God and he turned away from bad dealing (Job 1:1). In due course he spells out the way he sees his own life. He says, I've resisted the temptation to fancy other girls; I haven't plotted trouble for other people; I haven't made a pass at my neighbor's wife; I haven't dismissed claims of ill-treatment by my servants; I haven't eaten on my own rather than share with the needy or the widow or the orphan, or dressed well rather than share clothing with such people, or lived in a big house when they didn't have a roof over their head; I haven't trusted in my assets; I haven't smiled when trouble came to someone who didn't like me (see Job 31). You might think he is claiming rather a lot, but that opening statement describing him as a person of fantastic integrity suggests that the author of Job accepts his claim. And in the context of arguing that his suffering was undeserved, Job would be foolish to be claiming what wasn't true. In effect he claims integrity of mind, heart, and life.

FOR REFLECTION AND DISCUSSION

1. Given that we probably know ourselves less well than we think, how can we grow in self-knowledge?

2. Can you think of ways in which anxiety or disappointment or bitterness or hurt or sadness has led you astray ethically?

3. Are there ways in which your mind is shaped by your culture rather than by the Scriptures? Or maybe it's easier to think of ways in which someone else's mind is misshaped in this way!

4. Are you aware of any ways that other cultures help us see where we are shaped by our culture in ways that clash with the Scriptures?

5. Are there practical ways in which we can bind the teaching of the Scriptures onto our minds?

10

WEALTH

In chapter eight I noted how it's said that an ever-increasing proportion of income and assets is possessed by the top 10 percent or the top 1 percent or the top one-tenth of a percent of the people in a country such as Britain or the United States (and nowadays of developing countries). But it's also been said that there's nothing very new about that situation. If you were one of the top percent, should you feel guilty? Should you simply give your wealth away? Proverbs doesn't propose a redistribution of wealth, but it offers a wide variety of comments about money. Any one of them on its own could be misleading, but the total picture they suggest is illuminating.

First, Proverbs is not world denying. It's true to life and positive about wealth.

> The wealth of the rich person is his strong city;
>> their poverty is the ruin of the poor. (Prov 10:15)

> Even by his neighbor a poor person is repudiated,
>> but the friends of a wealthy person are many. (Prov 14:20)

> All the brothers of a poor person repudiate him—
>> how much more do his neighbors keep their distance from him.
>> (Prov 19:7)

> Valuable treasure and oil are in the dwelling of someone wise,
>> but a stupid person will consume them. (Prov 21:20)

Wealth does give you some security (Prov 10:15). It makes it possible for you to enjoy things you couldn't otherwise enjoy (Prov 21:20). It makes you popular, though this popularity is no doubt a mixed blessing (Prov 14:20). Proverbs is thus realistic about how life actually works; indeed, Proverbs is often simply analyzing how life does work, not commenting on whether it should work that way. And ethics needs to take into account how things do work in life. Further, Proverbs doesn't assume that the possession of wealth is original sin, as Karl Marx rather implied. It encourages us to seek wealth (though it doesn't imply that it's the most important thing to seek). So how are you to do so?

> Honor Yahweh with all your wealth,
> > with the first of all your revenue.
> Your barns will fill with plenty,
> > your vats will overflow with new wine. (Prov 3:9-10)

> Yahweh's blessing—it enriches,
> > and toil doesn't add to it. (Prov 10:22)

> A woman of grace takes hold of splendor,
> > and violent men take hold of wealth. (Prov 11:16)

> There is one who scatters and gets still more,
> > and one who holds back beyond what is upright, only to be in want.
> > (Prov 11:24)

> A person of blessing will be made fat;
> > someone who refreshes—he will also be refreshed. (Prov 11:25)

> Better a little with awe for Yahweh
> > than much treasure and turmoil with it. (Prov 15:16)

How are you to gain some wealth? Be bold (Prov 11:16): the saying compares with Jesus' parable that ridicules the man with a bag of gold who sits on it rather than investing it (Mt 25). Be generous (Prov 11:25): business involves being sharp, but it also profits from getting on with people. Be honest (Prov 15:16): another surprising comment that assumes we live in a moral universe (cf. Prov 10:2). Be reverent (Prov 10:22): prosperity comes from God so trusting and honoring him is important (cf. Prov 3:9-10). But be realistic (Prov 11:24): prosperity is unpredictable, and Proverbs' "rules" are broad generalizations not universals.

This consideration leads into some consideration of the shortcomings of wealth.

> Wisdom's profit is better than the profit of silver,
>> her revenue than gold. (Prov 3:14)

> Wealth doesn't avail on the day of wrath,
>> but faithfulness rescues from death. (Prov 11:4)

> Better a little with awe for Yahweh
>> than much treasure and turmoil with it. (Prov 15:16)

> One who gets dishonest gain troubles his household,
>> but one who is hostile to a gift will live. (Prov 15:27)

> Better one who is poor who walks with integrity
>> than one who is crooked with his lips and stupid. (Prov 19:1)

> Rich and poor meet;
>> Yahweh makes each of them. (Prov 22:2)

> Don't get weary in order to become wealthy;
>> out of your understanding, desist.
> Should your eyes flit upon it, it's gone, because it definitely makes itself wings;
>> like an eagle, it flies to the heavens. (Prov 23:4-5)

> Someone who increases his wealth by means of interest and profiteering,
>> amasses it for someone who will be gracious to the poor. (Prov 28:8)

> A rich person is wise in his own eyes,
>> but a poor person of understanding sees through him. (Prov 28:11)

> One who is evil in eye hurries for wealth
>> and doesn't acknowledge that lack will come to him. (Prov 28:22)

Wealth can come to seem all-important. But it's no use when the earthquake happens (Prov 11:4). It can't buy me love or wisdom (Prov 3:14) or forgiveness or God. It tends to be accompanied by turmoil (Prov 15:16) and to make people forget its moral connections (Prov 22:16). It tends to make people forget relationships (Prov 15:27): if money becomes all-important it affects friends and family. It tends to give people inflated ideas about their importance (Prov 22:2) and about their smartness (Prov 28:11). It's just not as important as honesty (Prov 19:1; 28:8, 22). It has a knack of disappearing (Prov 23:5).

In other words, seeking or possessing wealth tends to drive you to the opposite of the attitudes that will actually lead to your making some wealth. It drives you away from generosity, honesty, and reverence. So:

Rely on Yahweh with all your mind,
> don't lean on your own understanding.
In all your ways acknowledge him,
> and he himself will keep your paths straight. (Prov 3:5-6)

Honor Yahweh with all your wealth,
> with the first of all your revenue. (Prov 3:9)

The one who relies on his wealth—he falls,
> but the faithful flourish like foliage. (Prov 11:28)

Working for treasures by means of a lying tongue
> is a breath driven off, people seeking death. (Prov 21:6)

Don't get weary in order to become wealthy;
> out of your understanding, desist. (Prov 23:4)

Sheol and Abaddon don't get full,
> and the eyes of a human being don't get full. (Prov 27:20)

Emptiness and a lying word keep far from me,
> poverty and riches do not give me,
> let me grab the food that is my due,
Lest I get full and renounce
> and say, "Who is Yahweh?"
Or lest I get poor and rob
> and take the name of my God. (Prov 30:8-9)

So: be moderate (Prov 30:8-9). Don't place your reliance on it (Prov 11:28) but rather on God (Prov 3:5-6); you can't serve two masters (Mt 6:24). Give God the first of your income; don't wait until the end of the year to see if you have anything left (Prov 3:9). Don't be tempted to get rich by dishonesty, because in the end it doesn't pay (Prov 21:6). Don't work too hard for it (Prov 23:4) or get obsessed by it (Prov 27:20).

In turn that leads into some sayings in Proverbs about what to do with your wealth.

Honor Yahweh with all your wealth,
> with the first of all your revenue. (Prov 3:9)

A person of blessing will be made fat;

> someone who refreshes—he will also be refreshed. (Prov 11:25)

One who withholds grain—the community will curse him;

> but blessing will be on the head of one who sells it. (Prov 11:26)

One who oppresses a poor person insults his maker,

> but one who is gracious to a needy person honors him. (Prov 14:31)

One who is gracious to a poor person lends to Yahweh,

> and he will pay him his recompense. (Prov 19:17)

One who stops his ears to the cry of the poor person—

> he too will call and not be answered. (Prov 21:13)

One who is good of eye will be blessed,

> because he gives of his bread to the poor person. (Prov 22:9)

Honor God with it (Prov 3:9), be a blessing with it (Prov 11:25), serve the community with it (Prov 11:26). Be generous to the needy with it, because doing so honors God (Prov 14:31), because doing so is like lending to God, and he pays back (Prov 19:17), and because then you will meet with generosity (Prov 21:13; 22:9).

The answer to Marx's point about wealth causing evil is to do good with it. Often in the world there are people who have none and people who have lots that is doing nothing. Proverbs' solution is cash flow.

FOR REFLECTION AND DISCUSSION

1. How realistic do you think is Proverbs' teaching on wealth in our world?

2. Do you have any experience of its teaching being proved true or not coming true?

3. Are there ways in which Proverbs challenges you about your attitudes in connection with money?

4. Are there ways in which you should you change your life in light of Proverbs' teaching?

5. Are there ways in which your church should change the way it handles questions of money in light of Proverbs' teaching?

11

VIOLENCE

I write some while after two US citizens shot and killed fourteen people and injured many others in San Bernardino, a few miles down the freeway from where I live; more recently two Belgian citizens bombed and killed thirty-five people and injured over two hundred in Brussels. Is nowhere safe? Our leaders declare themselves committed to stopping such violence, but how are they to do so? The best comment on the Brussels event appeared on *The Onion*, a satirical website. It consisted of a simple tirade about how we have tried hard and long to understand this violence and we hereby give notice that we are giving up trying to understand it.

It's typical of the Old Testament to have a multiplicity of ways of approaching a tricky issue, and this feature of the Old Testament is particularly significant in connection with ethical questions. I do not have in mind here differences in *what* it says about the issue but with differences in *how* it says, though that difference has implications for the *what*. Its treatment of violence involves telling stories about it, making rules about it, thinking about it analytically, sharing God's warnings and promises about it, and praying about it.

First, the Old Testament tells stories about acts of violence.

> Yahweh recognized Abel and his offering, but Cain and his offering Yahweh did not recognize. It really enraged Cain and he went into a huff. . . . And while they were in the open country, Cain set upon Abel his brother and killed him. (Gen 4:4-5, 8)

Lemek said to his women,
Adah and Sillah, listen to my voice;
  as Lemek's women, give ear to my word.
Because I've killed someone for wounding me,
  a young man for injuring me.
If for Cain it's to be redressed sevenfold,
  for Lemek seventy-sevenfold. (Gen 4:23-24)

The earth was full of violence. . . . So God said to Noah, "The end of all flesh
has come before me, because the earth is full of violence through them. Here,
I'm going to devastate them, with the earth." (Gen 6:11, 13-14)

Like our news, the Old Testament is full of stories about violence, from vir-
tually the very beginning. You're only just outside the Garden of Eden, and
Adam and Eve's first son is killing their second son. God had warned Eve
about how painful it would be for her to have children, and I don't think God
was just talking about the physical pain of giving birth. The greater pain was
surely watching one son kill another. The violence increases through the narrative until the reason why God decides to send Noah's flood is that the world
is full of violence. And giving the world a new start after the flood doesn't
make a difference. Later in Genesis there's a great act of mass violence when
a foreigner seduces or rapes a girl and two of her brothers kill the entire
population of the city (Gen 34).

That's just Genesis. The book of Judges is full of such violent stories.
Christians sometimes express unease about them, as if by telling them the
Scriptures were approving of them, though the stories make clear enough
that they don't approve. But maybe the unease is the one implied by a story
a hospital chaplain told me a few days after the San Bernardino shootings.
Someone he met wanted to know why God hadn't stopped the San
Bernardino killers. She said she couldn't believe in a God who would let
that kind of thing happen. But God didn't create a world in which we'd be
unable to do wicked and stupid things. He gave the world and life over to
us for us to live in and to look after on his behalf, and then he weeps like
the mother or father of those terrorists over what we do in his world. In
Genesis God says that Eve will suffer through being a mother, and then
Genesis uses the same word when it says that God suffers as he watches the
world doing what it does.

Jesus comes and lets the world do its violent worst to him, and that doesn't make a difference either. There'll be wars and rumors of wars, Jesus says (Mt 24:6). Thinkers and politicians in the modern world thought we might be able to abolish violence, abolish wars. The First World War was the war to end all wars. Jesus is more plausible. There will be wars and rumors of wars. They are an aspect of how the world is. We'd like to think it's different, but it isn't. So the Bible tells stories about war and terrorism and violence and invites us to face facts.

Second, the Old Testament makes rules about violence. In between the stories in Genesis and the stories in Judges are all the laws, the sets of rules for life, in Exodus, Leviticus, and Deuteronomy, and violence is one of their subjects. They don't make the mistake of telling people to abolish violence, telling them not to make war. Elsewhere the Old Testament does tell people not to exercise violence on their own behalf. It declares that vengeance belongs to God, so you don't take vengeance, and Paul takes up that statement and affirms it (Deut 32:35; Prov 25:21-22; Rom 12:19-20). Dinah, the girl who got seduced or raped, had some other brothers apart from the ones who took revenge in connection with what happened to her. One of these brothers was Joseph, and he was also the victim of his own brothers' violence. He later has the chance to get his own back, and they assume he'll take the chance, but he refuses. "Why would I do that?" he asks. He knows that the truly human thing to do, the thing that you do if you have faith in God, is turn the other cheek (Gen 50).

In a sense, then, the Old Testament does have an ideal of nonviolence, but it knows that in reality people will get involved in violence and war, and its sets of rules for life therefore apply themselves to curbing the effects of it, controlling it a bit. Only an eye for an eye and a tooth for a tooth, the punishment to fit the crime, not I'll kill you because you hurt me, which was Lemek's idea.

There's a strange rule in the Old Testament about a particular aspect of something that happens in war.

> When you go out for battle against your enemies, and Yahweh your God gives them into your hand and you take them captive, and you see among the captives a woman who's attractive in appearance, you fancy her, you get her for yourself as wife, you bring her inside your house, she shaves her head, trims her nails, removes her captive clothes from her, lives in your house, and bewails

her father and her mother for a whole month, and after this you have sex with her and you become her husband and she becomes your wife: if you then don't want her, you're to send her off for herself. You will not at all sell her for silver. You will not do what you like with her, since you've humbled her. (Deut 21:10-14)

Suppose you fight in a war, you win, and you capture one of the enemy's women and take her home in order to marry her. If you then decide you don't like her, the rule says, you can't turn her into your slave. Either she's your proper wife, or you let her go as a free woman.

Looked at from one angle it's an inhuman rule. It presupposes you have the right to capture a woman in that way. Shouldn't it simply tell you not to do it? But the rule is being realistic. That kind of thing happens in war. It's no use trying simply to outlaw it. So let's try to curb the negative results. Let's see whether we can offer the woman some protection. It's an example of a rule that works with God's making allowance for human hardness of heart and an example of the rules in the Torah thereby being an expression of love for one's neighbor.

The Old Testament models a practicality about war, violence, and terrorism. It doesn't say abolish it. It says do what you can to constrain it.

Third, the Old Testament thinks about questions concerning war and violence. It tries to understand them. It analyses issues. It does it in books such as Proverbs, Job, and Ecclesiastes. Ecclesiastes is the great repository of realism about the fact that we aren't going to abolish war. There is

A time of being loyal, a time of being hostile,
      a time of battle and a time of peace. (Eccles 3:8)

It doesn't mean that there's a time when you should make war and a time when you should make peace. It means that there simply are times when the one happens and times when the other happens, as there is a time for being born and a time for dying (Eccles 3:2). Accept the limits of what you can understand and achieve in that connection and in other connections, Ecclesiastes says.

Proverbs incorporates a number of sayings about national leadership. While it speaks in terms of kings, its comments apply to cultures where we are used to elected presidents and prime ministers. It assumes that the existence of authority is a good thing. The task of the authorities is to exercise control over the forces of evil and disorder in society. Proverbs talks about the way kings work and about the power for good and for bad that they have.

An issue people discuss in the United States is the fact that we have a problem with violence that nobody else in the world has, and we can't seem to do anything about it. Why can't we? It's not that we are more wicked than anyone else. Is it because we have a more dysfunctional system of government than most countries? There are so many checks and balances between president and Congress and Senate, and there is so much lobbying and wheeling and dealing that no one can do anything. Is that part of our problem? There is no governing authority in our country?

The horrifying stories in the book of Judges close with a declaration about what underlay the problem in the book. "There was no king in Israel. Each person would do what was all right in his own eyes" (Judg 21:25).

What kind of king is Judges talking about? Is it referring to a human king? Indeed, later on it is the case that when Israel has got kings, there aren't as many horrible stories to tell. There is now some social order. But is Judges rather referring to the fact that Israel has been ignoring God as its king? Given the way Paul talks about God's authority being exercised via the imperial government (see Rom 13), maybe we don't have to choose. They had no human king and they were ignoring God their king. The role of government is one of the issues the Old Testament analyses and reflects on.

Fourth, in the Old Testament God shares with us his nightmares and his dreams, his warnings and his promises. He does so through the prophets. It may be the most important way in which the prophets are significant for ethics. The prophets say, "If you carry on the way you're going, this is where you are going to end up": and its picture of where you will end up is often a picture of being overwhelmed by war. That prospect became a reality for Israel within the Old Testament, and you could say it became a reality in Europe in the twentieth century, and maybe it's becoming a wider reality in the twenty-first century. Perhaps we are all paying now for the way the West has related to the Middle Eastern world.

> Israel put its maker out of mind,
>> and built palaces,
> While Judah made many fortified towns,
>> but I will send off fire on its towns and it will consume its strongholds.
> (Hos 8:14)

I saw the Lord standing by the altar. He said:

Strike down the capitals so the thresholds shake;
> break them off onto the head of all of them.
The last of them I shall kill with the sword;
> not one of them will flee as a fugitive,
> no escapee will survive. (Amos 9:1)

Fortunately, the prophets share God's dreams as well as God's nightmares, his promises as well as his warnings.

It will come about at the end of the time:
The mountain of Yahweh's house will have become established,
> at the head of the mountains, and it will lift up higher than the hills.
All the nations will stream to it;
> many peoples will come and say,
"Come on, let's go up to Yahweh's mountain,
> to the house of Jacob's God,
So he may instruct us in his ways,
> and we may walk in his paths."
Because instruction will go out from Zion,
> Yahweh's word from Jerusalem.
He will exercise authority among the nations,
> and issue reproof to many peoples.
They'll beat their swords into hoes,
> their spears into pruning hooks.
Nation will not carry sword against nation;
> they will no more learn about battle.
Jacob's household, come on,
> let's walk by Yahweh's light! (Is 2:2-5)

Isaiah has a vision of nations flocking to Jerusalem to learn from God, so that God will then sort out the issues that divide them, and they will be free to focus on growing food instead of fighting wars. "Gonna lay down my sword and shield / Down by the riverside / Ain't gonna study war no more."

The reason why you can face the facts about violence, terrorism, and war that appear in the Bible stories and that we watch unfolding on our screens is that the Bible knows that violence, terrorism, and war are not the end of the story. The fact that Jesus was willing to be terrorized and killed, to be a blood-stained victim, but then that he didn't stay dead but that God raised him from death is the guarantee that God will fulfill his vision. His dream will become reality.

Fifth, the Old Testament prays about violence. Mostly, it's what the Psalms do. We may think that we live in violent times, but the people for whom the Psalms were written evidently lived in violent times as well. It may be the thing they prayed about more than anything else. They knew insecurity, and they prayed about it. They knew what it was like to be under attack, and they prayed about it. They knew fear, and they prayed about it.

They didn't pray because it would make them feel better. Maybe sometimes it did make them feel better, though sometimes it didn't. But the point about prayer is not to make you feel better. The point about prayer is to get God to do something. It's to lay hold on God to do what you cannot do. Prayer is utterly realistic. It starts from the fact that we cannot do anything, and it batters on the chest of the one who can, the one who has shared with us his dream and his vision, and it urges him to do what he said he would do.

After the San Bernardino shootings, the *New York Daily News* got angry about politicians who told people in such places that their prayers were with the community. The paper's front page screamed, "God Isn't Fixing This," and the paper argued that we need gun control, not calls for prayer. Now I loved the way the paper called out the politicians over the platitude they express when they say, "Our prayers are with you." The platitude implies that distorted understanding of prayer, that prayer is designed to make you feel better, that prayer works horizontally. I'm also glad that the paper called for action, though it was ironic that in California we already have as tight gun control as anyone. But it's very often the case that the Bible believes in both-and, not either-or. Those sets of rules in the Torah point toward gun control and other action. But the Psalms also invite prayer. Prayer without rules might not get us anywhere; rules without prayer also won't get us anywhere.

FOR REFLECTION AND DISCUSSION

1. Have you got a story about violence to tell?

2. What rules or laws about violence would help with regard to that kind of story or others?

3. What are your reflections about violence in your context?

4. How can you picture God's nightmare and God's dream in relation to situations of violence that you know?

5. How can you pray about violence now?

12

SHALOM

The Hebrew word *shalom* is a bit like English words such as *relationship* and *community*, in that it is a warm word but with a range of meanings that make it impossible to define. It's thus translated in a number of different ways, including "peace," "well-being," "good health," "prosperity," "favor," "rest," and "safety." In Western thinking, people sometimes talk about the concept of "shalom," but one needs to distinguish between that concept of "shalom" in Western thinking and the meaning(s) of the word *shalom* in the Old Testament. I will try to keep the distinction clear by using "shalom" to refer to the Western concept and *shalom* to denote the Hebrew word. It's important to hold onto the fact that the Old Testament can be talking about "shalom" without using the word *shalom*, and it can use the word *shalom* without implying the concept of "shalom" in that Western sense.

The two main areas covered by *shalom* are peaceful relations between people and the broader reality of things going well for people. Here are some examples of the first meaning, peaceful relations:

> We've done only good with you, and sent you off in *shalom*. (Gen 26:29)

> They became hostile to him and couldn't speak with *shalom* to him. (Gen 37:4)

> I shall put *shalom* in the country and you will lie down with no one making you tremble. (Lev 26:6)

In those contexts one can take *shalom* to mean "peace." But even in this connection there is a difference between the two languages. When the Old Testament talks about peace, it is referring to peace between people, not inner peace. Hebrew doesn't have a word for inner peace, a feeling of peace. One way the Old Testament talks about inner peace is by urging people not to be fearful—"don't be afraid" is thus one of the most common exhortations in the Old Testament (e.g., Gen 15:1; 21:17; 26:24; 35:17; 43:23; 46:3; 50:19, 21). Another way of referring to inner peace is to use one of the several related words for confidence or a sense of security (e.g., Prov 1:33; 3:29; Is 30:15).

In contrast, *peace* in English can refer both to relationships between people and to a feeling we have inside, and the two may not be related—you can have peaceful relationships but not feel peaceful, or you can feel peaceful but not have peaceful relationships. Both *peace* and *shalom* are thus words with ranges of meanings; they illustrate the point I made just now. In English *peace* can denote inner peace or relationship peace, but not well-being, in Hebrew, *shalom* can denote well-being or relationship peace, but not inner peace. Here are some examples of *shalom* meaning that things are well:

> You will go to your ancestors in *shalom*. (Gen 15:15)

> He said to them, "Does he have *shalom*?" They said, "*shalom*."
> > [That is, "He said, 'Are things well with him?' They said, 'They're well.'"] (Gen 29:6)

> Yahweh bless you and keep you! Yahweh shine his face toward you and be gracious to you!
> Yahweh lift his face toward you and make *shalom* for you! (Num 6:24-26)

> I am giving him my pact, *shalom* [that things will be well]. (Num 25:12)

> Go, with *shalom* [things will be well]. (Judg 18:6)

Here are some examples from the Psalms:

> Yahweh gives vigor to his people;
> > Yahweh blesses his people with *shalom*. (Ps 29:11)

> The humble—they'll enter into possession of the country
> > and revel in abundance of *shalom*. (Ps 37:11)

> There's no integrity in my body by reason of your condemnation;
> > there's no *shalom* in my bones by reason of my wrongdoings. (Ps 38:3)

> I will listen to what the God Yahweh will speak,
> > because he will speak of *shalom*,

To his people and to those committed to him,
>   those who do not turn back to dimwittedness.
Indeed his deliverance is near for people who live in awe of him,
>   so that his splendor may settle in our country.
Commitment and truthfulness—they've met;
>   faithfulness and *shalom*—they've embraced. (Ps 85:8-10)

May Yahweh bless you from Zion;
>   you can look at the good things of Jerusalem,
All the days of your life,
>   and look at your grandchildren;
>   *shalom* [be] on Israel! (Ps 128:5-6)

Here are some examples from the prophets:

The effect of faithfulness will be *shalom*,
>   the service of faithfulness will be calm and confidence permanently.
My people will live in an abode characterized by *shalom*,
>   in secure dwellings, in carefree places to settle down. (Is 32:17-18)

I am Yahweh your God,
>   the one who teaches you to succeed,
Who directs you in the way you should go—
>   if only you had heeded my orders.
Your *shalom* would have been like a river,
>   your faithfulness like the waves of the sea.
Your offspring would have been like the sand,
>   the people who went out from you like its grains.
Your name would not be cut off,
>   not be annihilated, from before me. . . .
There's no *shalom*
>   (Yahweh has said) for faithless people. (Is 48:17-19, 22)

Chastisement to bring us *shalom* was on him,
>   and by means of his being hurt there was healing for us. (Is 53:5)

Because mountains may move away, hills slip,
>   but my commitment will not move away from you.
My pact of *shalom* will not slip,
>   the one who has compassion for you, Yahweh, has said.

Humble, tossing, not comforted—
> here I am, resting your stones in antimony.

I'll found you with sapphires,
> make chalcedony your pinnacles,

Your gateways into sparkling stones,
> your entire border into delightful stones.

All your children will be Yahweh's disciples;
> great will be your children's *shalom*.

In faithfulness you'll establish yourself;
> you can be far from oppression. (Is 54:10-14)

Seek the *shalom* of the town where I've exiled you; plead on its behalf with Yahweh, because in its *shalom* will be *shalom* for you. . . . Because I myself acknowledge the intentions that I'm formulating for you (Yahweh's declaration), intentions for your *shalom* and not for bad things, to give you a future, a hope. (Jer 29:7, 11)

Shalom in the sense of well-being is an all-embracing idea. When Julian of Norwich went through a death-like experience, God reassured her that "all shall be well, and all shall be well, and all manner of thing shall be well." God was giving her an assurance about *shalom*. The trouble is that when a word becomes all-embracing, it becomes so vague it loses meaning. Another problem is that, as a result, we can pour into it whatever we want to—as we do with words such as *community* and *relationship*.

If you were to ask a prophet or a psalmist or some other Old Testament figure to expound what *shalom* in the sense of well-being was, what might he or she say? A way to answer that question might be to think of it in connection with different aspects of being human. So well-being is a facet of

- *Community life.* Well-being means the community is functioning well. People are getting on with each other. They are able to dig wells and terrace hills so as to grow fruit trees. They are able to celebrate the festivals and to celebrate marriages and births, and to mark people's passing. They live fairly with one another and share fairly with one another.

- *Family life.* It means the different generations get on with one another. It means (adult) brothers and sisters get on with each other. It means that there is proper respect for sexual boundaries. It means people have satisfying work and that the work of the family gets done.

- *Bodily life.* It means individuals are able to walk and talk, to see and hear, to sleep and wake up. It means they can eat and drink. It means they nurse, grow, learn, mature, and move toward being "full of years." It means they can sit under their vine and their fig tree.
- *Inner life.* It means people experience joy, satisfaction, commitment, mercy, forgiveness, security, wisdom, mourning, comfort. Although the Old Testament would not talk about inner "peace," then, it would assume that inner peace was part of well-being.
- *Religious life.* It means they are engaged with God in praise (they know what God has done for them and they celebrate it), in prayer and protest (urging God to relieve them when they are under attack and in danger), in thanksgiving (to give public testimony to his answering such prayers), in obedience (acknowledging God in their lives), and in penitence (when obedience fails).

There is no suggestion in the Old Testament that it is our job to work for *shalom* in the world or seek to further *shalom* or seek to extend it, as there is no suggestion in the New Testament that we are to work for the kingdom of God or seek to further it or seek to extend it. *Shalom* is God's promise, not our responsibility. Yet promises of *shalom* come in ethical contexts in the sense that ethical failure means we surrender any right to look for *shalom* in our lives.

That lack applies to the way the Old Testament speaks (or rather doesn't speak) about seeking peace. The exceptions may prove the rule. Joseph is someone who seeks peace with his brothers, though in light of previous comments, it is noteworthy that Genesis doesn't use the word *shalom* in this connection. Further, when Joseph does (eventually) seek a restoration of peaceful relationships with his brothers, he does so as someone who is in a position of power. My guess is that one reason why the Old Testament doesn't speak much about Israel seeking peace is that Israel is usually in a position of weakness and subordination to major powers such as Egypt, Assyria, Babylon, Persia, and Greece. Its vocation is to trust God to bring about its *shalom.* The notion of seeking *shalom* in the Old Testament presupposes two more or less equal parties. A neat example is when Israel sends a message of *shalom* to a king, seeking to pass through his land without causing him any loss (Deut 2:26); unwisely he refuses. More shrewdly, another people get

Joshua to make *shalom* with them when they are the weak party by deceiving Joshua about who they are, and he has to keep his commitment of *shalom* with them even though they had lied their way into it.

FOR REFLECTION AND DISCUSSION

1. Where are the best expressions of *shalom* in your community?

2. Where is the biggest shortfall in *shalom*?

3. Where might ethical action issue in more *shalom*?

4. Is there anywhere where you have the power to seek *shalom*?

13

JUSTICE

I read recently that a reduction of state funding caused by the state of Louisiana's financial crisis has meant that there are many fewer public defenders available to represent poor people when they appear in the New Orleans criminal court. As a result, there are fifty-two people stuck in jail in New Orleans without representation. The issue at stake, says the city's chief public defender, is "Do poor people deserve equal justice? Do poor people deserve justice at all?" Ironically and also scandalously, a further significant source of funding for the courts comes from punitive court fees and fines. So another commentator observes that "a court is supposed to be where justice is done, not where revenues are generated." What principles in the administration of justice does the Torah emphasize?

First, the community needs to make sure it has a proper system for administering justice.

> You're to make yourself authorities and officials in all the communities that Yahweh your God is giving you for your clans. They're to exercise faithful authority for the people. You will not twist the exercise of authority. You will not honor persons. You will not accept a bribe, because a bribe blinds the eyes of smart people and twists the words of faithful people. You're to pursue absolute faithfulness. (Deut 16:18-20)

This principle meant appointing a group of people who could "exercise faithful authority" on the people's behalf. In other words, they have authority to make decisions, and they are under obligation to do so in a faithful way—a totally faithful way, with no compromises. They will find guilty people guilty and innocent people innocent. They won't be professional lawyers but neither will they be like a jury that sits just for one case, and neither will the situation be like a court where one judge decides things.

How are they to make their decisions? One basic guideline is that accusations should be accompanied by evidence, such as the testimony of witnesses. For a capital offense, in particular, there need to be two or three witnesses, not just one.

> At the mouth of two witnesses or three witnesses is a person to be put to death. He will not be put to death at the mouth of one witness. The hand of the witnesses is to be the first against him to put him to death, and the hand of the entire people afterward, so you burn away the bad thing from among you. (Deut 17:6-7)

Requiring two or three witnesses is not an infallible rule; people can be bribed (see 1 Kings 21). But it's better than nothing. And requiring witnesses to begin the execution process has a chance of making people of average honor hesitate. There are other safeguards.

> One witness will not stand up against someone regarding any waywardness or regarding any wrong, in connection with any wrong that he does. At the mouth of two witnesses or at the mouth of three witnesses the thing will stand up. When a felonious witness stands up against someone to avow defiance against him, the two people who have the argument are to take their stand before Yahweh, before the priests or the authorities who are there at that time, and the authorities will inquire well. There, the witness is a false witness: he has avowed a falsehood against his brother. You're to do to him as he intended to do to his brother, and burn away the bad thing from among you, while the remaining people will hear and live in awe, and will never again do the likes of this bad deed among you. Your eye will not pity: life for life, eye for eye, tooth for tooth, hand for hand, foot for foot. (Deut 19:15-21)

So in case of dispute, the two people are to come before Yahweh to the priests or the people on duty at the time, who are to inquire—which likely means inquiring of Yahweh rather than trying the case themselves. And if it is determined that someone has given false testimony, then the community is to apply to them the penalty that they sought for the person they accused. That's one of the situations in which the "eye for an eye" rule applies. It's a poetic formulation—Israelites would be too sensible to think that you poke someone's eye out to make good for their poking an eye out. It's a vivid way of saying that there should be no compromise in favor of the person who has falsely accused a fellow member of the community.

For a capital offense such as murder, there's another issue.

> You're to distinguish for yourself three towns within your country that Yahweh your God is giving you to take possession of it, so any killer may be able to flee there. This is the thing with the killer who flees there so he may live—one who strikes down his neighbor without knowing, and wasn't hostile to him in previous days, but who comes into the forest with his neighbor to chop wood, and his hand thrusts with the ax to cut down a tree and the iron slips off the wooden part and finds his neighbor and he dies. He can flee to one of these towns so he may live, so the blood-restorer doesn't pursue after the killer when his feelings are hot and overtake him, because the journey is long, and strike him down a fatal blow, when he wasn't liable to the death sentence because he hadn't been hostile to him in previous days. . . . But when an individual is hostile to his neighbor, lies in wait for him, sets on him, and strikes him down with a fatal blow so he dies, and he flees to one of these towns, the elders of his town are to send and get him from there and give him into the hand of the blood-restorer, so he dies. Your eye will not pity him. You're to burn away from Israel the blood of the person who is free of guilt, so things may be good for you. (Deut 19:2-6, 11-13)

When someone is murdered, it's the responsibility of a senior member of the family to see to the killing of the murderer. He is the "blood-restorer." The blood of murder victims cries out from the ground, as Abel's blood did. The cry can't just be ignored. It's as if things have got out of kilter in the community and the world, and they need leveling. But suppose a person who killed someone did so by accident? If the blood-restorer kills that person, it makes the situation worse. So Israel has some asylum towns where a person who did kill someone accidentally can hide. The blood-restorer isn't allowed to get him there, and there's time for some investigation of where the truth lies.

Supposing someone has been killed out in the country and no one knows who did the killing? The blood still cries out, the land is still defiled. So the people in the nearest town have to take responsibility for the murder and make a special offering in order to expiate the blood, to burn it away, to restore equilibrium (see Deut 21).

In the administration of justice, there's to be no accepting of bribes, and justice must be the same for everyone.

> You will not twist the exercise of authority in respect of a resident alien or orphan. (Deut 24:17)

> You will not bend a poor person's ruling when he's in an argument. A false statement: stay distant from it. Someone who is free of guilt and is in the right: don't kill him, because I do not treat the person who is in the right as in the wrong. A bribe: don't accept it, because a bribe blinds people who can see and overturns the statements of people who are in the right. A resident alien: you will not afflict him; you yourselves know the feelings of a resident alien, because you were resident aliens in Egypt. (Ex 23:6-9)

There is the obvious temptation to favor the people who are big in the village—people such as the members of the group of elders. But there is also an opposite temptation.

> You will not do evil in making a decision: you will not honor the person of someone who is a poor person and you will not respect the person of someone who is big; you will make a decision for your fellow with faithfulness. (Lev 19:15)

> You will not carry an empty report. Don't put your hand in with a faithless person to become a felonious witness. You will not follow a majority to act badly. You will not avow in an argument so as to bend after a majority, so as to bend it. Neither will you defer to a poor person in his argument. (Ex 23:1-3)

It could be tempting to be so sympathetic to the poor or so suspicious of the big guys or so concerned to avoid the temptation to favor the important people that you side with the poor just because they are poor. If someone with nothing steals a sheep from someone who has many, shouldn't one be sympathetic? Yes, but not so as to pervert justice.

There isn't an appeal court in Israel, but there is a higher court. The Torah recognizes that sometimes the local elders may not be able to see the right decision, so then they are to go to the sanctuary and consult the Levites, the assistant ministers whose job includes teaching and looking after the sanctuary, and to go and see the person who's on duty that day.

> When a matter is too hard for you to decide, between one instance of bloodshed and another, between one judgment and another, or between one assault and another (matters of argument in your communities), you're to set off and go up to the site that Yahweh your God chooses and come to the Levitical priests, to the person in authority who's there at that time, and inquire. They'll tell you

the word of decision, and you're to act in accordance with the word that they tell you, from that site that Yahweh chooses. (Deut 17:8-10)

When someone gives his neighbor silver or things to keep but it's stolen from the man's house, if the thief is found, he's to make good double. If the thief isn't found, the owner of the house is to draw near to God [to testify] that he didn't lay hand on his neighbor's work. Over any breach of trust, over an ox or donkey or sheep or garment or any loss about which someone says, "This is it," the thing involving the two of them is to come to God. The one whom God says is in the wrong is to make good double to his neighbor. (Ex 22:7-9)

It looks as if the priest's job wasn't to go over the case and work out the answer on the basis of his superior knowledge or insight. Rather it was to consult God, maybe by using the Urim and Tummim, the Yeses and Noes—some equivalent to tossing a coin, or rather tossing two coins, in the belief that God would make sure the coins fell right.

FOR REFLECTION AND DISCUSSION

1. Do you know someone who has been treated unjustly by the legal system? How and why did it happen?

2. What are the big obstacles to fair operating of the legal system in your community?

3. Are there ways in which the legal system in your community works against poor people or foreigners?

4. Are there ways in which election to office skews the legal system in your community?

5. Are there ways in which wealth perverts the operation of the legal system?

6. What could you do about unfairness in the legal system in your community?

14

REPARATION

In Western countries, we commonly think of wrongdoings such as theft, assault, or fraud as transgressions of the law that are to be investigated by the state. People have committed a crime and will be punished by law. They might have to pay a fine or they might have to go to prison. The Old Testament is more inclined to see such wrongdoings as offenses against another person (and against God), and the obligation upon wrongdoers is to put things right with the other person (and with God). The community's job is to supervise that process.

So on one hand there's no such thing as imprisonment or fines as a punishment for a crime, because there really isn't a concept of crime. There are exceptions that prove the rule; from time to time a king may put someone in jail, but that's because they've offended the king. And there's no allowance for revenge or vengeance in the sense of someone taking their feelings out on a person who has wronged them. Again there are exceptions that prove the rule, such as Lemek's seventy-sevenfold revenge (which we noted in chapter eleven, on violence)—but that's not the kind of action Israel approves of. When words such as *vengeance* come in Old Testament translations, we would do better to think of the action they refer to as redress or compensation. The place of punishment and vengeance is taken by the idea that someone who wrongs someone else must put the wrong right.

A basic principle in community relationships is that there should be honor and honesty between people. To put it in our terms, we know what a pound or a kilo is, and we know what an ounce or a gram is, and it's always the same.

Further, for most of Old Testament times people worked by barter or by valuing things in silver pieces of a known weight; a sheqel was a weight in silver before it was a unit of currency. In this connection, too, it was important that weights were always the same. The principles of honor, honesty, and fairness are an outworking of mutual love, love for one's neighbor.

> You will not have in your bag two stones, big and small. You will not have in your house two measures, big and small. You're to have a stone that's perfect and faithful, a measure that's perfect and faithful, in order that your days may be many on the land that Yahweh your God is giving you. Because anyone who does these things, anyone who does evil, is an offense to Yahweh your God. (Deut 25:13-16)

The basic principle is the one stated in the rule about an eye for an eye and a tooth for a tooth, to which we have already seen the Torah refers in more than one connection. Another of these connections is when you have to make good for something you deprive someone of.

> Someone who strikes down an animal is to make good for it, life for life. An individual who causes an injury to his fellow: as he did, so it's to be done to him, fracture for fracture, eye for eye, tooth for tooth. As he causes an injury to the person, so it's to be caused to him. (Lev 24:18-20)

If you kill someone else's animal, you have to give him one of yours. That rule could be taken literally. What about the words concerning fracture for fracture, eye for eye, and so on? I noted in chapter thirteen that this formulation looks more figurative than literal—it's almost poetic or parabolic. Whereas it makes sense to think in terms of literally replacing an animal such an ox or a sheep that a family depends on for its livelihood, it doesn't help the family to injure the head of the other family because he injured the head of your family. More likely the idea is that the head of the other family is to make up for the injury. If father can't drive the plow until his leg heals, then the head of the other family must do so. Whatever is the injury, he has to make up for it in this way.

> When someone opens a cistern or when someone digs a cistern and doesn't cover it, and an ox or a donkey falls into it, the cistern's owner is to make good. He's to give back silver to its owner, but the dead thing will be his. When someone's ox injures his neighbor's ox and it dies, they're to sell the live ox and divide

the silver, and also divide the dead thing. If it was known that the ox was in-clined to gore in previous days and its owner doesn't keep it in, he must defi-nitely make good, ox for ox, but the dead thing will be his. (Ex 21:33-36)

When men fight and they hit a pregnant woman and her children come out but there's no harm, he's definitely to make compensation, as the woman's husband may lay on him, or give it by arbitration. If there's harm, you're to give life for life, eye for eye, tooth for tooth, hand for hand, foot for foot, burn for burn, wound for wound, bruise for bruise. When someone strikes his servant's eye or his handmaid's eye and devastates it, he's to send them off as a free person because of their eye. If someone makes his servant's tooth or his handmaid's tooth fall out, he's to send them off as a free person because of their tooth. (Ex 21:22-27)

Someone who strikes a man down so he dies is absolutely to be put to death. Someone who didn't set a trap, but God made him fall into his hand: I shall set a site for you where he may flee. But when someone asserts himself against his neighbor so as to kill him with shrewdness, you're to take him from beside my altar to die. Someone who strikes down his father or his mother is absolutely to be put to death. Someone who kidnaps a person, and he sells him or he's found in his possession, is absolutely to be put to death. Someone who slights his father or his mother is absolutely to be put to death. (Ex 21:12-17)

A variant on that principle concerns when you get someone to look after an animal and something happens to it.

When someone gives his neighbor a donkey or ox or sheep or any animal to keep and it dies or is injured or is taken off, with no one seeing, there's to be an oath to Yahweh between the two of them that he hasn't laid his hand on his neighbor's work. Its owner is to accept it, and he's not to make good. But if it's actually stolen from him, he's to make good to its owner. If it gets mauled at all, he's to bring it as evidence. For something mauled, he's not to make good. (Ex 22:10-13)

If the other person can't really be blamed for what happens, then he's not liable—but the two people have to come before God about whether he is telling the truth. If the animal gets mauled, he doesn't have to make good. It's not his fault. But if it gets stolen because of his negligence . . .

When someone steals an ox or sheep and slaughters it or sells it, he's to make good with five from the herd for the ox or four from the fold for the sheep. . . .

He's definitely to make good; if he doesn't have it, he's to be sold for his theft. If
the thing stolen (either ox or donkey or sheep, alive) is actually found in his
possession, he's to make good double. (Ex 22:1, 3-4)

A similar principle emerges from the rule about a man injuring his
neighbor. If you maliciously and irresponsibly attack your neighbor and he
dies, that's one thing. It's a murder rap. But if he's just incapacitated, you have
to accept responsibility for the consequences. You pay the medical bills, and
(again) you do his plowing until he's able to do so again.

When people get into an argument and one strikes his neighbor with a stone
or with his fist and he doesn't die but he falls into bed, if he gets up and walks
about outside on his staff, the one who struck him can be free of guilt, only he's
to pay for his sitting around, and definitely to get him healed. (Ex 21:18-19)

On the other hand, that same set of rules declares that a life for a life applies more literally to murder. You don't just have to put things right in connection with the human being whom you've wronged. The imposition of a
death penalty presupposes you've done something wrong against God or
against the very principles on which the community's life is based. So the
Torah talks in terms of the death penalty in connection with murder, with
kidnapping, and with a serious assault against a parent or cursing a parent.
All these offenses involve taking someone's life away.

When God is starting the world going again after the great deluge, he lays
down some principles for ongoing life. They include:

Your blood, belonging to your lives, I will require;
    from the hand of every living thing I will require it.
From the hand of a human being,
    from the hand of an individual for his brother,
    I will require the life of a human being.
One who pours out the blood of a human being,
    through a human being his blood will pour out.
Because it was in God's image
    that he made a human being. (Gen 9:5-6)

There's no doubt here that murder is a capital offense, and that the person
who is offended is God. It's God who "requires the life" of someone who deliberately kills someone else. There's some ambiguity about the rest of the

ruling, so it's not really a proof text for capital punishment. Does God mean that the murderer's blood will pour out "through a human being" in the sense of "on account of a human being"—the human being whose blood the murderer has shed? Or does he mean "by means of a human being"—that the community is responsible to see that the murderer is executed? And in the latter case, is God saying he requires this action, or is he commenting on the way one murder will lead to another? The last line is apparently then implying that nevertheless something positive does find expression in that grim dynamic; it is the fact that God made humanity in his image that makes murder wrong. It is an assault on God, as an attack on a portrait of a king is an attack on the king. But if God is saying that humanity is responsible to take action against murderers, the implication of the last line might be different. It could rather be that God made humanity in his image to rule the earth, and one aspect of its ruling the earth on God's behalf is to take action against the defacing of that image.

It can seem dispiriting when the meaning of a scriptural passage is subject to debate, but there is often a silver lining to this cloud. In this case there are two silver linings. One is that God's main concern is to stop people killing each other, not to have to cope with the consequences when they do kill each other. The other is that the ruling presupposes that it's possible to be certain when someone is guilty of murder, though the Old Testament itself recognizes that often it's not possible—no one saw it happen. In countries that practice capital punishment, from time to time people get executed for murders they never committed. Maybe it would be as well to be on the safe side and not execute anyone because it's the punishment you can't undo.

The rule about execution also applies to consensual adultery, though not in connection with rape.

> When a man is found sleeping with a woman who's married to a husband, they are to die, both of them, the man who slept with the woman and the woman. So you will burn away the bad thing from Israel. When there's a girl who's a young girl betrothed to a man, and a man finds her in the town and sleeps with her, you're to take the two of them out to the gateway of that town and pelt them with stones so they die (the girl on account of the fact that she didn't cry out in the town, and the man on account of the fact that he humbled his neighbor's wife). So you will burn away the bad thing from among you. But if the man finds the betrothed girl in the fields and the man takes hold of her and

sleeps with her, the man who slept with her is alone to die. You're not to do anything to the girl. There's no wrong that deserves death attaching to her, because this thing is like an individual who sets upon his neighbor and kills him, because he found her in the fields. Should the betrothed girl have cried out, there was no one to deliver her. (Deut 22:22-27)

There's something bad in Israel that needs burning away when people have committed adultery. It strikes at the foundations of community life and at the foundation principle of the relationship between God and Israel. To put it another way, there's nothing more basic than faithfulness in relationships between God and Israel and in relationships between Israelites, and adultery compromises that principle.

Yet it's striking that the Old Testament tells quite a few stories about actions such as adultery to which the death penalty is attached, but it never speaks of someone being judicially executed. It seems that Israel was no more literal about these rules than it was about the rules concerning an eye for an eye, which is the principle it illustrates. The death penalty was a theory, not a practice.

This odd fact links with a broader issue that is hard for Western readers to recognize, which we noted in the introduction to this book. Although we refer to the Torah as law, it's not a collection of statutes for implementation in a court. When kings came to the throne in the Middle East, it was common for them to issue collections of rules that can be compared with rules in the Torah. These kings were then not saying "these are the laws you must implement" or even "these are the laws I intend to implement." They were saying something more like "these are illustrations of the kind of principles that I accept." If you're feeling a bit cynical or disheartened, you can compare them with election promises. So when we read in the Old Testament that different wrongdoings are subject to the death penalty, the implication is "this is a really terrible thing."

There is another qualification to the principle of "an eye for an eye." In the case of theft, the person in the wrong has not merely to make up for what he stole or defrauded. He's to make up double.

When someone gives his neighbor silver or things to keep but it's stolen from the man's house, if the thief is found, he's to make good double. If the thief isn't found, the owner of the house is to draw near to God [to testify] that he didn't lay hand on his neighbor's work. . . . The one whom God says is in the wrong is to make good double to his neighbor. (Ex 22:7-9)

Presumably that's intended as a deterrent. If all you have to do is return something you stole, you have nothing to lose by stealing. In another version of a rule for cases such as these, the thief is simply to add one-fifth to the value of the thing he took by fraud.

> When a person does wrong and commits a trespass against Yahweh and is deceptive toward his fellow in connection with something entrusted or something deposited with him or by seizing, or he defrauds his fellow, or he finds something lost and is deceptive about it and swears in falsehood, regarding one of all the things that a human being may do so as to do wrong by them: when he does wrong and is liable, he's to give back the thing that he seized or the thing that he got by fraud or the thing that was entrusted to him or the lost thing that he found, or anything regarding which he swore in falsehood. He's to make good for it in terms of its total sum, and add to it a fifth of it. He's to give it to the person to whom it belongs, on the day of his reparation. (Lev 6:2-5)

There are thus differences between different versions of many of the rules in the Torah. These differences reflect how the rules came into being in different historical or social contexts. For instance, I take the rules in Exodus to reflect the life of a village community in the time of the Judges, whereas the rules in Leviticus or Deuteronomy come from life in urban Jerusalem several centuries later.

FOR REFLECTION AND DISCUSSION

1. In your context, what are the trickiest ways in which people operate with dishonest "stones" or "measures"?

2. Are there ways in which in your context people need to rework their assumptions about how people have to make up for their wrongdoing?

3. Are there points where in your context penalties of more than an eye for an eye are imposed?

4. Are there ways in which Christians, at least, should expect to bring God into judicial procedures?

5. What are the points where in your context more attention needs to be paid to burning away what's bad as well as restoring things for the sake of people who have been wronged?

15

SABBATH

In our Sunday services we regularly pray for the unemployed, and someone in our congregation, when they lead that prayer, always adds "and the under-employed." It makes me want also to add "and the overemployed," not least in our context where many people work two or three part-time jobs because they cannot get a "proper" job, and where they may well have to work longer hours because their various part-time jobs don't come with health care.

God's job as creator was a thoroughly full-time one. You can actually count eight aspects of the work involved in creation, which have to fit into the six days that are available in order to get the job finished in a week. But God does it, and then sits back and admires his work.

> God saw all that he had made, and there—it was very good. And there was evening and there was morning, the sixth day. So the heavens and the earth were finished, with all their forces. On the seventh day God had finished his work that he had been doing, so on the seventh day he stopped from all his work that he had been doing. God blessed the seventh day and made it sacred, be-cause on it God stopped from his entire work of creation that he had been doing. (Gen 1:31–2:3)

Of course it's a picture, and in some sense he could have done it all in one go, instantly, and in another sense he didn't stop at all—he still had to keep the world going. An Israelite farmer would understand: you can't not feed the animals or not milk the cows for a day. But you can stop initiating, stop cre-ating, give up the things that you can leave until tomorrow. For human beings, stopping is an act of faith. Suppose the ground is too hard to plow if you leave it one more day? It's an act of trust in God not to work for a day. The manna story illustrates the point.

> Yahweh said to Moses, "Here, I'm going to rain bread for you from the heavens so the people may go out and glean a day's allocation on its day, in order that I may test it, whether it will walk by my instruction or not. On the sixth day they will prepare what they bring in, and it will be double what they glean each day." . . . On Friday they gleaned double bread, two gallons for a single person. All the assembly's leaders came and told Moses. He said to them, "It's what Yahweh spoke. Tomorrow is a stopping, a sacred Sabbath [a *shabbat*, a "stop"] for Yahweh. Bake what you will bake and boil what you will boil, and lay up for yourselves all that's surplus for keeping until morning." . . . On the seventh day some of the people went out to glean, but they didn't find any. (Ex 16:4-5, 22-23, 27)

It was impossible enough to believe that God would supply them with food in the wilderness day by day. But believing that they could gather twice as much on Friday and that it would not go bad and that anyway there wouldn't be any there on Saturday . . .

Those first two references to God making the seventh day special say nothing about it being a day of rest. The main point is that it's a day that's different. When God eventually lays the law down about the Sabbath in the Ten Commandments, making it a day that's different is again the point.

> Be mindful of the Sabbath day to make it sacred. For six days you can serve and do all your work, but the seventh day is a Sabbath for Yahweh your God. You will not do any work, you, your son or your daughter, your servant or your handmaid, your animal, or your resident alien who is in your communities. Because in six days Yahweh made the heavens, the earth, the sea, and all that's in them, and settled down on the seventh day. That's why Yahweh blessed the seventh day and made it sacred. (Ex 20:8-11)

On the Sabbath you don't work. I see little indication in the Old Testament that work was an idol for people. In Western culture it is an idol. I'm thinking now of people who love their work and don't want to stop, not of people who fear they won't have enough to feed their children if they don't work seven days. The ethical implication of the Sabbath is thus its implication for the way we look at work.

What of the point about including your children, your servants, your animals, and the resident alien? The next version of the Sabbath command nuances the point.

> For six days you can do your work, but on the seventh day you're to stop, in order that your ox and your donkey may find relief and the offspring of your handmaid and the resident alien may find refreshment. (Ex 23:12)

In effect it declares that these people and the animals weren't made for the Sabbath. The Sabbath was made for them. One can imagine it would be tempting for the head of the household to make sure that the inner family had their day off but to do so by assuming that the servants and the resident aliens did the work that needed doing, such as cooking and feeding the animals. It's in this connection that God first speaks about the Sabbath being a day for finding refreshment, and the people he says are to find refreshment are not the inner family but those other, more marginal people (and the animals!). If we don't make it possible for people to feed their families without working seven days, in our own way we are breaking the Sabbath. And at least in this connection, it may not matter if different people keep different Sabbaths; the point is that people should have the opportunity for refreshment.

Remember that you know what it's like to be a servant, the next version of the Ten Commandments reminds Israel.

> Keep the Sabbath day so as to make it sacred, as Yahweh your God has ordered you. For six days you can serve and do all your work, but the seventh day is a Sabbath for Yahweh your God. You will not do any work, you, your son or your daughter, your servant or your handmaid, your ox or your donkey or any of your animals, or the resident alien who is in your communities, in order that your servant and your handmaid may rest like you. You're to be mindful that you were a servant in the country of Egypt, but Yahweh your God got you out of there with a strong hand and an extended arm. That's why Yahweh your God has ordered you to make the Sabbath day. (Deut 5:12-15)

You were servants in Egypt. It should be easy to be sympathetic with your servants.

I'm the priest-in-charge of a church. I work hard on Sunday, at least until I get home for a large sherry sometime between 12:30 and 4:00. Another set of instructions put a challenge before people like me, because they reaffirm the rule about the Sabbath in the context of God's issuing instructions about building the portable sanctuary in the wilderness, when Israel is on its way to the Promised Land.

> Yahweh said to Moses: "You yourself, speak to the Israelites: Nevertheless, my Sabbaths you're to keep, because it's a sign between me and you through your generations, for acknowledging that I Yahweh have made you sacred. . . . Because in six days Yahweh made the heavens and the earth, and on the seventh day he stopped and found refreshment." (Ex 31:12-13, 17)

Working for God doesn't give you an excuse for working seven days. This version of the rule adds that the Sabbath is a sign of Israel being God's people. It made them stand out. Nobody else observed the Sabbath in the sense of having a work-free day once a week. It's still the case that Jewish observance of the Sabbath raises questions for the Gentile world. Among other things, it exactly raises the question whether we have our attitude to work right. (Boldly, this version of the Sabbath command even adds that the first Sabbath was the day when God found refreshment.)

The principle that keeping Sabbath is a distinctive mark of God's people links with way Nehemiah got steamed up about Sabbath breaking in Jerusalem.

> I saw people in Judah treading winepresses on the Sabbath and bringing grain heaps and stacking them on donkeys, and also wine, grapes, figs, and every load, and bringing them into Jerusalem on the Sabbath day. I testified on the day when they sold provisions and when the Tyrians who lived there were bringing fish and all merchandise and selling on the Sabbath to Judahites and in Jerusalem, and I argued with the important people in Judah: "What is this bad thing that you're doing, and profaning the Sabbath day?" . . . When the gateways of Jerusalem grew dark before the Sabbath, I said that the doors should shut, and I said that they should not open them until after the Sabbath. Given that I put in place some of my boys at the gateways, no load would come in on the Sabbath day. The merchants and the people selling all merchandise stayed the night outside Jerusalem once or twice, but I testified against them: "Why are you staying the night opposite the wall? If you do it again, I'll lay hands on you"; from that time they didn't come on the Sabbath. I said to the Levites that they should purify themselves and come keep watch over the gateways to make the Sabbath day sacred. (Neh 13:15-17, 19-22)

The Jerusalemites were living just the same way as the merchants from Tyre, that great business city that knew what was really important. Except that it didn't. So Nehemiah, who was a businesslike and fearless guy, took practical steps to make sure of preserving the distinctive nature of life in Jerusalem. He wasn't the first. The merchants in Bethel in Amos's day couldn't wait for the Sabbath to be over so they could start swindling again.

> Listen to this, you who trample the needy person,
>> who make the humble people in the country cease,
> Saying, "When will the new month be over,
>> so we can sell wheat,
>> and the Sabbath, so we can lay out grain—
> Making the barrel measure small but the sheqel big,
>> falsifying the scales by deceit." (Amos 8:4-5)

The implication is that the Sabbath stands for things working God's way, for a bit of realization of the new Jerusalem (or the new Bethel), for things being characterized by fairness and justice and concern for the needy. Conversely, there were people whom others might think couldn't be part of the people of God such as eunuchs and foreigners. Yes, they can belong. They just have to keep the Sabbath.

> To the eunuchs who keep my Sabbaths,
>> and choose what I want, and hold onto my pact . . .
> And the foreign people
>> who attach themselves to Yahweh, to minister to him,
> And to give themselves to Yahweh's name,
>> to be servants to him,
> Anyone who keeps the Sabbath rather than treating it as ordinary,
>> and holds strongly to my pact,
> I will bring them to my sacred mountain,
>> and let them rejoice in my prayer house. (Is 56:4-7)

Of course it would be possible to keep the Sabbath but be living wickedly the rest of the week. That doesn't work.

> Incense is an offense to me,
>> new month and Sabbath, the calling of a convocation. (Is 1:13)

FOR REFLECTION AND DISCUSSION

1. What would keeping Sabbath look like in your context?

2. What are the main obstacles to keeping Sabbath in your context?

3. Whose Sabbath could you make easier?

4. What does finding refreshment mean for you?

5. Does the question of trust make keeping Sabbath hard for you?

6. Does your pastor have a rest day?

16

ANIMALS

When Yahweh has let Job and his three friends argue things out for long enough, and the three friends have run out of steam, and Elihu the young upstart has also had his say, Yahweh finally decides to respond to Job's plea to say something.

Where were you when I founded the earth?
    —tell, if you know and understand. . . .
And who shut the sea in with doors,
    when it gushed from the womb it came out of? . . .
Since your days began, have you ordered morning,
    let the dawn know its place,
For it to grasp the earth by the corners,
    so that faithless people shake out of it? . . .
Who cut a channel for the torrent,
    and a way for the bolt of thunder,
To rain on land with no people,
    wilderness with no one in it,
To satisfy the devastated devastation,
    and make a crop of grass flourish? . . .
Can you hunt prey for a lion,
    and fill the appetite of whelps,
When they crouch in dens,
    lie in wait in a bivouac?

Who prepares its provision for the raven
>   when its young cry for help to God
>   and wander without food? (Job 38:4, 8, 12-13, 25-27, 39-41)

What Yahweh says isn't what Job was looking for. It's a long disquisition about the physical and animate world, and about humanity's relationship to it. One major point that underlies the disquisition is the fact that the world doesn't revolve around humanity. Genesis 1 makes that point, though it adds that God gives us some responsibility for the world. In Job, God is even more radical. We are not even part of the picture. We were not there when the world was created. We were not the ones who set the rules for it. We don't tell day when to break. The world is full of things that we don't know or understand. God doesn't make the rain fall where we need it but where it will make a nice crop of grass grow. God feeds lions and ravens, as we cannot.

Who sends off the wild donkey, free,
>   and who looses the ropes of the wild mule,
Whose home I made the steppe,
>   its dwellings the salty land?
It makes fun of the uproar of the township;
>   it doesn't listen to the shouts of a driver.
It ranges mountains as its pasture,
>   and searches after any green thing.
Is an antelope willing to serve you,
>   will it lodge by your feeding trough?
Can you hold an antelope with a harness to the furrow,
>   will it till the vales behind you?
Can you rely on it because its energy is great,
>   and abandon your toil to it?
Can you trust it that it will bring back your seed,
>   and gather it to your threshing floor? (Job 39:5-12)

Further, then, God sends off the wild donkey over the steppe where it can range on the mountain pasture—instead of making itself useful to human beings. Likewise the antelope, whose energy could be harnessed to humanity's requirements.

Without the need to be polemical as God is with Job, the Old Testament suggests an ecology of creation that sees human beings and animals as one community. God is like a farmer who provides all that his animals need, and by the same acts God provides for humanity. The alternating of sun and moon, of day and night, structures life for humanity and for animals. A basic thing that human beings and animals share is life itself. We share breath. God gives breath to both human beings and animals, and God in due course takes it away.

> You're the one who sends out springs in wadis,
>> so that they go about between the mountains.
> They water every animal of the field;
>> donkeys break their thirst.
> By them the birds of the heavens dwell;
>> from among the branches they give voice.
> You're one who waters mountains from his lofts
>> —from the fruit of your deeds the earth has its fill.
> You're the one who grows grass for the cattle,
>> and plants for the service of human beings,
> To make bread go out from the earth,
>> and wine that rejoices a person's heart,
> To make the face shine with oil,
>> and bread that sustains a person's heart.
> Yahweh's trees get their fill,
>> the cedars of Lebanon that he planted,
> Where birds nest,
>> the stork—the junipers are its home.
> The lofty mountains belong to the ibex,
>> the cliffs are a shelter for the rock badgers.
> He made the moon for set times;
>> the sun knows its setting.
> You bring darkness so that it becomes night:
>> in it every creature of the forest moves about.
> The lions roar for prey,
>> yes, in seeking their food from God.
> When the sun rises, they gather,
>> and crouch in their abodes.
> Human beings go out to their work,
>> and to their service until evening.

How the things you made multiplied, Yahweh;
> you made them all with smartness. . . .
All of them look to you,
> to give their food at its time.
You give them, they gather;
> you open your hand, they have their fill of good things.
You hide your face, they're fearful;
> you gather up their breath, they breathe their last,
> and go back to their dirt.
You send out your breath, they are created,
> and you renew the face of the ground. (Ps 104:10-24, 27-30)

To put it another way, we share blood with animals, and blood is a symbol of life—because when you lose your blood, you lose your life. For human beings and for animals, life is a gift we receive from God. One marker of that fact is that you have to be respectful of an animal's blood as you are of a person's.

An individual person from the Israelites or from the people who reside as aliens among you who catches a game animal or a bird that may be eaten is to pour out its blood and cover it with dirt. Because its blood is the life of all flesh. It simply is its life. So I've said to the Israelites, "You will not eat the blood of any flesh, because its blood is the life of all flesh." (Lev 17:13-14)

At the same time, the Old Testament recognizes that the fate of the animal world is bound up with that of the human world, sometimes in a good way, sometimes in a bad way. People's violence leads God to all-but annihilate humanity—and the animals are implicated in the catastrophe, without any comment on the rationale.

Yahweh saw that humanity's bad state on the earth was great. The entire inclination of its mind's intentions was simply bad, all day. Yahweh regretted that he had made humanity on the earth. It pained his heart. Yahweh said, "I shall wipe out the humanity that I created from the face of the ground, from humanity to animals to moving things to birds in the heavens, because I regret that I made them." (Gen 6:5-7)

My guess is that the rationale is the same as for the way women and children are implicated in the catastrophes of which God warns Israel. Western people like to think that every human being is a separate individual with a separate fate, but it isn't so. We are bound up together in the bundle of life, as Abigail put it (see 1 Sam 25:29). The same applies to animals in relation to us. The theme recurs in the story of the calamities in nature that Moses brings on Egypt (see e.g., Ex 9). They affect animals, too.

In the flood story, the good side to the coin is that some of the animals are kept alive with the one human family, so that all the species don't die out. And when God makes a pact never to devastate the world again, it's explicit that the animals are part of the pact.

> Of every pure animal take with you seven of each, a male and its mate, and of an animal that's not pure, two, a male and its mate, also of the birds in the heavens seven of each, male and female, to keep offspring alive on the face of the entire earth. (Gen 7:2-3)
>
> Noah built an altar for Yahweh, took some of every pure animal and of every pure bird, and offered up burnt offerings on the altar, and Yahweh smelled the nice smell. (Gen 8:20-21)
>
> God said to Noah and to his sons with him: "Here, I myself am going to implement my pact with you, with your offspring after you, and with every living being that's with you: birds, animals, and every living thing on the earth with you, all that got out of the chest, every living thing on the earth. I shall implement my pact with you and all flesh will not be cut off again by the water of a deluge." (Gen 9:8-11)

There's thus another ambiguity in the story of the great deluge. God keeps alive a pair of all the animals that Israelites are not allowed to sacrifice or eat but seven pairs of the ones they can sacrifice and eat, and the first thing that happens after the flood is that Noah sacrifices some of them. To judge from Genesis 1, killing and sacrificing wasn't part of the original plan. But it's firmly established now. The fate of many animals is subordinate to the relationship between humanity and God.

God does protect animals from us in other ways. I noted in chapter fifteen that they are to enjoy a Sabbath rest; we can't work them when we are stopping work.

> The seventh day is a Sabbath for Yahweh your God. You will not do any work, you, your son or your daughter, your servant or your handmaid, your animal, or your resident alien who is in your communities. (Ex 20:10)

They are also to share in the natural growth that will be the sustenance of human beings and animals in the Sabbath year.

The country's Sabbath will be food for you, for you yourself, for your servant
and for your handmaid, for your employee and for your resident alien living
with you, for your animals, and for the creatures that are in your country: all
its yield will be for eating. (Lev 25:6-7)

Deuteronomy suggests another way in which we can't just treat them as if
they are machines: "You will not muzzle an ox when it's threshing" (Deut 25:4).

Paul will later ask, does God really care that much about oxen? (1 Cor 9:9).
To which the answer seems to be "Well, yes, actually." (Though no doubt in
the back of God's mind was also an interest in supporting ministers, which
was Paul's concern in that context.) And we can't indulge in culinary delicacy
that ignores the proper relationship of the life-giving mother and her offspring: "You will not cook a kid goat in its own mother's milk" (Ex 23:19).

You can't seize a bird's eggs and seize the mother who's sitting on them—
she must be allowed to hatch some more another day.

When a bird's nest happens to be before you on the road, in any tree or on the
earth, with young ones or eggs and the mother sitting on the young or on the
eggs, you will not take the mother along with the offspring. You're absolutely
to send off the mother, but you may take the offspring for yourself. (Deut 22:6-7)

To put it positively, one could almost say that we should love our animals as
we love ourselves.

A faithful person knows his animal's appetite,
but the compassion of the faithless is cruel. (Prov 12:10)

FOR REFLECTION AND DISCUSSION

1. Are there ways in which you treat animals as having no rights?

2. Are there particular ways in which animals suffer because of human
   beings in your culture (apart from by being eaten, but you can think
   about that, too).

3. How do pets, zoos, and wildlife parks fit into the kind of considerations that these scriptural passages raise?

4. How can we hold together sharing life with animals and eating them,
   in the way Jews do by draining the blood?

17

WORK

There's an old Babylonian story about creation that includes an account of how the gods got fed up of having to do all the work so they created human beings to do it for them. If you read the Babylonian story, you'll be glad that it isn't in the Bible (in general, the gods in the Babylonian story aren't very nice), and you'll be glad that we have Genesis instead. But it's worth noting that Genesis agrees with the Babylonian story about some things, and one of the motifs it accepts is that we were indeed created to work in the world for God.

> God created human beings in his image. He created them in the image of God. He created them male and female. God blessed them, and said to them, "Be fruitful, be numerous, fill the earth and subjugate it, hold sway over the fish in the sea, over the birds in the heavens, and over every creature that moves on the earth." (Gen 1:27-28)

Work didn't come in only after things went wrong in the world, though the unpleasant side to work did come in then. One of the obvious things about God in Genesis 1 is that he's a worker. Indeed, as I noted in chapter fifteen, like a human being God does a week's work and then has a day off—or rather, we are like God in doing a week's work and then having a day off. Work is not everything; at the end of a work project it's good to stop and stand back and admire what we've achieved.

One of the things about being made in God's image is that we are workers. The second creation story makes the same point in a different way: "Yahweh God took the human being and set him down in Eden Garden to serve it and keep it" (Gen 2:15). The first man is created in order to work in God's orchard.

More precisely, he is created to "serve" God's orchard, to look after it. And the first woman is created to help him do so. Marriage was designed to facilitate work. Which sounds like really bad news, until you remember that work itself wasn't designed to be tough and arduous but to be fulfilling and worthwhile. It became tough and arduous only because of decisions the first couple took in their workplace.

> The ground is cursed because of you. In pain you'll eat from it all the days of your life. Thorn and thistle it will grow for you, and you'll eat plants of the wild. By the sweat of your face you'll eat bread, until you go back to the ground. (Gen 3:17-19)

The work they were given was to manage the world on God's behalf. Instead, they let the world manage them, and that's how things went wrong. And the rest of the Old Testament's teaching about work presupposes that work can be hard work. It's tempting therefore to shirk work, but laziness won't pay in the end, as Proverbs notes (among other truths about work):

> Go to the ant, lazybones,
>> look at its ways and get wise.
> One that has no commander,
>> officer, or ruler,
> Produces its food in summer,
>> gathers its provisions at harvest.
> How long will you lie down, lazybones,
>> when will you get up from your sleep?
> A little sleep, a little slumber,
>> a little folding of the hands to lie down,
> And your poverty will come walking in,
>> your want like someone with a shield. (Prov 6:6-11)

> A lazy hand makes for poverty,
>> but the hand of diligent people makes rich. (Prov 10:4)

> One who stores up during summer is a sensible son,
>> but one who sleeps during harvest is a shameful son. (Prov 10:5)

> Really, one who is slack in his work—
>> he's brother to someone destructive. (Prov 18:9)

> The lazy person buries his hand in the bowl;
>> he can't even bring it back to his mouth. (Prov 19:24)

> The door turns on its hinge,
>> the lazy person on his bed. (Prov 26:14)

Laziness may not seem so terrible a fault, but in the end it is as devastating as direct destructiveness, because the result of both is that you have nothing (Prov 18:9). In an engaging picture, a lazy person can be so lethargic that he can put some food on his fork but not manage to get it to his mouth (Prov 19:24), like a little child who falls asleep during a meal. In another such picture, a lazy person turns over in bed as instinctively as a door on its hinges (Prov 26:14). You have to be prepared to take a longer view.

> After fall the lazy person doesn't plow,
>> but he asks at harvest and there is nothing. (Prov 20:4)

> The lazy person says, "A lion in the street,
>> in the middle of the square I shall be slain!" (Prov 22:13)

> Establish your work outside,
>> get it ready in the fields for yourself;
>> afterward build your house. (Prov 24:27)

> I passed by the field of someone who was lazy,
>> and by the vineyard of one lacking sense.
> There: it all had come up in weeds,
>> chickpeas covered its surface,
>> its stone wall lay in ruins.
> When I myself looked, I applied my mind;
>> when I saw, I grasped a lesson.
> A little sleep, a little slumber,
>> a little folding of the hands to lie down,
> And your poverty will come walking about,
>> your want like someone with a shield. (Prov 24:30-34)

> A lazy person says, "There's a cougar on the road,
>> a lion among the squares." (Prov 26:13)

> You should really know the faces of your flock,
>> apply your attention to your herds,
> Because wealth isn't forever
>> or a crown for generation after generation.

The hay goes away and the new grass appears
>   and the growth of the mountains is gathered.
The lambs are for your clothing,
>   the goats for the price of a field,
Enough goats' milk for your food,
>   for food for your household and life for your young girls.
>   (Prov 27:23-27)

We can be geniuses at finding excuses not to work (Prov 22:13; 26:13). Even if we are prepared to work, we have to be discerning about priorities (Prov 24:27). It's a long time from sowing to harvest, but unless you take appropriate action in the fall, and appropriate action in connection with the less glamorous side to work, there is nothing to harvest in summer (Prov 20:4; 24:30-34). Something similar applies to the shepherd (Prov 27:23-27). Fortunately, our appetite tells us we had better resist the temptation to be lazy:

One who serves his land will have his fill of food,
>   but one who follows empty pursuits lack sense. (Prov 12:11)

The appetite of a laborer labors for him,
>   because his mouth is pressing on him. (Prov 16:26)

Laziness makes deep sleep fall,
>   but a slack person gets hungry. (Prov 19:15)

Don't give yourself to sleep lest you become poor;
>   open your eyes, be full of food. (Prov 20:13)

One who serves his land will be full of food,
>   but one who pursues empty things will be full of poverty. (Prov 28:19)

FOR REFLECTION AND DISCUSSION

1. In what sense is work a matter of ethics?
2. Do Christians you know think about work differently from non-Christians you know?
3. How (if at all) does your work contribute to the fulfillment of God's purpose for the world?
4. What (if anything) makes your work seem worthwhile to you?
5. What (if anything) makes you tempted to avoid work?

PART THREE

RELATIONSHIPS

Much of ethics is about how we relate to other people. The Old
Testament makes that focus quite a practical matter. It doesn't
talk much about loving everyone or being advocates for groups
who need action taken on their behalf. It talks more about your
relationships with the people you are in contact with—your
friends, your neighbors, the woman or the man in your life,
your parents, your children. It does also talk about nations and
cities and about people who don't belong and about leadership.

18

FRIENDS

A tricky thing about coming to work in California twenty years ago was moving away from my friends in England. My first wife was wheelchair-bound with multiple sclerosis, and my friends were vital to my staying sane and resourced and supported through the tough aspects of living with that reality. At a key moment, one of them helped me think through the decision to change jobs. I was wondering about giving up my post in England and coming to one I was being invited to consider in California, and it seemed a complicated decision-making process. This friend simply suggested that I should see that this question was actually two separate ones, and as soon as I did so, I knew that resigning from the position I had was right; the question about where to go to would need more thinking about. It was just one of the moments when my friends were worth their weight in gold.

The best known friendship story in the Bible is that of David and Jonathan. I'm not clear that David was very good at being a friend or that Jonathan got much out of the friendship, but I'm clear that Jonathan was a great friend and that David got a lot out of it. For them, friendship meant a harmony of purpose, and for Jonathan it meant a self-giving and a risk-taking. No wonder that, in his lament for Jonathan after his death in battle, David described Jonathan's love or loyalty as the most extraordinary relationship of his life.

My brother Jonathan,
>   you were very lovely to me.
> Your loyalty was extraordinary to me,
>   more than the loyalty of women. (2 Sam 1:26)

The most poignant account of friendship is that between Jephtah's daughter and her girlfriends. Jephtah has accidentally promised to offer her as a sacrifice to God, and it apparently occurs to no one to ask God whether he might be willing to regard that as a mistake. All she asks for is the chance to spend two months with her friends. What did they talk about? What happened to the friends afterward?

> She said to her father, "May this thing be done for me. Let me go for two months so I can walk and go down on the mountains and bewail my girlhood, I and my friends." He said, "Go," and sent her for two months. She and her friends went and bewailed her girlhood on the mountains. At the end of two months she came back to her father, and he performed the pledge that he had made in connection with her. (Judg 11:37-39)

Friends are people who share the suffering of others:

> When they were ill,
>   my clothing was sack.
> I humbled myself with fasting,
>   and my plea would turn back to my heart.
> I walked about as if it was my friend, as if it was a brother;
>   as if I were a mother grieving, mourning, gloomy. (Ps 35:13-14)

The most distressing friends in the Old Testament are the three who hear of the catastrophes that have befallen Job and come to sit with him, like people observing the Jewish custom of sitting shiva with someone who has lost a loved one.

> Three friends of Job heard about all these bad things that had come upon him, and they came each one from his place: Eliphaz the Temanite, Bildad the Shuhite, and Tsophar the Naamatite. They met together by agreement to come to express their sorrow to him and to comfort him, but they raised their eyes from afar and didn't recognize him. They raised their voice and cried. They ripped, each one, his coat, and they threw dirt over their heads, to the heavens. They sat with him on the ground seven days and seven nights with no one speaking a word to him because they saw that his suffering was very great. (Job 2:11-13)

The trouble is that once Job opens his mouth with his laments, protests, and questions, they can't handle the way his questions undermine their assumptions about life and God, and all they want to do is shut him up. So Job remonstrates:

> As for one who refuses commitment to his friend,
>> he abandons awe for Shadday.
> My brothers have broken faith like a wadi,
>> like the canyons with wadis that pass away. (Job 6:14-15)

> Be gracious to me, be gracious to me, you're my friends,
>> because God's hand has touched me.
> Why do you pursue me like God,
>> and why aren't you full of my flesh? (Job 19:21-22)

> Yahweh said to Eliphaz the Temanite, "My anger rages against you and against your two friends, because you haven't spoken to me what is established truth, like my servant Job. So now get yourselves seven bulls and seven rams, go to my servant Job, and offer up a burnt offering on your behalf. Job my servant can plead for you, because I will show regard to him." (Job 42:7-8)

A wadi is a stream that has water in it only when rain has fallen in the mountains. Job's friends' commitment is like that of a wadi that runs out of water just when you need it. The person on whom God's hand has come down is the person who needs his friends to be gracious, to take his side. Yet for all his tough words to them, Job shows he does not give up on his friends. Rather astonishingly, when God eventually tells them to get Job to pray for them, he agrees.

It's clearly important who you let be your friends. To start with, they had better be people who live in awe of God and who do the kind of things that God says to do:

> I'm a friend to all who live in awe of you
>> and to the people who keep the things you've determined. (Ps 119:63)

Sayings from Proverbs again illustrate the nature and importance of friendship. Your friends had better be people who are wise, not stupid, because they will help you get wise (Prov 13:20; 14:7; 27:17). Friends are people who are careful with their speech (Prov 16:28; 17:9). They should be people who'll talk straight with you (Prov 27:5-6; 28:23).

> The one who walks with the wise gets wise,
>> but the friend of stupid people experiences evil things. (Prov 13:20)

Get away from the stupid person;
>   you won't have known knowledgeable lips. (Prov 14:7)

A crooked person stirs up arguments,
>   and a gossip separates a friend. (Prov 16:28)

One who seeks a relationship covers over rebellion,
>   but one who repeats a matter separates a friend. (Prov 17:9)

Open reproof is better
>   than concealed friendship. (Prov 27:5)

The wounds of a friend are trustworthy;
>   the kisses of an enemy are importunate. (Prov 27:6)

Iron sharpens iron,
>   and a person sharpens the edge of his friend. (Prov 27:17)

One who reproves a person in the end will find more grace
>   than one who makes his tongue smooth. (Prov 28:23)

In other words, your friends are going to influence your ethics. Hang out with angry people, you'll end up angry; hang out with indulgent people, you'll end up self-indulgent (Prov 22:24-25; 28:7). Beware the way money attracts "friends" (Prov 19:4, 6).

Wealth makes many friends,
>   but a poor person becomes separate from his friend. (Prov 19:4)

Many seek the face of a ruler,
>   and everyone befriends the person with a gift. (Prov 19:6)

Don't befriend a person characterized by anger,
>   don't go about with someone hot-tempered,
Lest you learn his ways
>   and get a snare for your life. (Prov 22:24-25)

An understanding son guards instruction,
>   but one who befriends gluttons disgraces his father. (Prov 28:7)

Conversely, don't trade on friendship:

Let your foot hold back from your neighbor's house,
>   lest he gets his fill of you and repudiates you. (Prov 25:17)

Like a madman who is shooting
> fiery arrows of death,
So is someone who deceives his neighbor
> and says, "I was joking, wasn't I?" (Prov 26:18-19)

One who blesses his neighbor in a loud voice in the morning early:
> it will be counted for him as humiliating. (Prov 27:14)

It is unwise to push one's luck with one's friends.

FOR REFLECTION AND DISCUSSION

1. Is there a friend who has shaped you?

2. Who are your best two or three friends? What sort of people are they?

3. Are there ways in which they are a good or bad influence on you?

4. Do you have an important experience of friendship?

5. Are you aware of being a good or a bad influence on a friend?

19

NEIGHBORS

We live in a condo or condominium, a building whose ownership is shared by the people who live there (there are thirty-nine units in ours). The residents share responsibility for seeing that the building is kept under repair and we agree together on what the rules are (e.g., only one dog, or other pet, per apartment). Living in a condo has its challenges. What do you do when your neighbor makes a lot of noise? When he or she is scared about intruders in the garage and wants to spend thousands of dollars on security cameras, which you think are a waste of money? When someone gets behind in paying their monthly contribution to the maintenance and repair funds? When you suspect someone has a cat as well as a dog? When a neighbor calls you late at night because waste water is backing up in her sink? There are lots of opportunities for being neighborly and for testing neighborliness when you live in a condo. It's a little community.

Most Israelites lived in a village, and it was their community—bigger than our condo, though no bigger than some other condos near us. A village, that is, might comprise a couple of hundred people from three or four extended families. Your friends would be other people in the village. Your prospective husband or wife would be someone from one of the other extended families in the village. The practicalities of life in the village would depend on people working together and getting on with each other when they need to dig a well or to terrace some hills for growing olives or grapes there. You would celebrate the festivals each year with the rest of the village if it was too far to go to Jerusalem, and you would celebrate weddings together.

Jesus gets one of his two top commandments from Leviticus's instructions about neighborliness.

> You will not take the stand against your neighbor's life. I am Yahweh. You will not be hostile to your brother in your mind; you will firmly reprove your neighbor so you do not carry liability because of him. You will not take redress, and you will not hold onto things in relation to members of your people, but love your neighbor as yourself. I am Yahweh. (Lev 19:16-18)

The basic idea comes toward the end, that you love your neighbor as yourself. What does *love* mean, and what does *as yourself* mean? And who is my neighbor? A smart-ass theologian (or perhaps a serious inquirer) asked Jesus who counted as his neighbor (Lk 10:25-37). Unsurprisingly, Jesus gave him a slightly puzzling response: Learn from this Samaritan: he knew the answer. It's not very complicated.

For most of us, most of the time, your neighbor is—well, your neighbor. In an Israelite village, people had lots of chances to love their neighbors. They too might be making too much noise late at night. They might need a loan. Their son might be looking as if he was trying to take advantage of your daughter. They might not be pulling their weight in those village tasks of digging a well or terracing the hillsides. One neat aspect of the command is thus that your neighbor is local and concrete. Of course you should also love the world and people who live far away, though God never told Israel to love the Egyptians or the Assyrians, and the New Testament never tells people to love the world—in fact it says the opposite (1 Jn 2:15-17). God didn't tell them to hate the Assyrians or the Egyptians either. These peoples were responsible for themselves. The individuals who live near you are the place to start and not to neglect.

So what does *love* mean? The Hebrew word for love does cover warm feelings, but the way Leviticus spells things out, when it tells you to love your neighbor, *love* is mostly an action word. It means caring for (not just caring about). It means doing something. I noted in chapter one that Middle Eastern peoples used their word for love to describe the faithfulness of one people to another, not least in the relationship of big powers and little powers. Big powers were supposed to express love by protecting the security or safety of their underlings, little powers were supposed to express their love by being loyal to their lords and masters.

What about *as yourself*? Maybe it means "as you love yourself," though if so, the implication is not that you need to focus first on loving yourself so you can then move on to loving others. Indeed, the opposite dynamic may work better. Love your neighbor, and you may end up loving yourself, too. But maybe it means "as a person like yourself." Your neighbor is a person with needs and feelings and prejudices like you. Love them on that basis. But don't flatter them, because you might be tripping them up (Prov 29:5).

What does this love look like? Leviticus spells it out in a number of sample ways. It means you won't try to get rid of him (you might be trying to do so in order that you can grab his land or his wife). You won't harbor hostile thought about him. The immediate implication is not that hostile thoughts are wrong, though that might also be true. It's that they need to be brought out into the open. Reproving your neighbor for wrongdoing is an expression of love. Just be careful that you don't implicate someone else in what you say, someone who maybe has told you something in confidence, and you end up in trouble (Prov 25:9-10). And be wary of getting involved in a case that does come to the elders, when you don't really know what you are talking about.

Your reproof is also an expression of self-love, because if he's doing something wrong and you don't say anything, you are complicit in his wrongdoing. On the other hand, if the wrong he is doing affects you personally, you won't take redress. If (for instance) he has left the lid off the well and your sheep has fallen in, it's not your job to punch him in the face or steal one of his sheep. If you want action taken, you have to ask the elders to decide what should happen. And finally, you therefore won't hold onto things, because your resentment is likely to come out one way or another in due course. You need to let go of things. That's what love involves.

These examples of loving one's neighbor show that the idea is not that you love your (nice) neighbor but can then hate your enemy (the Torah never tells people they can hate their enemies). The neighbor you're challenged to love is the neighbor who is your enemy (which is what the Samaritan did, because Jews and Samaritans were often enemies). That's why Jesus was filling out the Torah when he told people to love their enemies.

It also doesn't just mean loving your neighbor who is big in the community. It means loving the lowly person, from whom you are going to get no advantage.

Conversely, you have to be wary of becoming the neighbor who is an enemy. Community depends on trust, and if you plan something against your neighbor, you're doing something dangerous. Community depends on people living at peace, and someone who is violent by temperament and encourages his neighbor to be violent is also a danger. Elsewhere, the Torah gives other examples of neighborliness and non-neighborliness:

> You will not move aside your neighbor's boundary marker, which previous generations laid down, in your domain which you will have as yours in the country that Yahweh your God is giving you to take possession of it. (Deut 19:14)

> You will not see your brother's ox or his sheep straying, and hide from them. You're definitely to get them back to your brother. If your brother is not near to you or you don't know him, take it home to your house so it may be with you until your brother inquires about it and you can give it back to him. You're to act in this way with his donkey and to act in this way with his clothing and to act in this way with anything lost by your brother, which gets lost from him and which you find. You can't hide. You will not see your brother's donkey or his ox falling on the road and hide from them. You must definitely get it up with him. (Deut 22:1-4)

> When you come into your neighbor's vineyard, you may eat grapes in accordance with your appetite until you're full, but you will not put them into your container. When you come into your neighbor's standing grain, you may pluck ears with your hand, but you will not put a sickle to your neighbor's standing grain. (Deut 23:24-25)

You won't move the boundary stone between your neighbor's land and yours so as to enlarge your land. You won't shrug your shoulders when you see an ox or sheep or donkey straying ("Well, it's not my business; I don't know whose it is, anyway"). You won't look the other way when your neighbor's ox or donkey has collapsed under its load and needs someone's help to get it on its feet again. You can eat a handful of grapes from your neighbor's vine or pluck some heads of grain from his field, but you can't collect a bag full or put your sickle to it.

Proverbs fills out the idea of neighborliness, too.

> Don't say to your neighbor, "Go, and come back,
>> and tomorrow I'll give [it to you]," when it's with you. (Prov 3:28)

> Don't devise evil against your neighbor,
>> when he's living trustingly with you. (Prov 3:29)

One who despises his neighbor is an offender,
>   but one who is gracious to the lowly: his blessings! (Prov 14:21)

A violent person misleads his neighbor,
>   and makes him go in a way that isn't good. (Prov 16:29)

A person lacking in sense pledges his hand,
>   standing surety before his neighbor. (Prov 17:18)

There are neighbors to act like neighbors
>   and there's one who loves, who sticks firmer than a brother.
>   (Prov 18:24)

Don't become a witness against your neighbor without reason;
>   will you mislead with your lips? (Prov 24:28)

Contend your cause with your neighbor,
>   but don't reveal the secret of another person,
Lest someone who hears it reproach you,
>   and the charge against you doesn't turn away. (Prov 25:9-10)

A man who flatters his neighbor
>   spreads a net for his feet. (Prov 29:5)

If you owe your neighbor some grain and you've got it to hand, give it to him now. On the other hand, you don't have to be stupid. If you're thinking about standing surety for your neighbor, think twice. If you give everything away, you will have left your own family in the lurch. Then there are people who go the second mile (as Jesus puts it): there are neighbors who act like neighbors, and there is the person who loves, who sticks firmer than a brother. In other words, he loves his neighbor as he loves himself or as person like himself.

FOR REFLECTION AND DISCUSSION

1. Has a neighbor ever loved you? How?

2. Have you ever loved a neighbor? How?

3. Do you have a neighbor who needs love?

4. Have you ever reproved a neighbor and got into trouble for it?

5. Have you ever been reproved by a neighbor? How did you react?

6. Have you ever taken advantage of a neighbor? Or been taken advantage of?

20

WOMEN

A friend of mine who is ordained recently moved from one part of the United States to another, where she found that the local churches "have no female readers, acolytes, chalice bearers, no females anywhere." There will be many of them in the pews, but not with any involvement in leading worship. This morning another friend told me of someone who had left the denomination he loved because it took a similar stance; his daughter has gifts for leading music in worship and there was no opportunity for her to exercise them there.

In the Old Testament there were no women priests as there were among other peoples, though there were women prophets. And there are indications that questions about women's roles are not just modern Western ones. Like the church in the modern West, the Old Testament had to deal with the interaction between social expectations and another vision.

A man called Zelophehad had no sons but five daughters. But only men could inherit land. So their family land would pass to their nearest male relative. "Well, that's not fair!" you can hear them saying, though the reason they think it's not fair is striking. It's because their father's name (and thus their family's name) would then disappear from Israel. Their family would cease to exist. The land would be known as the land of their Uncle Eliphaz (or whatever it was). "Treat us as if we were one of our father's brothers, instead. Let us inherit," they urge.

> They stood before Moses, before Eleazar the priest, and before the leaders and the entire assembly, at the entrance of the appointment tent and said, "Our father died in the wilderness. . . . He had no sons. Why should our father's

name disappear from among his kin-group because he had no son? Give us a holding among our father's brothers." Moses presented their case before Yahweh, and Yahweh said to Moses, "The daughters of Zelophehad are speaking correctly. Do give them a holding, a domain among their father's brothers. Pass their father's domain over to them." (Num 27:1-7)

When they ask their question, Moses is a wise man, refuses to comment, and rather refers the case to God. If the way he gets his response from God involves some process like consulting Urim and Tummim (something that would give you a yes or a no), then the daughters can't blame Moses for the result. But the answer is yes. (The story of Job also closes with Job arranging for his daughters to inherit alongside their brothers.)

Later, the leaders of their clan point to a problem.

They said, "Yahweh ordered my lord to give the country to the Israelites as a domain by lot, and my lord was ordered by Yahweh to give our brother Zelophehad's domain to his daughters. But they may become wives of someone from the members of the other Israelite clans, and their domain will disappear from our ancestral domain." . . . So Moses ordered the Israelites at Yahweh's bidding: "The Josephite clan are speaking correctly. This is the thing that Yahweh has ordered concerning Zelophehad's daughters: They may become the wives of whoever is good in their eyes, yet they're to become wives of a kin-group in their father's clan. The domain of the Israelites will not go around from clan to clan, because the Israelites are to attach themselves, each individual, to his clan's ancestral domain." (Num 36:2-3, 5-7)

If the daughters inherit and then marry someone from another clan, they will take their land with them to the other clan. That can't be right! Moses sighs and again asks himself and God why he got saddled with the job of sorting things out for these people, then he consults God again. Again God agrees that the clan leaders have a case, affirms that it doesn't mean going back on the earlier decision, but in effect says that the daughters have to choose. They can have the land and marry inside their own clan (which gives them plenty of choice). Or they can marry outside their clan, but forfeit their claim on the land. The story goes on to describe how they all chose the compromise.

The story of the five daughters raises issues that compare with a rule that comes earlier in Numbers. How do you deal with a situation when a man suspects his wife of having an affair?

When an individual's wife goes off and breaks faith with him, and someone has slept with her and they had sex but it was concealed from the eyes of her husband and she's kept it secret, but she's made herself taboo, yet there's no witness against her and she was not caught, but a jealous spirit has come over him and he's become jealous in respect of his wife when she has made herself taboo; or a jealous spirit has come over him and he's become jealous in respect of his wife when she hasn't made herself taboo: the man is to bring his wife to the priest, and to bring as an offering for her a tenth of a barrel of barley flour; he will not pour oil on it and he will not put frankincense on it, because it's a grain offering of jealousy, a grain offering of mindfulness, which makes someone mindful of waywardness. The priest is to present her and get her to stand before Yahweh. The priest is to get sacred water in a clay container. The priest is to get some of the dirt that's on the dwelling floor and the priest is to put it in the water. The priest is to get the woman to stand before Yahweh and to bare the woman's head and put on her palms the grain offering of mind-fulness, the grain offering of jealousy. In the priest's hand is to be the bitter water that brings a curse. The priest is to get her to swear: he's to say to the woman, "If no one has slept with you, and if you haven't gone off in taboo while married to your husband, you can be free of guilt from this bitter water that brings a curse." . . . When he's got her to drink the water, if she's made herself taboo and broken faith with her husband, the water that brings a curse, be-coming bitter, will come into her, her womb will swell and her thigh fall, and the woman will become the exemplar for a vow among her people. But if she hasn't made herself taboo and she's pure, she'll be free of guilt and she'll be fruitful. (Num 5:2-19, 25-28)

The rite to cover that situation is a kind of sacrament, or a kind of negative sacrament, with a kind of psychological slant. The problem might be that the man has "a spirit of jealousy"—he's suspicious when there is no reason. Or the problem might be that the woman has been unfaithful, and she won't admit it. The bet that the rite makes is that she won't go through the rite if really she is guilty, or that if she does, God will ensure that it "works" and she pays the price. One reason that God will ensure it is that by having an affair she has made herself taboo or unclean. She hasn't just done something wrong by her husband. She's done something wrong by God. She took vows before God, and she's broken them. But if she is innocent, then the rite will not "work," and her husband will be reassured and he will have to shut up.

There's compromise in that rule, too. It's not very egalitarian—it deals only with a man suspecting his wife, not with a wife suspecting her husband. So it's an example of the way many rules in the Torah are realistic. In most societies, men have formal control of resources and power. If a man thinks his wife has committed adultery and decides to throw her out (or if he just wants to get rid of her and provides himself with the excuse to throw her out by making such an accusation), it puts her in a vulnerable position. So a rule like this one, which looks unfair, can protect her. It's all very well to say that things should be equal for the women's sake, but it's also important to be realistic for the women's sake.

There are other aspects of the rules in the Torah that handle the vision for women and men in a similar way. When you compare many of the rules in Deuteronomy with the earlier versions in Exodus, a striking feature is that they make explicit that the rules apply to women as well as men, to daughters as well as sons, to mothers as well as fathers, to maidservants as well as male servants. The rule about freeing a bondservant after six years applies to women as well as men; daughters can no more be sacrificed than sons; being responsible to avoid apostasy and being liable to the death penalty applies to women as well as men; the rule about rebelling against one's parents and the parents' obligation to take action about it applies to mothers as well as fathers; women as well as men take part in the festivals (Deut 12:31; 15:12; 16:9-15; 17:2-5; 18:10; 21:18-21).

In the way it deals with the position of women, the Torah works with that tension between God's creation ideal and God's making allowance for human stubbornness, of which Jesus speaks. The question in the contexts in which we ourselves live is, what's the profile of human stubbornness, how does it place constraints on us, and how can we pull toward the creation vision? One of the passages about divorce, where Jesus discusses the tension between God's creation ideal and the need to make allowance for human stubbornness, relates how the disciples spot that he's really urging people to go for the creation ideal and forgo the right to divorce. "Better not to marry if you can't divorce, then," they comment (Mt 19:10). It's hard to go for God's creation ideal. It's tempting to go for whatever is the easier standard.

FOR REFLECTION AND DISCUSSION

1. How does your congregation expect women to be able to exercise ministry? Are there ways to work more toward a creation vision?

2. What constraints does your society place on women? Are there ways in which your congregation can counteract those constraints and model an alternative?

3. In what ways is your society or your congregation unfair to women, or how does it work with a double standard?

4. Where are the points in your congregation at which women still have to compromise on the creation vision?

5. How do they live with having to do so?

21

GOOD HUSBANDS, GOOD WIVES

"When a man takes a new wife he will not go out in the army. . . . For a year he's to be free for his household so he may enable his wife whom he's taken to rejoice" (Deut 24:5). What a great ideal, one might think! Likewise, if there's trouble out in the community or at work, then you can always look forward to going home for respite and relaxation. But what if things are tough at home, one way or another? Some comments from Proverbs, mostly from a husband's angle:

> Animosity stirs up strife,
>> but love conceals all acts of rebellion. (Prov 10:12)

> A gold ring in a pig's nose
>> is a beautiful woman turning away from discernment. (Prov 11:22)

> A strong woman is her husband's crown,
>> but a shameful one is like decay in his bones. (Prov 12:4)

> The wisest of women builds her house,
>> but stupidity tears it down with her own hands. (Prov 14:1)

> Better a helping of greens when love is there
>> than a fattened bull when hatred is with it. (Prov 15:17)

> Better a dry crust and quiet with it,
>> than a house full of contentious sacrifices. (Prov 17:1)

> He finds a wife, he finds good things,
>> and obtains favor from Yahweh. (Prov 18:22)

A stupid son is a disaster to his father,
>   but a woman's arguments are a continuing drip. (Prov 19:13)

House and wealth are the property of parents,
>   but a woman with good sense comes from Yahweh. (Prov 19:14)

Under three things the earth shudders,
>   and under four that it cannot bear:
Under a servant when he becomes king,
>   under a mindless person when he's full of food,
Under a woman who has been repudiated when she marries,
>   and under a servant when she replaces her mistress. (Prov 30:21-23)

To judge from Proverbs, there are two things that can ruin a marriage. One is the man committing adultery. The other is the wife nagging. It wouldn't be surprising if these two problems are related, though there are various ways in which the relationship might work. If the wife suspects that her husband fancies someone else's wife or is chatting up the nubile teenager next door, it won't be surprising if she gets fed up and goes on at him. If the wife is inclined to nag him about snoring or traipsing sheep droppings into the house, it won't be surprising if he starts wondering if his neighbor's wife is easier going. The Old Testament does imply that wives might also commit adultery and maybe that husbands could nag: "I'm fed up with pita and olive oil for my lunch packet when I go out plowing for the day." But the stereotype that a man's eye wanders and a woman nags was prevalent in Western culture for a long time, so it wouldn't be surprising if it was the pattern in Israel.

The advice to the man, then, is that he needs to be wary about adultery. The Torah says that it's wrong. Proverbs' emphasis is that it's stupid.

Drink water from your own cistern,
>   running water from within your own well.
Should your fountains gush outside,
>   your streams of water in the squares?
They should be for you alone,
>   so that there is none for strangers with you.
May your spring be blessed,
>   may you rejoice in the wife of your youth,
She is a doe to love,
>   a graceful deer.

Her breasts should satisfy you all the time;
>be crazy on her love always.

So why be crazy on a stranger, son,
>and embrace the bosom of a foreigner? (Prov 5:15-20)

If a man walks on coals,
>will his feet not burn?

So it is with someone who has sex with his neighbor's wife;
>no one who touches her will go free.

People don't despise a thief
>when he steals for the sake of his appetite, when he's hungry.

But if he's found out, he'll pay back sevenfold;
>he'll give all the wealth of his household.

The person who commits adultery with a woman is lacking in sense;
>one who so acts is destroying himself.

He'll meet with injury and disgrace;
>his reproach will not be wiped away.

Because jealousy [arouses] a man's fury;
>he won't pity on the day of redress.

He won't have regard for any compensation;
>he won't agree, even if the inducement is great. (Prov 6:28-35)

People who have affairs commonly think that this new relationship is a wonderful life-giving gift. Proverbs says, "No it isn't. Actually it's death dealing. It's likely to ruin your life. It's like walking on hot coals. And don't think you can resolve the matter man-to-man by apologizing and buying him a drink. The entire community will be scandalized by your action, and he will want to kill you." The advice Proverbs then gives is that before he gives in to temptation the man should renew his attention to his wife. If he takes the right approach to her, she's quite likely to blossom and become an extremely satisfying partner.

The man who provides the most vivid negative embodiment of Proverbs' teaching is David. He's got wives enough already and his fancying Bathsheba and following up on fancying her (2 Sam 11) does seem extraordinarily stupid. And it ruins his life and those of some other people. The man who is the most impressive embodiment of Proverbs' ideal is Joseph (see Gen 39). Admittedly he is not yet married, but the woman with whom he might have had an affair is married. So it counts as adultery whether the married partner is the man or the woman.

While one piece of advice to the woman is to remember what nagging does, another is to set about being the kind of woman described in Proverbs 31:10-31. It is in her interests in her own right, and it will also make him proud of her.

Who can find a resourceful woman?
> —her value is far above rubies.

Her husband's mind relies on her,
> and he lacks no spoil.

She deals him good, not bad,
> all the days of her life.

She looks for wool and flax,
> and works with delight with the palms of her hands.

She becomes like a trader's ships,
> when she brings her bread from far away.

She rises while it's still night,
> and gives a bite to her household,
> and an allocation to her girls.

She schemes about a field and gets it;
> from the fruit of the palms of her hands she plants a vineyard.

She wraps her hips in vigor,
> and firms up her arms.

She checks that her trading is good;
> her lamp doesn't go out at night.

She puts out her hands to the spindle,
> and her palms take hold of the wheel.

She opens her palm to the humble person,
> puts out her hands to the needy person.

She isn't afraid for her household because of snow,
> because her entire household is dressed in crimson.

She makes coverlets for herself;
> her clothing is linen and purple.

Her husband is acknowledged at the gateways,
> as he sits with the country's elders.

She makes fabric and sells it,
> and gives a sash to the merchant.

Vigor and magnificence are her clothing;
> she can make fun of a future day.

She opens her mouth with smartness;
>   committed instruction is on her tongue.
She watches over the goings of her household;
>   she doesn't eat the bread of laziness.
Her children rise up and declare her blessed;
>   her husband praises her:
"Many women produce resources,
>   but you surpass all of them."
Grace is false, beauty is hollow,
>   but a woman who lives in awe of Yahweh—she's to take pride.
Give to her from the fruit of her hand;
>   her deeds should praise her at the gateways.

She is a notably resourceful woman. He knows he can rely on her. She deals in goods and cloth and real estate. She thinks ahead, knows when she needs to prepare for winter and does so. She can tell her household staff what they need to do. Proverbs also throws in that she opens her hands to the lowly and needy, and that she lives in awe of Yahweh. In other words, she fulfills the aim that Proverbs has for everyone. The first paragraph in the book assumes that smartness, ethics, and faith are interwoven. This last paragraph of the book does the same.

The woman who is the most impressive embodiment of Proverbs' ideal is Abigail (see 1 Sam 25), though it's not clear that either of her husbands had much good sense. Her first husband is Nabal. His name can have various meanings; one of them is "villain." Presumably it wasn't the meaning his parents had in mind when they chose the name. But his reaction when David asks him for protection money suggests he's not very wise. It's Abigail who realizes the danger they are in and who in lightning time produces two hundred loaves of bread, two skins of wine, five prepared sheep, five measures of roasted grain, one hundred raisin blocks, and two hundred fig blocks, puts them on donkeys, and sets off to take them to David. And she wins David's favor. When Nabal conveniently drops dead, Abigail is available for a marriage of convenience.

FOR REFLECTION AND DISCUSSION

1. In your context, are women and men equally likely to commit adultery?

2. In your context, are women and men equally likely to nag?

3. In your context, are there other important threats to faithfulness in marriage?

4. In your context, what most holds women back from living up to the vision in Proverbs 31?

5. What strike you as the significant other insights for husbands and wives in these Scriptures?

22

WHO YOU CAN'T HAVE SEX WITH

The Old Testament includes all sorts of rules about marriage. There's a rule about who you must marry: namely, if you seduce a young girl you have to be prepared to marry her.

> If a man seduces a young girl who's not betrothed and sleeps with her, he's to make the actual marriage payment for her as a wife for himself. If her father absolutely refuses to give her to him, he's to weigh out silver in accordance with the marriage payment for young girls. (Ex 22:16-17)

> When a man finds a girl who's a young girl who's not betrothed and takes hold of her and sleeps with her and they're found out, the man who slept with her is to give the girl's father fifty in silver and she can be his wife. Since he humbled her, he can't send her off through his entire life. (Deut 22:28-29)

While the Old Testament disapproves of sex between two people when neither is married, it doesn't take as serious a view of that wrongdoing as it does of adultery. A man who seduces a girl does have to accept responsibility for wrongdoing and to put things right with her father and her. The father would be looking forward to a significant gift from the family into whom his daughter married, but now there's a risk that no family will want her to join it or that no other man in the village will want to marry her—maybe people shouldn't take that view, but communities do. And in their culture there's no recognized way of a single girl staying single and being fine, thank you very much. She'd be stuck with her parents forever. The obligation that rests on the man need not mean she has to marry him if she and her father don't wish it, but if she likes this guy, marrying him might be the least bad option. If she doesn't want to, then at least she and her father can take the money and run. The point is that the seducer is under obligation to be willing to marry the girl and to forgo any right ever to divorce her, though again the obligation that rests on him doesn't mean she can't leave him if she wishes to.

Suppose a man marries a girl and then decides he doesn't like her, and accuses her of not having been a virgin.

> The girl's father and her mother are to get the evidence of the girl's virginity and bring it out to the town's elders at the gateway. The girl's father is to say to the elders, "I gave my daughter to this man as wife but he came to dislike her. Here, that man has made accusations, saying 'I didn't find the evidence of virginity in your daughter.' This is the evidence of my daughter's virginity." And they will lay out the cloth before the town's elders. Then that town's elders are to get the man, chastise him, charge him a hundred in silver, and give it to the girl's father, because he caused an Israelite young girl to have a bad name. And she will be his wife; he will not be able to send her off through his entire life. But if this thing was truthful, if the evidence of virginity was not found for the girl, they're to bring the girl to the entrance of her father's house, and the people of her town are to pelt her with stones so she dies, because she's done something villainous in Israel by whoring in her father's household. So you will burn away the bad thing from among you. (Deut 22:13-21)

Like lots of the rules in the Torah, this rule looks unrealistic on both sides—how are the girl's parents to prove she was a virgin, or how are they to be unable to do so? Those problems suggest it's another example of a rule that we misunderstand if we interpret it simply as a provision for literal implementation. It's a declaration about something important in the form of a rule. Keeping yourself for your eventual husband (or wife) is important. Resisting the temptation to try to get out of a marital commitment you have made is important. It's also the kind of rule that exists because of human hardness of heart.

> When a man takes a wife and becomes her husband, if she doesn't find grace in his eyes because he finds something indecent in her, and he writes her a divorce document, puts it in her hand, and sends her off from his household, and she leave his household, goes, and comes to belong to another man, but the other man dislikes her, writes her a divorce document, puts it in her hand, and sends her off from his household, or when the other man who took her as

his wife dies, her first husband who sent her off cannot take her again as his
wife after she's been made taboo, because it would be an offense before Yahweh.
You will not do wrong to the country that Yahweh your God is giving you as a
domain. (Deut 24:1-4)

It's in connection with this rule about divorce papers that Jesus formulates
the "hardness of heart" principle underlying the Torah. The beginning of the
Torah in Genesis, he points out, implicitly rules out divorce. This Deuteronomic rule presupposes that divorces do happen in the sense that as an em-
pirical fact men throw out wives and leave the women of unclear status and
in danger of being homeless and supportless, and of drifting into prostitution.
At least it's something, if she has a document that makes her status clear. In
Deuteronomy 24, however, this requirement that a woman be given a divorce
document is only the premise of the concern expressed in the ruling itself.
What happens if the man wants to remarry his ex-wife? It's not clear why the
Torah prohibits it, though forbidding it might have the effect of holding a
man back from divorcing his wife too easily.

The Torah incorporates rules about who a man can't have sex with and
who he therefore obviously can't marry. Essentially, it's any of your close
relatives, the people who live in the same house or in the house next door.
What might seem odder to Western readers is that in the same context Leviticus includes a ban on having sex with a menstruating woman, with another man, or with an animal. It looks as if Leviticus has bundled together a
miscellaneous collection of rules about sex so that they all come together. The
rules have different rationales, though all of them have something to do with
safeguarding order or structure or stability in the family and community. "No
individual person will approach any close relative so as to expose their nakedness. I am Yahweh" (Lev 18:6).

Leviticus goes on to make explicit who counts as a close relative: your
father, your mother, your father's wife (that is, a second wife who is not
your mother), your full sister or half-sister, your daughter-in-law, your aunt,
your uncle, your sister-in-law. Further,

You will not expose the nakedness of a woman and her daughter. You will not
take her son's daughter or her daughter's daughter and expose her nakedness.
They're relatives. It's a deliberate wickedness. You will not take a wife alongside
her sister so as to cause pressure, so as to expose her nakedness beside her

during her lifetime. You will not approach a woman during her taboo flowing, so as to expose her nakedness. You will not have sex with the wife of your fellow, so as to become taboo through her. You will not give any of your offspring for passing across to the Shameful King; you will not treat the name of your God as ordinary. I am Yahweh. You will not sleep with a male as one sleeps with a woman. It's an offensive act. You will not have sex with any animal so as to become taboo by it, and no woman is to present herself before an animal so as to lie down with it. It's a perversion. (Lev 18:17-23)

Leviticus then lays down the death penalty for adultery and lays down this sanction or other sanctions for some of the previously noted relationships and for others:

Someone who sleeps with a male as one sleeps with a woman—the two of them have performed an offensive act. They are absolutely to be put to death. Their shed blood is against them. Someone who takes a woman and her mother: it's a deliberate wickedness. They are to burn him and them in fire. There will not be a deliberate wickedness among you. Someone who has sex with an animal is absolutely to be put to death, and you're to kill the animal. A woman who approaches any animal to lie down with it: you're to kill the woman and the animal. They are absolutely to be put to death. Their shed blood is against them. Someone who takes his sister, his father's daughter or his mother's daughter, and he sees her nakedness and she sees his nakedness: it's a shameful thing. They shall be cut off before their people's eyes. He's exposed his sister's nakedness. He will carry his waywardness. When a man sleeps with a woman who's unwell and exposes her nakedness, he has bared her flow and she herself has exposed her blood flow. Both of them shall be cut off from among their people. You will not expose the nakedness of your mother's sister or your father's sister, because he's bared his flesh. They will carry their waywardness. Someone who sleeps with his aunt has exposed his uncle's nakedness. They will carry their waywardness. They will die childless. Someone who takes his brother's wife—it's a defilement. He's exposed his brother's nakedness. They will be childless. (Lev 20:13-21)

One plausible rationale for these rules is that sexual behavior and marriage need to work for the upbuilding of the family and the community, not for its collapse. The rules about who you can marry have nothing to do with genetics but with what causes disorder, scandal, division, and disruption in the family and the community. The stability of community and family, and their future, depend on the proper structuring of the family, with an established sense of how the generations relate. In a Western context, we emphasize the individual more than the family or the community, and the idea that I should subordinate my attraction and my longing to the need of the community seems odd.

That Western feeling lies behind our puzzlement at the idea of parents being involved in the arrangement of a marriage. This involvement need not mean that the parents make a decision that the boy or girl opposes, yet it worries us. It compromises the principle that's so important to us, that I and I alone make the key decisions in my life in light of what seems best for me and seems to me most likely to make me happy. But our affirmation of that principle doesn't seem to generate happiness for us. And it seems to produce fractured families and communities.

Another rationale likely comes from a conviction that the way God created the world had a built-in order about it to which we should adhere. Animals are designed to have sex with animals. Men are designed to have sex with women; in Western culture we may not like that one, but at least it's worth our seeing its rationale. And further, death and life are opposites. The problem with that principle is that in practice death and life can get confused. Questions about abortion concern (among other things) the boundary between nonlife and life at the beginning. And questions about life-support systems concern (among other things) the boundary between life and non-life at the end. The Torah didn't have to chafe about those questions in the same way as we do, but its ban on sex during menstruation also presupposes the fact that the boundary between life and death gets confused. Menstruation is a sign of life, because it indicates that a woman could conceive. But it involves blood, which makes it a sign of death; lose too much blood and you die. So menstruation is uncanny and mysterious. It has to be taken seriously. Treating menstruation as simply an inconvenience or having sex during menstruation doesn't take it seriously. The implication of the rule is not that we should simply avoid doing what it proscribes. It resembles other rules in the Torah like observing the Sabbath or not cooking a kid goat in its mother's milk. It's designed to make us think about the way we think and to rethink the way we act.

The story of Samson is the great Old Testament account of how to get into a mess through sex. There's not so much ethical ambiguity in the story. Samuel's unnamed mother is unable to have children, but Yahweh's envoy comes to tell her that she will have a son who is to be consecrated to God from birth (a *nazir*) and who will begin to deliver Israel from control by the Philistines; which he does. But the plan for him to be consecrated doesn't work out very well. Is it a good idea to decide ahead of time on such a plan for a young man? But Samson's mother is the first woman in his life and the best, a wise and spiritually astute woman. Samson grows, Yahweh blesses him, and Yahweh's spirit begins to stir him (Judg 13:24-25).

He fancies a Philistine girl and asks his parents to arrange for their marriage (Judg 14:1-2). Is such involvement of parents a good idea? The story indicates that an arranged marriage is indeed not bound to be one in which the couple have no say or take no initiative. Samson's parents, however, think it's a good idea to marry someone from your own people: are they right? There is no objection in the Old Testament to marrying a foreigner, but it's important that the foreigner is someone who has come to acknowledge Yahweh (see Ruth the Moabite and Uriyyah the Hittite). Samson seems moved only by the girl's attractiveness. Or is this his way of picking a fight with the Philistines, as actually happens, and as Yahweh wants to happen?

The girl is put under frightening pressure by the boys in her village, to which she eventually yields and deceives Samson about their ploy with her. Samson kills thirty Philistines, the prospective marriage collapses, Samson destroys the villagers' food supply, they kill the girl and her father, Samson wreaks slaughter among the Philistines, they attack Judah, the Judahites surrender Samson, Samson gets free, and kills another thousand (Judg 14:8–15:20).

After a second capture and escape following a visit to a Philistine whore, Samson falls for another Philistine girl, Delilah, who is again put under pressure by her countrymen to deceive Samson into revealing the secret of his strength and thus to surrender him to them (Judg 16:1-22). He ends up in prison, but there his shorn hair begins to grow back. During a Philistine festival he is able to pull down the temple on himself and on the Philistine worshipers, so that "the people whom he put to death when he died were more than he put to death when he lived" (Judg 16:30).

A most grim Old Testament story relates a horrifying experience on the part of David's daughter Tamar. Her half-brother Amnon is attracted to her, but he can't see what to do about it. His uncle and friend Yonadab is smart and knows what to do. He cooks up a plan to get Amnon alone with Tamar so he can rape her.

He said to him, "Prince, why are you down like this, morning by morning? Won't you tell me?" Amnon said to him, "Tamar, my brother Absalom's sister— I'm in love with her." Yonadab said to him, "Lie on your bed and act ill. Your father will come to see you and you're to say to him, 'May Tamar my sister please come and give me bread to eat. May she prepare the food before my eyes in order that I may see and eat from her hand.'" . . . So Tamar went to Amnon her brother's house; he was lying down. She got dough and kneaded it and made pancakes. . . . Tamar got the pancakes that she'd made, brought them to Amnon her brother in the room, and brought them up to him to eat. . . . He took hold of her and humbled her and bedded her. (2 Sam 13:4-6, 8, 10-11, 14)

So this most grim story about sex is also a most grim story about friends.

FOR REFLECTION AND DISCUSSION

1. In your context, what are the biggest factors that make people go wrong in their sexual relationships?

2. In your context, how do people decide who to marry, and does the system work?

3. In your context, are there ways in which attitudes to sexual relationships cause breakdown in the community?

4. Is there a particular rule from the Torah on this subject that you think has something to teach us?

5. If the difference in cultures makes some of the Torah's rules not directly helpful, are there nevertheless other ways in which we can learn from them?

23

PEOPLE WHO CAN'T UNDERTAKE A REGULAR MARRIAGE

When the US Supreme Court declared that same-sex marriage was acceptable, and at about the same time the Episcopal Church made its own declaration along those lines, I felt I needed to ask our congregation what it thought, so as to know what to do if a same-sex couple should ask to get married in our church. So I preached about the issues, and we had a congregational meeting to discuss the question. I asked people to join in a secret ballot to indicate whether they agreed that the church could be used for a same-sex marriage, whether they dis-agreed, or whether they were not sure. There were more or less exactly the same number of yeses and noes and don't knows. I think I laughed. So in effect we agreed that as a congregation we didn't know what we thought and that when and if the situation arose, I would bring the case to the church council. It hasn't arisen yet, and there seems a good chance it won't arise on my watch.

I noted in chapter twenty-one the rulings in Leviticus: "You will not sleep with a male as one sleeps with a woman. It's an offensive act," and, "Someone who sleeps with a male as one sleeps with a woman—the two of them have performed an offensive act. They are absolutely to be put to death. Their shed blood is against them" (Lev 18:22; 20:13). We have also seen how those rulings come in the context of many other rulings that proscribe acts that don't seem outrageous to us and that lay down the death penalty for many acts for which we wouldn't expect to impose the death penalty; neither did Israel impose it in practice, but the rulings come with that metaphorical sanction to show that the Torah sees them as serious matters.

In the debate on same-sex marriage, it's been suggested that the way God makes promises to eunuchs in Isaiah 56 points to the way in our context God might relate to a person who is attracted to someone of the same sex. In that chapter "eunuchs" likely denotes Judahites who are genitally deformed or have been emasculated, perhaps with their cooperation or perhaps not. Emasculation would likely have happened in order that they could safely supervise (for example) the Babylonian king's harem. God promises them an honored place in the community of Israel, even though they can't contribute to its future by begetting children.

> The foreigner who attaches himself to Yahweh
> > is not to say,
> "Yahweh will quite separate me
> > from among his people."
> The eunuch is not to say,
> > "Here am I, a dry tree."
>
> Because Yahweh has said this,
>
> To the eunuchs who keep my Sabbaths,
> > and choose what I want, and hold onto my pact—
> I will give to them,
> > within my house and within my walls,
> A memorial and name
> > better than sons and daughters.
> I will give him a permanent name,
> > one that will not be cut off. (Is 56:3-5)

How might one decide whether to infer that the acceptance of eunuchs by God would mean that God might similarly accept homosexuals and same-sex marriage?

One aspect of the answer is that one needs to set the question in the context of an understanding of sex and marriage developed from the Scriptures as a whole. I suggest that such an understanding would see marriage as

- service focused (the first man and woman were to serve God and serve the world together)
- independent (you leave your parents)
- heterosexual
- procreational (the first human beings were to be fruitful)

- monogamous
- egalitarian
- covenantal and thus lifelong
- sexually expressed
- amorous
- publicly recognized by the community

The implication is that a marriage falls short of this vision if it involves

- people living largely separate work lives
- people failing to separate from their parents
- two people of the same sex
- two people who avoid having children
- polygamy
- husband or wife having authority over the other
- husband or wife having a still-living former spouse
- celibacy
- a platonic relationship
- a clandestine relationship

A same-sex marriage thus does fall short of the vision. But so do lots of other forms of marriage. In Western culture we disapprove of polygamy but not of some of the other shortfalls. Some traditional societies accept polygamy but not same-sex marriage. What tips me over the edge in still wanting not to agree with the secular Western culture and simply accept same-sex marriage is that it implies a mistaken vision of marriage. We are inclined to think that any form of sexual expression that doesn't impose itself on the other person is fine, and that we can define marriage as we like, and that same-sex marriage is just as good in terms of God's creation vision as heterosexual marriage. I know a heterosexual couple who live separately with each of their parents but who apparently have a faithful sexual relationship which has now produced two children. Just yesterday I was asked by someone if it was okay for a woman to choose artificial insemination and raise a child by herself. The average Western Christian understanding of "regular" heterosexual marriage almost as much as the secular understanding is miles away from this vision that emerges from the Scriptures.

FOR REFLECTION AND DISCUSSION

1. How does your church regard (say) people who have been divorced who marry again?

2. Does the way it treats same-sex marriage differ, and if so is there a basis for the different treatment?

3. What lifestyle should the church expect of someone who is attracted to other people of the same sex?

4. How can the church support heterosexual and homosexual people who live celibately?

24

PARENTS AND CHILDREN

Thirty years ago my first wife and I lived as a nuclear family with our two sons, but our sons spent almost as much time in our neighbors' houses as in our own, and their education was formally in the hands of their schools and their Sunday schools but also in the hands of their friends and the television. Further, we lived fifty and a hundred miles away from our widowed mothers. Twenty years ago at about the time our sons got married I moved six thousand miles away, and over these twenty years I have seen them and their wives and my grandchildren maybe once a year. The way the family works in a traditional society like Israel's differs from the way the Western family works. We shouldn't assume that their way is better at every point—it had its strengths but also its weaknesses. But it gives us an alternative pattern in light of which to look afresh at our own.

First, the family is the place where people learn things.

These words that I'm ordering you today are to be on your mind. You're to drive them home to your children and speak of them when you're staying at home and when you're going on a journey, when you lie down and when you get up. You're to tie them as a sign on your hand. They're to be bands between your eyes and you're to write them on the doorposts of your house and on your gateways. (Deut 6:6-9)

When your child asks you in the future, "What were the affirmations, the decrees, and the rulings that Yahweh our God ordered you?" you're to say to your child, "We were Pharaoh's serfs in Egypt, and Yahweh got us out of Egypt with a strong hand. Yahweh put great, bad signs and proofs against Egypt, against

Pharaoh and against his entire household, before our eyes, and he got us out of there in order that he might bring us in to give us the country that he swore to our ancestors. Yahweh ordered us to act on all these decrees, to live in awe of Yahweh our God for our good at all times, to keep us alive, this very day. It will be our right standing, when we keep this entire order before Yahweh our God by acting on it." (Deut 6:20-25)

You're to put these words onto your mind and onto your person. Tie them as a sign on your hand. They're to be bands between your eyes. You're to teach them to your children by speaking of them when you're staying at home and when you're going on a journey, when you're lying down and when you're getting up, and you're to write them on the doorposts of your house and on your gateways, in order that your days and your children's days may be many on the land that Yahweh swore to your ancestors to give them. (Deut 11:18-21)

The family is the place where children learn about life in general, about God and his ways with us, and about the story of God's involvement with his people. A huge responsibility thus rests on Israelite parents for the ethical upbringing of children. There is an even more solemn aspect to this relationship because the children often pay a price for the parents' wrongdoing.

> We became orphans with no father,
>   our mothers actual widows. . . .
> Our parents did wrong and are no more,
>   and we were the ones who carried their wayward acts. (Lam 5:3, 7)

In more everyday circumstances, conversely, when the children go prodigal, it can have disastrous consequences for the family (Prov 29:3). Here and elsewhere, "children" needn't mean little children. At least as much, it means teenagers, young adults, and grown-ups with children of their own.

Parents have responsibility for their children's safety in practical ways:

> When you build a new house, you're to make a wall for your roof so you don't put shed blood on your household when someone falling down falls from it. (Deut 22:8)

Parents have responsibility for their children's safety in other ways, too, Proverbs comments:

> Don't reject Yahweh's discipline, son,
>   don't despise his correction.

Because the one Yahweh gives himself to, he corrects,
> just like a father the son he favors. (Prov 3:11-12)

Son, guard your father's command
> and don't turn your back on your mother's teaching.
Fasten them into your mind always,
> bind them onto your neck.
When you're going about, it will lead you,
> when you lie down, it will keep watch over you,
> when you wake up, it will talk to you.
Because the command is a lamp and the teaching is a light,
> and the rebuke that disciplines is the way to life. (Prov 6:20-23)

The person who is sparing with his club repudiates his son,
> but one who loves him gets him up early with discipline. (Prov 13:24)

Discipline your son and he'll give you peace,
> and give much delight to your spirit. (Prov 29:17)

Parents are to correct their children as Yahweh does, and vice versa (Prov 3:11-12). It can actually mend relationships within the family (Prov 29:17). This correction includes corporal punishment (Prov 13:24). In this connection, too, one needs to remember that the Old Testament is not talking about infants but about teenagers and young adults.

One of David's great ethical failures lies here, and his family paid the price for it when he also failed to take decisive action over who was to succeed him as king. His third son, Adonijah, attempted to get himself crowned king; the background to his ambition was the way his father had never corrected him about anything.

Adonijah son of Haggit exalted himself, saying, "I will be king"; he prepared for himself chariots and horsemen, and fifty men to run before him. His father had never at any time displeased him by asking, "Why have you done thus and so?" He was also a very handsome man. (1 Kings 1:5-6)

To judge from what we read of David's other sons, Amnon, Absalom, and Solomon, he was not the only one. They illustrate Proverbs' comments on what can happen to someone who spurns his father's discipline, or never receives it; physical discipline can eradicate some stupidity:

A stupid person spurns his father's discipline,
> but one who heeds reproof shows shrewdness. (Prov 15:5)

The ear that listens to life-giving reproof
> lodges among the wise. (Prov 15:31)

Stupidity is bound up in a youth's mind;
> the club of discipline will take it far away from him. (Prov 22:15)

Listen to your father who begot you,
> and don't despise your mother when she is old. (Prov 23:22)

One who robs his father and his mother
> and says, "It's not an act of rebellion"—
> he's a companion of one who destroys. (Prov 28:24)

Someone who gives himself to wisdom rejoices his father,
> but someone who keeps company with immoral women destroys
> wealth. (Prov 29:3)

Club and reproof give wisdom,
> but a youth let loose shames his mother. (Prov 29:15)

A circle that humiliates its father
> and doesn't bless its mother! (Prov 30:11)

The eye that mocks a father
> and despises a mother's teaching:
The ravens in the wadi will gouge it out,
> and young eagles will eat it. (Prov 30:17)

Again, it will be middle-aged "children" who may be tempted to despise
and not to listen to their father and mother when they are old (Prov 23:22—
the aphorism is a good example of the way one needs to interweave the two
parts of a line). It will be middle-aged children who rob their parents and
deny they have done anything wrong (Prov 28:24).

It is at least in part because children learn about ethics from their parents
that they are to live in awe of their parents and to respect the elderly:

An individual is to live in awe of his mother and his father and keep my Sabbaths. I am Yahweh your God. . . . You're to get up in the presence of the grey-
haired, respect the person of the elderly, and live in awe of your God. I am
Yahweh. (Lev 19:3, 32)

When an individual has a defiant and rebellious son who doesn't listen to his father's voice or to his mother's voice, and they discipline him but he doesn't listen to them, his father and his mother are to get hold of him and take him out to the town's elders, to the gateway of his place. They're to say to the town's elders, "This son of ours is defiant and rebellious. He doesn't listen to our voice. He's a wastrel and a drunkard." All the town's people are to pelt him with stones so he dies. So you will burn away the bad thing from among you; all Israel will hear and live in awe. (Deut 21:18-21)

Living in awe of one's parents means doing what they say (Prov 6:20-23). It means keeping the Sabbath when they say keep the Sabbath (Lev 19:3). It means not being a wastrel and a drunkard, and if a son refuses to learn that principle, then it is the wider community's responsibility also to get involved in disciplining him (Deut 21:18-21). Some further lines from Proverbs:

A wise son [listens to] a father's discipline,
> but an arrogant person doesn't listen to a rebuke. (Prov 13:1)

A good man endows grandchildren;
> the strength of the offender is stored up for the faithful person.
> (Prov 13:22)

Discipline is evil to the one who abandons the path,
> but the one who repudiates reproof dies. (Prov 15:10)

Grandchildren are the crown of elders,
> but their parents are the glory of children. (Prov 17:6)

One who destroys a father or drives out a mother
> is a son who brings shame and disgrace. (Prov 19:26)

One who humiliates his father and his mother:
> his lamp will go out at the approach of darkness. (Prov 20:20)

Wisdom means not being too confident of your ability to shape life for yourself rather than heed your parents' discipline (Prov 13:1). So parents are their children's glory, and if they are, their grandparents will be able to be proud of them (Prov 17:6). On the other hand, shame and disaster come to someone who throws out their parents (for example, in their old age when they cease to be useful) or who humiliates them (Prov 19:26; 20:20). So ethics pays; wickedness gets its reward (Prov 13:22; 15:10).

One of my students once asked a question that arose from reading Christian parenting manuals. (I didn't know there were Christian parenting manuals, as I didn't know there were Christian dating manuals, though on reflection I should have guessed because, after all, the Scriptures include them.) One of these manuals urged parents not to neglect the use of physical punishment in discipline and correction of children. "I have been told," my student said, "that if I didn't spank my children (some say only until they become verbal, others at any sign of willful rebellion regardless of age) that I was disobeying God's command. These comments are usually fleshed out with tales of woe about parents who have ignored God's command and the unfortunate results. Also in the conversation the other famous parenting proverb ('Train up a child in the way he should go and when he is old he will not depart from it') is evoked as a form of guarantee. In other words if you parent this way your child will turn out great—if not you're in for a load of trouble. Is this a legitimate use of the proverbs? If not, how are the proverbs to be used? (Do you think I would have a less rebellious spirit if I had been spanked as a child?) Does the New Testament talk about disciplining children in this way?"

Another student later commented, "One of the problems with this viewpoint is that the verses cited as "mandates" or "commandments" are proverbs. "Do not withhold discipline from your children; if you beat them with a rod, they will not die. If you beat them with the rod, you will save their lives from Sheol" (Prov 23:13-14). What would happen if we regarded the entire book of Proverbs as commandments meant to be fulfilled literally by God's people today? Here are a few examples of the sorts of things we would be required by "biblical mandate" to do:

- Beat stupid people (fools) as well as our children (Prov 10:13; 14:3; 18:6; 26:3)
- Beat scoffers (Prov 19:25) and those who need inward purification (Prov 20:30)
- Cut off the tongues of perverts (Prov 10:31)
- Subject lazy people to forced labor (Prov 12:24)
- Own many oxen if we want to have food to eat (Prov 14:4)
- Cast lots in order to resolve disputes (Prov 18:18)

- Commit suicide by slicing our throats if our appetites are too large (Prov 23:2)

My own additional comments were:

- For a New Testament angle, see Hebrews 12:4-11.
- Remember again that the "child" who is disciplined is called a youth: the word includes teenagers and young adults, married as well as single.
- Note that the word for "discipline" or "correction" in Proverbs is the word that also means "instruction" (e.g., Prov 1:2, 3, 7, 8). It doesn't need to imply physical punishment if the context doesn't suggest that.

And now (Kathleen Scott Goldingay reminds me) I should again note that proverbs are more like observations about the way people have seen that things work out than divinely dictated categorical imperatives.

FOR REFLECTION AND DISCUSSION

1. In light of this material, what are your reflections on your relationship with your parents?

2. And on your relationship with your children, if you have any?

3. And on what you see of other peoples' relationship with their parents?

4. And on what you see of other peoples' relationship with their children?

25

NATIONS

The nations on far shores parted into their countries, each with its language, by their kin-groups among their nations. (Gen 10:5)

All the kin-groups on the earth will find blessing by you. (Gen 12:3)

All the nations on the earth will bless themselves by your offspring. (Gen 22:18)

Yahweh your God dried up the Jordan water before you . . . in order that all the peoples of the earth might acknowledge how strong is Yahweh's hand. (Josh 4:23-24)

Hazor was head of all these kingdoms. (Josh 11:10)

Old Testament Israel is a complicated entity. It is a kin-group, a people, a nation, an assembly, a congregation, a kingdom. It has a language and a country. It thus shares most of its forms with other peoples. In most of its forms, at least, Israel is designed to be a working model of what it means to be a human community and to be a means of blessing to other human communities, not least because the way God blesses it makes other communities pray to be blessed as it is blessed (e.g., Gen 12:1-3; 22:17-18).

First, being a kin-group suggests being naturally related to one another and living together in light of that relationship. A kin-group is an extended family—a vastly extended family. So the term suggests the assumption that the members of a nation will relate to one another in the way one would like to see the members of a family relate to one another. Within Israel, being a kin-group laid obligations on its members. When some members of the kin-group got into trouble one way or another, the other members were expected to come to its aid. If some members of the family were doing poorly economically, other members of the family were under moral obligation to lend them the necessities to enable life to continue, until their situation improved (Deut 15). When your brother's animals were in trouble or were lost, you didn't ignore the problem as if it didn't concern you (Deut 22:1-4).

Indeed, Genesis 9–10 sees all the peoples of its world as related to one another as if they were one vast extended family. They are all descended from Noah via his three sons. The implication would be that nations relate to each other as members of the human family. There is thus something manifestly wrong about treating a brother-sister people as if it is not a member of the family (Amos 1:9-10).

Second, etymologically, the Hebrew word for "people" likely also suggests the assumption that the members of a people are in some broad sense related to one another. They are ethnically one. They belong together genealogically. The Canaanites were a people (actually they were several). The Philistines were another people. The Israelites were yet another. And alongside the notion of being a blessing to other peoples is the idea of other peoples ending up under a curse. The first example is the hapless Canaan, who will find himself under a curse and in the lowest servitude to the descendants of Shem as a punishment laid upon his father for rather mysterious wrongdoing (Gen 9:20-27). An important aspect of the ethical significance of this passage is that it became the basis for seeing black peoples as implicated in this curse, which meant it was okay to enslave them and treat them in crushing fashion. Readers may be puzzled as to how interpreters derived this conviction from Genesis 9.

An ethical implication of this sorry tale about the interpretation of the Scriptures is that the interpretation of the Scriptures is an ethical undertaking—often an unethical undertaking. It can be the means of avoiding being ethical. We are all in danger of interpreting the Scriptures in a way that works in our favor and to the disfavor of other people.

A further insight emerges from this sorry tale about biblical interpretation. When Western people think about "race," we think especially of the way people groups are characterized by differences in skin color. It's a modern way of looking at race. When the Old Testament talks about race in connection with different peoples, it assumes that there are indeed distinctions between peoples, but skin color doesn't come into it. Now whether or not the men still have a foreskin, that's a different matter (e.g., Judg 14:3; Is 52:1)!

Third, nations are thus aware of distinctions and bounds over against other nations, and the growth of the nations in their separate identity in Genesis 10–11 is an outworking of God's creation blessing of humanity. That growth can become something selfish; the existence of nations is a means of trade flourishing, and this flourishing can be a blessing and a means to the domination of one nation over another. The growth of nations can be a means of self-assertiveness. In Genesis 11, people who are one in language seem nevertheless to be oddly apprehensive about their security in the world, and they build a tower as a bolster for their security. It is a security independent of God, and God sees it as dangerous. The God we have read about so far in Genesis hardly finds this development personally threatening. But he is concerned: who knows what they may do in God's world (see Gen 11:6)?

Fourth, diversity of languages links with diversity of peoples, though not in a neat way. There is a negative aspect to the existence of languages—it complicates communication. There is also a positive aspect—it complicates communication. Many large modern nations have one official language, though other large modern nations have more than one. The Old Testament almost begins with that story about how a group of people lose their common language and cease to be able to live and work together (Gen 11:1-9), and the Old Testament almost closes (in its Jewish order) with a story about the loss of language (Neh 13:23-27). Explicitly in Nehemiah, and perhaps implicitly in Genesis, having a common language is an aspect of having a common identity or culture or faith or life. It is also a symbol and a means of the capacity to communicate with one another and thus to work together and live together.

Yet oneness of language can be a means of oppression; English was one of the means whereby Britain controlled its far-flung empires. But encouraging diversity of language can also be a means of oppression, as happened in apartheid South Africa. And languages such as German and French cross national boundaries into Austria and Belgium.

Fifth, calling a people a country or land draws attention to the fact that it also has a geographical aspect. In Israel's world as in ours, one could call Moab or Edom or Babylon a country. Land and nationhood are tied together. The exceptions (the Romani, the Kurds, and the Jews themselves) test the rule, but in the end confirm it. A human being is not merely a soul but an embodied person, and so a nation is intrinsically related to its soil. God's plan in Exodus for the punishment of the Canaanites for their waywardness was to throw them out of their land—and such a punishment is close to causing them no longer to exist. It was God who gave the Philistines their land, and who gave the Syrians theirs (Amos 9:7). The Israelites could not simply take over the land of other peoples because they wanted it or even because God wanted to give it to them; it would not be fair (Gen 15:16). The Israelites could ask to travel through Edom (Num 20:14-21), but they knew they had to promise that they would not try to take over the Edomites' territory: "this land is not my home, I'm just a-passing through."

So the Old Testament does not take a negative view of the distinctiveness and separateness of peoples. It sees all of them coming to worship in Jerusalem, and even then they do not lose their identity. Yahweh plans that there should be a highway from Egypt to Assyria with Israel as its truck stop (Is 19:23-25); he doesn't plan that Assyria and Egypt should cease to exist as distinct entities.

Sixth, Israel was also a congregation, a religious entity. The religious affiliation of nations again brings complications. Sometimes Israel could coexist with its neighbors or with the superpower that controlled its destiny, and live with its theological differences over against them. The story of Naaman is a remarkable example (see 2 Kings 5:17-19). The Judahites could accept Persia's patronage of their temple (Ezra 1). Over the past two millennia, there have been long periods when the city of Jerusalem could embrace Jews, Christians, and Muslim communities living in harmony, though in modern times it no longer seems possible. In other words, it may or may not be possible for a nation to comprise several congregations.

Seventh, the Old Testament is also familiar with empires or superpowers, though it doesn't have a word for it. The first empire of which it speaks is Nimrod's (Gen 10:8-12). Genesis 14 tells a story about the city-states in the Jordan Valley that lived for some years under the control of imperial powers to the north, which were likely interested in them because of their position on trade routes. In due course the city-states rebelled and provoked the imperial powers to come to put them in their place. They made the mistake of taking Abraham's nephew among their captives, which incited Abraham to undertake a spectacular rescue mission and put the empire in its place.

Sometimes the Old Testament simply uses the plural word *nations* to refer to the empire.

Hey, the horde of many peoples,
>   that roar like the seas' roar,
The din of nations,
>   that make a din like the din of mighty water!
Nations make a din like the din of much water,
>   but he reprimands it and it flees far away. (Is 17:12-13)

These verses come near the center of the great systematic survey of individual nations in Isaiah 13–23. Here at the center the prophet comments on the destiny of an unnamed great nation—it was Assyria in Isaiah's day, but later it will be Babylon, Persia, Greece (Rome, Turkey, Britain, the United States, China . . .). Whereas the Old Testament implies that the development of individual peoples is an outworking of God's creation purpose, it's doubtful whether it sees any inherent goodness in the development of empires. The most devastating theological critique of them issues from the vision in Daniel 7, where they are monsters that emerge from the disorderly and tumultuous ocean. Elsewhere the Old Testament sees the superpower as subject to a number of dilemmas or temptations.

Sit in silence, enter into darkness,
>   Miss Kasdim [Babylon].
Because you will not again have them call you
>   mistress of kingdoms.
I was angry with my people, I treated my domain as ordinary,
>   I gave them into your hand.
You didn't show compassion to them;
>   upon the aged you made your yoke very heavy.
You said, "I shall be here permanently,
>   mistress always."
You didn't receive these things into your mind;
>   you were not mindful of its outcome.
So now listen to this, charming one,
>   who sits in confidence,
Who says to herself,
>   "I and none else am still here,
I shall not sit as a widow,
>   I shall not know the loss of children."

The two of these will come to you,
>   in a moment, on one day.
The loss of children and widowhood
>   in full measure will have come upon you.
In the multiplying of your chants,
>   and in the great abounding of your charms,
You've been confident in your bad dealing;
>   you said, "There's no one looking at me."
Your smartness, your knowledge,
>   it turned you back.
You said to yourself,
>   "I and none else am still here."
But bad fortune is going to come upon you
>   whose countercharm you won't know. . . .
You're collapsing in the multiplying of your plans;
>   they should indeed stand up and deliver you,
The people who observe the heavens,
>   who look at the stars,
Who make known for the months
>   some of what will come upon you. . . .
They've wandered, each of them his own way;
>   there's no one delivering you. (Is 47:1-11, 13, 15)

The reason the superpower exists is because people like power and they like stuff. The bigger and the more powerful you are, the more stuff you can accumulate. You can safeguard against your (perhaps irrational) fear of not having enough, or you can indulge your (certainly misguided) assumption that having more of everything will enhance your life. Your power does mean you can be a servant of God to effect God's purpose in the world. But you're likely to fulfill that role only unconsciously. You will not think in those terms. You will just enjoy power and stuff. So it is because you're tough that you can serve God, specifically in putting down peoples that God wants to put down. But your temptation is then to be ruthless, whereas God expects you to combine toughness with compassion (see chap. 2). And then, because you enjoy success through toughness and drive, your further temptation is to think that you will maintain your position of power forever. In practice, empires rise and fall, but no superpower ever thinks it will fall. Yet it will, and maybe the very fact that it thinks it is as eternal as God is the reason why it must, and the reason why it does. So it's wise for a superpower to keep in mind its position as God's servant, to resist attachment to power and stuff, to keep in mind their vulnerability, and to hold onto its own humanity by holding onto compassion.

FOR REFLECTION AND DISCUSSION

1. How far does your nation function like a family? How might it do so more?

2. How intrinsic is language to its nationhood?

3. Does your nation have a personality or a character or a gifting, and can you see how some other nation you know has a personality or character or gifting?

4. What is your perception of your nation as a superpower or of the superpower that dominates your situation?

26

MIGRANTS

It's quite reasonable for a nation to establish borders, as it's quite reasonable for a family to have a home. But a home is then the place into which the family welcomes other people and offers them hospitality, and a nation's territory is not by nature a basis for exclusion but a basis for inclusion. Which leads into a consideration of the place of aliens in a country.

> Sarah died at Arba Township (i.e., Hebron) in the country of Canaan. . . . Abraham set off from being in the presence of his dead and spoke to the Hittites: "I'm a resident, a settler, living with you. Give me a burial holding with you, so I may bury my dead." (Gen 23:2-4)
>
> Moses resolved to live with the man, and he gave Tsipporah his daughter to Moses. She gave birth to a son and he named him Gershom, because (he said) "I've become a resident alien in a foreign country." (Ex 2:21-22)

The Old Testament's word for a resident alien is *ger*, which means someone who is staying in a place that is not their own country or their own area. The word applies to Israelites who move to a part of the country other than their own, as well as to foreigners. I myself am a resident alien in the United States. When people ask where I come from, I say England, but I add with mock defensiveness, "But I'm not an illegal immigrant, I've got a green card." It puts me in a privileged position. I've just read the story of a Filipina graduate, a qualified teacher, who has lived in the United States for forty years working as a nanny and caretaker of old people in order to send money home to pay for the education of her seven children. She hasn't seen them over all those years, partly because going home would risk being unable to get back into the United States. Many of the vegetables and salads that I eat have been harvested by Mexicans and other Latinos and Latinas, many of whom are in the same position. That observation is not even to start talking about the plight of migrants from the Middle East taking refuge in Europe from conflicts back home.

I've been interested in several aspects of the reaction in the United States to the latter crisis. One is a declaration from this side of the Atlantic that Europe needs to set about solving this problem. Another is a fear of letting migrants come to the United States because of a correct awareness that some of them may be terrorists. Another is my diocese's determination, of which I feel a bit proud, that we as a diocese must set about finding ways of welcoming migrant families who come to settle in our area.

In Israel, too, people become resident aliens not because they've been offered a job somewhere else or simply fancy life in a different country. In some way life has become impossible in the place where they belong. Elimelek and Naomi, in what becomes the story of Ruth, leave Judah for Moab because of a famine. When Ephraim, the northern kingdom of Israel, falls to the Assyrians, some Ephraimites come to Judah as resident aliens there. They would never be able to possess land in Judah to replace the land they lost in Ephraim, but they might find a way of living. In an earlier period, many resident aliens found employment in the building of the temple (1 Chron 22).

In Israel, as in the modern world, migrants are in a vulnerable position. The Torah therefore emphasizes the need to treat them in the proper way. Negatively, people are not to take advantage of them.

> A resident alien: you will not afflict him; you yourselves know the feelings of a resident alien, because you were resident aliens in Egypt. (Ex 23:9)

> Be mindful of the Sabbath day to make it sacred. For six days you can serve and do all your work, but the seventh day is a Sabbath for Yahweh your God. You will not do any work, you, your son or your daughter, your servant or your handmaid, your animal, or your resident alien who is in your communities. Because in six days Yahweh made the heavens, the earth, the sea, and all that's in them, and settled down on the seventh day. That's why Yahweh blessed the seventh day and made it sacred. (Ex 20:8-11)

> When a person is a resident alien with you in your country, you will not wrong him. The person who is a resident alien with you is to be for you like a native

from among you. You're to love him as someone like you, because you were resident aliens in the country of Egypt. I am Yahweh your God. (Lev 19:33-34)

You will not defraud a humble and needy employee from your brothers or from your resident aliens who are in your country, in your communities. You're to give him his payment on the day. The sun will not go down on it, because he's humble and he's basing his life on it, and he will call out to God against you, and there will be wrongdoing counted against you. (Deut 24:14-15)

People are to make it possible for them to share in the Sabbath, not to use them as a way of getting things done on the Sabbath. If they are day laborers, they are to be paid when they have done their day's work. To ill-treat them is just as bad as (say) committing adultery.

So I shall come near to you to exercise authority and be an eager witness against the diviners, the adulterers, the people who swear falsely, the people who defraud the employee of his wages, the widow and orphan, and those who turn aside the resident alien and who are not in awe of me. (Mal 3:5)

Yahweh is loyal to the faithful;
> Yahweh keeps watch over the resident aliens.
He relieves orphan and widow,
> but subverts the way of the faithless. (Ps 146:8-9)

Yahweh your God—he's the God over the gods, the Lord over the lords, the God great, mighty, and awe-inspiring, who doesn't honor a person and doesn't accept a bribe. He makes a ruling for the orphan and the widow and he is loyal to the resident alien by giving him bread and clothing. So you're to be loyal to the resident alien, because you were resident aliens in the country of Egypt. (Deut 10:17-19)

So one bit of the rationale for treating them properly is that Yahweh keeps an eye on what happens to them. Another is that the Israelites know what it's like to be resident aliens, so they should be sympathetic to their needs. Indeed, that sympathy should push them beyond holding back from taking advantage of them into deliberately helping them find sustenance, even though it costs.

When you reap your harvest in your fields and you overlook a sheaf in the fields, you will not go back to get it. It's to belong to the resident alien, to the orphan, and to the widow, in order that Yahweh your God may bless you in all the action of your hands. When you beat your olive tree, you will not go over it after you. It's to belong to the resident alien, to the orphan, and to the widow. When you cut the grapes from your vineyard, you will not pick it over after you. It's to belong to the resident alien, to the orphan, and to the widow. You're to be mindful that you were a serf in the country of Egypt. That's why I'm ordering you to do this thing. (Deut 24:19-22)

Yet further, they will go beyond charity: they will embrace resident aliens into the community. The men will be welcome to accept circumcision and thus share in Passover like native Israelites (Ex 12): there's nothing more inclusive. Resident aliens are to share in Shavu'ot (Pentecost) in the same way (Deut 16:9-12). The same expectation applies to the Sukkot harvest festival, when all Israel rejoices: resident aliens are to be brought into the rejoicing (Deut 16:13-15). The same expectation applies to solemnity of the Day of Atonement (Lev 16).

You're standing today, all of you, before Yahweh your God—your heads, your clans, your elders, your officials, every individual in Israel, your little ones, your wives, your resident alien who is within the camps, from the person who chops your wood to the one who draws your water—for you to pass over into the pact of Yahweh your God and into its vow, which Yahweh your God is solemnizing with you today, in order that he may set you up today as a people for him and that he may be God for you, as he spoke to you and as he swore to your ancestors, to Abraham, to Isaac, and to Jacob. (Deut 29:10-13).

Assemble the people—the men and the women, the little ones and the resident alien who is in your communities—in order that they may listen, and in order that they may learn and live in awe of Yahweh your God, and keep all the things in this instruction by acting on them. (Deut 31:12)

They are to be treated as full members of the community. They are part of the covenant people. They are privileged and responsible to listen to the Torah and live by it. So when Moses gives the Israelites their instructions for confirming the covenant when they get to the promised land, the Israelites are to include in the ceremony the resident aliens who have been with them on the journey (Deut 31:12). They are all to listen to the exposition of Yahweh's expectations of them; these expectations apply to them all. The Sabbath command is again significant here. Resident aliens are to observe the same rules about which people they can have sex with or marry (Lev 18:6-23). The same penalties for cursing Yahweh's name apply to them, and the same rules about assault: "there's to be one ruling for you; it's to be as with the resident, so with the native, because I am Yahweh your God" (Lev 24:22).

In this connection, a key consideration that the Old Testament presses on Israel is that its people have to see themselves as resident aliens, in more than one sense. It's true about them as human beings. "This world is not my home, I'm just a-passin' through." The Israelites did not know that they were on the way to eternal life; they did know that they were beings with a limited lifespan that contrasts with God's eternity.

> I'm a sojourner with you,
>   a transient like all my ancestors. (Ps 39:12)

> Who am I, and who is my people? . . . Because we are resident aliens before you, transients like all our ancestors. Our days are like a shadow on the earth, and without hope. (1 Chron 29:14-15)

They are also resident aliens as Israelites because it is Yahweh's land that they are living on. You can't own land in the Old Testament. Land belongs to God. In addition, their own experience in Egypt means they know what it's like to be a resident alien.

> The land will not be sold permanently because the land belongs to me, because you're resident aliens, settlers, living with me. In the entire land that's your holding, you're to grant restoration for the land. (Lev 25:23-24)

Israel's land, in particular, belongs to God. If you defile the land, you have caused a lot of trouble between you and God. You're like someone who is renting an apartment; you have to treat it in a way that recognizes you do not own it. The land belongs to God, you can only reside on it.

> When there's a wrong that carries a death sentence against a man and he's put to death, and you hang him up on a tree, you will not let his corpse stay the night on the tree. Rather, you're to make sure you bury him that day, because someone hanged up is a slight to God, and you will not make taboo your land that Yahweh your God is giving you as a domain. (Deut 21:22-23)

If you're not an Israelite (or if you are an Israelite who has moved somewhere else) you can't even reside on it in the same sense as other people can. The definition of a resident alien is that it is someone living in a country or an area other than their own, who therefore cannot permanently own land. The land as a whole has been allocated to Israel (other people have their own land) and the area that a clan such as Judah occupies has been allocated to it and divided among its extended families. There is no "spare" land. As a resident alien in the United States, I can own my house and the land it sits on. In Old Testament Israel, I wouldn't be able to.

Why would it matter? In a traditional society it matters hugely, because a family's land is its livelihood. There is no supermarket down the road and not much opportunity to earn a salary that would enable one to buy things there. Resident aliens are acutely dependent on the generosity of the village where they live if they are to eat as well as if they are to have somewhere to sleep.

So it's important that the people in the village remember the reasons for caring about resident aliens. They are to remember that, fortunately, Yahweh keeps watch over resident aliens—so they had better do so. They are to remember their own (or their ancestors') experience of being resident aliens in Egypt. They know what it feels like to be a resident alien. Indeed, Abraham had been a resident alien when he lived in Canaan because it was never the ancestors' land until Yahweh gave it to them in the time of Joshua. And Moses had been a resident alien with a Midianite family before he was commissioned by Yahweh.

FOR REFLECTION AND DISCUSSION

1. What do you think it would look like to love resident aliens in your community?

2. Are there resident aliens in your community who are needy because of their position?

3. Are there ways in which resident aliens are treated wrongly in your community?

4. Are there ways in which you could welcome resident aliens into your fellowship and enable them to learn about what God has done for us?

5. What difference does it make to us to see ourselves as resident aliens with God?

27

CITIES

The Bible's first city is named after Adam's grandson. Cain has killed his brother and been sentenced to wander the earth as a fugitive.

> Cain slept with his woman, she got pregnant, and she gave birth to Enoch. He was building a city, and he named the city after his son Enoch. To Enoch was born Irad, Irad fathered Mehuyael, Mehuyael fathered Metusael, and Metusael fathered Lemek. Lemek got himself two women; the name of one was Adah, the name of the second Tsillah. Adah gave birth to Yabal; he was the ancestor of everyone who lives with a tent and livestock. His brother's name was Yubal; he was the ancestor of everyone who plays guitar or pipe. Tsillah, she too gave birth, to Tubal Cain, forger of all copper and iron. Tubal Cain's sister was Naamah. (Gen 4:17-22)

The city begins as a refuge from the insecurity of an open and hostile world. The city will in due course become a metaphor for community, but archaeological work in Canaan also draws attention to this more primary facet of its significance, because the dominant architectural feature of the Israelite city is its walls. It is first and foremost a stronghold, a refuge from enemies (the metaphor functions this way in Psalms 46 and 48). But Cain's insecurity had been willed by God. The story of the city has an inauspicious beginning.

The end of the story in Genesis 4 is also inauspicious. First there is the proud violence of Lemek, which we noted in chapter eleven. The city is a place where violence flourishes, not least family violence. But Genesis also tells us that the city's development is the context in which families grow (Enoch, Irad, Mehuyael, Metusael, Lemek) before it is the context in which the order of marriage becomes imperiled when Lemek takes two wives. The city is the context in which art and technology begin to develop (the invention of musical instruments, the forging of tools) even though the first recorded use of such discoveries is in the glorifying of human violence (in Lemek's proud verses about the execution of his wrath on an enemy) as the city becomes a place where vengeance has to be subjected to constraint. There are huge differences between preindustrial cities and the vast cities of the industrial era, but they also have common features. Both kinds of cities facilitate the development of art and technology. They are the context where specialized activities and crafts evolve, though the underside of this latter is the emergence of a class structure in society. They are also the context where writing develops: if there had been no city, it seems there would have been no history, no theology, no science, no Bible.

The negative aspects to the city hinted in Genesis 4 are also factors underlying the formulating of the Torah in Israel. It is therefore illuminating to consider the Old Testament's regulations for the city in light of its stories about the city, and specifically to look at Deuteronomy, whose material was put together in urban Jerusalem. It reflects a more developed state than that of the regulations in Exodus and a more "everyday life" set of concerns than that of the priestly material represented by Leviticus.

There runs through Deuteronomy a series of concerns that are illuminated by the awareness that this is teaching for an urban culture. Most of them we have noted in discussing matters such as the administration of justice, womanhood, and family order, but here we can note how these concerns together relate to life in the city.

First, Deuteronomy emphasizes honesty and truth in society. There is to be no swindling of customers by merchants (Deut 25:13-16). There is to be machinery for handling tricky legal cases in a fair way (Deut 17:8-13). The same law is to apply to rich and poor—which is not how it feels to many inner-city people, particularly when race is factored in. Deuteronomy 19 includes a rule to limit the taking of redress by establishing places where a person guilty of accidental homicide may find refuge from the vengeance of his victim's family.

Second, the teaching is concerned for the needy, in particular for groups whom we might call the underclass, people who have fallen out of the regular support systems of society. In Israel these comprise especially people who have no land by which to support themselves (we might see being without land as the Israelite equivalent to being without a job). They include Levites, widows, orphans, immigrants, poor people generally, and people whom debt has taken into servitude (e.g., Deut 14–15).

Connected with that concern, third, is Deuteronomy's stress on brotherhood. When it seeks to motivate people to take action on behalf of those needy groups, it keeps reminding them that such people are their brothers (e.g., Deut 15). It reminds people in government not to forget that they are the brothers of those they govern (e.g., Deut 17:14-20). As an institution, the city combats the more "natural" division of humanity by families and clans: where people live now counts as much as who they are related to. As Deuteronomy sees it, the community needs to be the family writ large. It might be saying retrospectively to Cain and Abel, "Come on, you're brothers."

Fourth, as if to anticipate the charge of being sexist in its stress on brotherhood, it adds a concern for womanhood. Its teaching repeatedly mentions attitudes to mothers, wives, and daughters, and their rights and responsibilities, as well as those of fathers, husbands, and sons (e.g., Deut 15; 18). It points to the fact that women need protecting in the city. In *The Origin of the Family, Private Property, and the State*, Friedrich Engels traced the subjugation and oppression of women to the breakup of the communal kin group and the transformation of the nuclear family into the basic economic unit of society, because this turned women's work into a private service for their husbands. It was thus an urban phenomenon.

Related to this concern for womanhood in Deuteronomy, fifth, is a concern about family order and sexual relations, which we considered in chapter twenty-two (see e.g., Deut 22). Sex easily goes wrong in the city.

Sixth, and most strikingly, a recurrent theme in Deuteronomy is happiness. Only in Psalms and in Proverbs among the Old Testament books does the verb *rejoice* occur more than it does in Deuteronomy. Its teaching keeps returning to the joy of festivals and the joy of food, and perhaps invites us to see the joys of the city as God-given and its unhappiness as to be fought in the name of the God of joy.

The reason why these ideals come to expression in Deuteronomy is that they are not actually embodied in Israel's urban life. Another noteworthy feature of Deuteronomy is that it starts where society is. Its vision can seem insufficiently radical by the standards of some parts of both Testaments, but one reason is that in seeking to pull society toward ideals it ought to affirm, Deuteronomy manifests a practical concern that begins from society as it is in its sinfulness or "hard-heartedness" (Mark 10:5). Politics and social policy combine ideals and the art of the possible. Deuteronomy implies that we should both be realistic about how things and people are, and also be visionary about the ideals we affirm, and then be specific in the way we bring the two together. Bringing together ideals and realism is the vocation of society's lawmakers, economists, and planners. People concerned about the city often pay their respects to the Old Testament by nodding toward the eighth-century prophets, but the Deuteronomists provide at least as suggestive a role model for practical involvement in society. If Christians want to play a part in the shaping of urban policy, we need to nurture the economists, lawyers, planners, and civil servants in our churches.

Deuteronomy is not just a legal or ethical work but a theological one built on Israel's being Yahweh's people and Yahweh's being Israel's God. This factor underlies its concern about right and wrong forms of worship in the sanctuary that Yahweh chooses. In a culture in which palace and temple stood together at the apex of the city, this urban document could not ignore religious issues. It is easy for city and religion to be interwoven to the exclusion of God. That theme also emerges in Genesis. We looked briefly at Genesis 11 in chapter twenty-five, but we may consider it further here.

> Now the entire earth was of one language and common words. As people moved on in the east they found a valley in the region of Shinar and lived there. They said, one to his neighbor, "Come on, let's make bricks and bake them thoroughly"; so they had brick in place of stone, and tar in place of cement. They said, "Come on, let's build ourselves a city and a tower with its top in the heavens, and make a name for ourselves so we don't disperse over the face of the entire earth." But Yahweh went down to see the city and the tower that the human beings had made. Yahweh said, "Here, one people with one language for all of them, and this is the first thing they do. So now nothing that they may scheme to do is closed off from them. Come on, let's go down and make a babble of their language there, so one person won't be able to hear his neighbor's language." So Yahweh dispersed them from there over the face of the entire earth and they left off from building the city. That's why it was named Babel, because there Yahweh made a babble of the language of the entire earth, and from there Yahweh dispersed them over the face of the entire earth. (Gen 11:1-9)

Apart from the telling note in Genesis 10:8-12 about Nimrod, the first mighty warrior who was also a great city builder, the Bible's second major city is Babel. People decide to settle in Shinar (Babylon) and build themselves a city there. It's to have a skyscraper, a tower reaching to the heavens so that the people would not be scattered all over the world. Again the city is a refuge from the insecurity of an open world and from the destiny willed for them by God. They were supposed to fill the world, and the previous chapter has described the scattering of peoples as part of humanity's filling the world after the flood, but these people resist that destiny. They want to stop in one place and find a unity grounded in fear. It may not exclude religion but rather make use of religion, as a government may expect to use an established church in the United Kingdom and as politicians do in the United States. The city is a place to reach for the heavens. There are echoes of the Babylonian ziggurat and a reflection of the fact that a characteristic feature of a city is the presence of monumental buildings, which urban economics make possible. One aim of this project is for the builders to make a name for themselves. The city represents human ambition and pride, which can be positive as well as negative attributes.

This city is a monument to human creativity and inventiveness as its builders work out how to use manufactured brick in the absence of natural stone. But Genesis may speak ironically, because brick means mud, shaped and dried in the sun. In Israel it was a common enough building material for private houses, but it was inferior to the stone hewn from a quarry, which was preferred for important buildings. Further, the builders lacked proper cement and had to fix their mud bricks together with tar. The ambiguity about Genesis's portrayal of the city perhaps corresponds to the ambiguity of Israel's experience of the city, and of ours.

Building a city was also a dangerous enterprise, as God saw it. "Who knows where else it may lead?" God asks. The city builders threaten to become like gods. So those who were afraid of being scattered are scattered by God, and they give up building the city. It becomes a place of non-communication. World peace and the success of the United Nations might be demonic in effect rather than divine.

The scattering was an act of judgment, but it opened up the possibility of God's purpose being realized in the filling of the world rather than people stopping in one place. It plays a part in the implementing of God's vision for humanity. It thus points us toward the prophets and their vision of judgment on the city and the transformation of the city. The prophets lived in the midst of calamity, in vision or in reality. Their vocation was to prepare people for calamity, to interpret it, and to respond to it. "Classical prophecy" begins with the appearance of the Assyrians on Israel's northern horizon and with the need for Israel to discover what God was doing with the nation in this context. The first of the prophetic books opens by presupposing that disaster has overtaken the cities of Judah: Isaiah's aim is to try to explain it and to help Judah learn the lesson (see Is 1). Prophets do call for repentance, but too hasty a desire to link them to programs for social reform may obscure their significance in a way that reduces their importance for us in the long term. Isaiah focuses on declaring to the people of God the fact and the significance of the judgment that hangs over their city. The city of David, which became Yahweh's city, the holy city, is now the bloody city, and Isaiah declares that "Yahweh Armies has a day in store for all the proud and lofty, for all that is exalted; . . . for every high tower and every fortified wall" (Is 2:12, 15). It is a warning rather than a program for reform.

A prophetic ministry involves drawing attention to facts and threats so as to make it difficult for government or nation to ignore clouds on the horizon. Prophets took part in public debate by trying to make people face facts. Another prophet was sent to tell a huge foreign city, a bloody city notorious for double-dealing, greed, and aggressiveness, that it was about to be overturned (Jon 3:1-3). He didn't invite Nineveh to repent, but to his disgust it did so, and his awful fear was fulfilled. God relented. "Am I not allowed to care about this great city with its hundred and twenty thousand people who do not know their right hand from their left," he asks, "let alone the cows?" (Jon 4:11). Jonah's story suggests that pagan cities can be saved as well as Israelite ones, though they do need to repent, not just be reformed.

Nor does this approach apply only to individual cities. Isaiah 24 offers a nightmarish portrayal of a ruined city that stands not for a particular place but for the world's urban civilization, high and lofty but defiled and desolated. A fortified town has been turned into a heap of rubble never to be rebuilt. Its memorial is those lifeless tells that scatter Israel's landscape, mute witnesses to the collapse of an urban civilization (cf. Is 25:2; 26:5). The ruined city is a symbol of humanity under judgment: compare Jesus' tirades against cities (e.g., Mt 11:20-24), and the diatribe in Revelation 18.

Such negatives are not all there is to the Bible's vision for the city. Isaiah 1 closes with a transition from the city under judgment to the city transformed. The judgment is itself the means of transformation. "Afterward you will be called 'Justice City,' 'Faithful City'" (Is 1:26). This Zion will be raised on high by God himself, not by human will. Such promises are to be spurs to human action (cf. Is 2:5), but to demythologize them into merely veiled exhortations regarding what we are to achieve is a besetting temptation to be resisted. They are promises of what God purposes to achieve, causing this Zion to attract the world as a place where it may discover the keys to truth and peace (Is 2:2-4; a significant promise when the news from Jerusalem is persistently disheartening). This promise for the city recurs throughout Isaiah (e.g., Is 26:1; 45:13; 52:1) and also in Revelation 21–22, where the city is a place of splendor, strength, community, provision, security, generosity, healing, and holiness, accessible to all as a place where God is known in glory, love, and grace. Whereas the Bible began in a garden, from which humanity was soon excluded, and might have been expected to conclude in the garden, it ends in the city, or in a place with the virtues of both, a garden city watered by a life-giving river and nurtured by fruiting trees. The city is one of a series of human devices such as sacrifice, monarchy, and temple that are taken up by God, even though they did not arise from God's initiative, and are worked into God's purpose so graciously that we would not be able to conceive of worship or of Jesus or of the fulfillment of God's final purpose without them.

God has a dream for the city. There is reason for hope even when there is no scope for action and when justice looks defeated. That consideration takes us to one more element in the Old Testament's approach to the city. In the late twentieth century, Western people started rediscovering the prayers of protest in the Psalms (often misleadingly called the lament psalms). While praying these psalms has enabled people to talk to God about the hurts in their own lives, the ethical significance of such psalms is to enable us to voice to God our protests on behalf of other people who are hurting. It is an aspect of weeping with people who weep. Praying from the position of the people whose need we take into our heart is the way the Psalms go about intercession. And the pain, suffering, and oppression that lie at the background of the Psalms are often those of the city (compare also Lamentations).

> Lord, swallow up, divide their speech,
>> because I see violence and contention in the city.

Day and night they go round it, on its walls;
>   harm and troublemaking are inside it.
Malice is within it;
>   injury and deceit do not leave its square. (Ps 55:9-11)

The city was supposed to be a place of refuge and safety, but it's not, so the Psalms challenge God to do something about that reality. The Bible does not tell us to pray for the city; it shows us how to do so. And prayer is the distinctive gift that the church adds to the efforts of social and community workers, politicians, and civil servants, on behalf of the city. It is the church exercising its indispensable ministry on the city's behalf. If it abandons it, we fall short at the crucial point; we are then simply activists alongside other activists who may fail because we neglect to lay hold on the resources for the city that lie in God. The Psalms do not point us toward the horizontal kind of prayer in which we exhort ourselves to play our part in bringing in the reign of God, nor even just the semi-vertical kind of prayer that asks God to enable us to fulfill our commitment to justice and peace, nor the kind of prayer that assumes God is real enough but is sitting in the gallery watching what goes on, keenly interested, but not active in the arena itself. The Psalms point us toward the disinterested kind of prayer that begins from human helplessness and lays hold on divine power and mercy because they are all there is; at many points in the city they *are* all there is. But such prayer lays hold of God's dream and urges him to implement it.

FOR REFLECTION AND DISCUSSION

1. Are there ways in which the Old Testament's positive portrayal of the city illumines your perception of the city?

2. Are there ways in which the Old Testament's negative portrayal of the city illumines your perception of the city?

3. Are there ways in which we need to learn from the Old Testament's rules for the city?

4. Are there ways in which the Old Testament's talk of the city points you toward hope or fear or prayer?

28

LEADERS

Leadership is an obsession and an idol in the world and in the church. It's another of those words like *community* that is undefined and undefinable; you can only say it's a word with warm associations. We are sure that it's important, which will be one reason why our faith in the value of leadership has an extraordinary capacity to survive our disappointment with actual leaders.

Saul, David, and Solomon illustrate the point. Each of their stories opens up ethical questions. One aspect of the background to Saul's story is the horrifying account of life in Israel that appears in the second half of the book of Judges. I noted in chapter eleven that people sometimes express dismay at the Bible's telling such appalling stories, and I think I discern two reasons why they do so. One is the feeling that the Bible is supposed to describe an alternative world, a better world than the one we live in. So why is it telling stories about a world that may seem even worse than the one we live in? This sense of puzzlement might mean that people would like the Bible to be more like comfort food, so that reading it becomes an exercise in escapism. Yet the sense is right that the Bible should (and does) lay before us God's promise of a better world. The other reason for a sense of dismay at the Bible's horrifying stories is that it doesn't keep saying "So this was really wicked, wasn't it?" in the way an old-fashioned Sunday school teacher would, and people infer that the Bible doesn't disapprove of the actions it records. Really, it simply assumes that we don't need to be told that this or that action was wicked. It's self-evident.

Judges itself does make the point in the note that recurs at the end of the book: "At that time there was no king in Israel. Each person would do what was all right in his own eyes" (Judg 21:25).

Israel lacked proper leadership. Leadership does have the capacity and the vocation to set bounds to the way people behave, and in Saul's day you don't hear about the kind of horrifying events that you read about in Judges. But when people asked Samuel to appoint them a king, one of his objections was ethical. Leaders live better than their people. They live in bigger houses, they have better health plans, they go on more interesting vacations, they are enrolled in better pension schemes, they drive bigger cars. Are you prepared to pay for those, Samuel asks? Yes, the people say. That's how important leadership is to them. The ethical challenge to leaders is to resist taking advantage of that willingness on their people's part.

> Samuel spoke all Yahweh's words to the people who were asking for a king from him. He said, "This will be the authority of the king who will reign over you. Your sons he'll take and make into his chariotry and into his cavalry for himself, and they'll run before his chariotry, making them divisional officers and unit officers for himself, and for plowing his fields and reaping his harvest and making his battle equipment and his chariot equipment. Your daughters he'll take as perfumers, cooks, and bakers. Your fields, your vineyards, and your olive groves, the best, he'll take and give to his servants. Of your seed and your vineyards he'll take a tenth and give to his courtiers and to his servants. Your servants and your maidservants, your best young men and your donkeys, he'll take and make into his work force. Of your flock he'll take a tenth and you yourselves will become servants to him. You will cry out on that day on account of your king whom you've chosen for yourselves, but Yahweh will not answer you on that day." (1 Sam 8:10-18)

The ethical high point in the story of Saul's kingship comes (unfortunately) at the beginning, in the story we looked at in chapter four; afterward it's all downhill. Having been out plowing, he comes home and hears that the Ammonites are threatening to gouge out the eyes of everyone in Yabesh-in-Gilead, in Israelite territory that the Ammonites would like to annex (1 Sam 11). God's spirit falls on Saul, he gets really angry, and he leads the Israelites in a bold and successful attack on the Ammonites and delivers the people of Yabesh.

Two ethical insights from Saul's story derive from the fact that he didn't really want to be king. Like Moses, he tried to avoid it. This is always a wise move, though it tends to be unsuccessful. It has some ethical significance for the people who appoint leaders. Don't appoint people who want to be leaders. Appoint people who don't. At least then you are not simply playing into their desire for self-aggrandizement and thereby imperiling them and imperiling their people. Unfortunately, like every other principle about leadership, this principle (that you appoint people who don't want to be leaders) may not work. Saul didn't want to be king, but once he was king, he grew to like it. Instead of being thrilled and relieved when Samuel put him on notice, he tried desperately to hold onto his position. The ethical principle for leaders: don't get attached to the job because the job has become the means of your self-fulfillment.

David did want to be king, and he was good at it. His ethical high point is less racy, but it is at least as profound. "David reigned over all Israel, and David exercised authority in faithfulness for all his people" (2 Sam 8:15). "Exercising authority in faithfulness" is the basic biblical expression for what we call social justice; we noted the significance of the phrase in chapter five. "Exercising authority in faithfulness" is the central vocation of leadership. On one hand, it involves power, authority, the making of decisions. On the other, it involves being faithful to the mutual commitment that is supposed to obtain within the community. Authority without faithfulness would be demonic. Faithfulness without the exercise of authority would be wishy washy and fruitless.

Unfortunately, within a couple of chapters David's story goes south when he spots a woman bathing in what she thinks is the privacy of her roof, summons her, has sex with her, and ends up having her husband killed. "But the thing that David did was bad in Yahweh's eyes" (2 Sam 11:27). You bet it was. David has the position and he uses it. He has the power and he uses it. His life is never the same afterward. The two ethical challenges of leadership in David's story are the ease with which leaders can use power to their own ends, and the way sex is often the downfall of a leader. And the frightening further ethical reality it expresses is how easily one wrong act leads to another and another and another, so that you eventually find yourself doing something (in David's case, arranging for the death of one of your top soldiers) that at the beginning you could never have imagined.

The highlight ethical moment in King Solomon's story again comes near its beginning (there is a worrying pattern here). Two women come to him as the equivalent of Israel's Supreme Court (1 Kings 3). They had both had babies, one baby had died, and now they both claimed to be the mother of the live baby. "Bring me a sword, I'll cut him in half," says Solomon. "Okay," says the mother who is lying. "No, give her the baby," says the real mother. You can't train people in ethics so that they are able to render a Solomonic judgment of this kind. Ethics requires imagination and inspiration.

The achievement and the problem with Solomon was that he turned Israel into a proper Middle Eastern state operating by Middle Eastern rules. He fulfilled Samuel's warnings. He undertook stupendous building projects for achievements in Jerusalem and elsewhere, but it involved his people in "tough servitude"; they were like oxen pulling an unreasonably heavy load (1 Kings 12:4).

When his people looked back on Solomon's life, they wanted to know if his son and successor, Rehoboam, was going to work the same way. The elders advised Rehoboam to be a servant to his people. I have hinted that the Bible doesn't share our enthusiasm for leadership—it's more interested in servanthood. Rehoboam is the king who has the chance to be a servant leader. Unfortunately, he blows it, thinking that a display of apparent strength will get him further than a display of apparent weakness.

> Rehoboam went to Shechem, because all Israel had come to Shechem to make him king. . . . Jeroboam came with the entire congregation of Israel and they spoke to Rehoboam: "Your father—he made our yoke tough. So you, now, lighten something of your father's tough servitude and of his heavy yoke that he put on us, and we'll serve you." He said to them, "Go for three more days, and come back to me." The people went, and King Rehoboam took counsel with the elders who had been standing before Solomon his father when he was alive: "How do you counsel me to give back word to this people?" They spoke to him, "If today you'll be a servant to this people, and serve them, and answer them and speak good words to them, they'll be your servants for all time." (1 Kings 12:1, 3-7)

Unfortunately Rehoboam ignores the advice.

Deuteronomy anticipates what will go wrong with kingship and seeks to forestall it.

> When you come into the country that Yahweh your God is giving you and you take possession of it and you're living in it, and you say "I intend to set a king

over me, like all the nations that are around me," you may indeed set over you a king whom Yahweh your God chooses. From among your brothers you may set a king over you. You cannot put over you an individual who's a foreigner, who's not your brother. Only, he will not acquire many horses for himself and he will not get the people to go back to Egypt in order that he may acquire many horses, when Yahweh has said to you, "You will never again go back that way." He will not acquire many wives for himself, so his mind does not turn aside, and he will not make very much silver and gold for himself. When he sits on his royal throne, he's to write for himself a copy of this instruction on a document, from before the Levitical priests. It's to be with him and he's to read out of it all the days of his life, in order that he may learn to live in awe of Yahweh his God, by keeping all the words of this instruction and these decrees by acting on them, so his mind doesn't rise above his brothers and so he doesn't depart from the order, right or left, in order that he may stay a long time over his kingdom, he and his sons, within Israel. (Deut 17:14-20)

It would be logical for the Torah simply to ban the idea of having kings, but Deuteronomy knows that its people are stubborn and knows it is no use being totally unrealistic. So it allows for kings and tries to regulate the working out of the idea. First (it says), God is going to decide who will be king. We see this principle working out in the stories of Saul and David. Second, it keeps emphasizing that the king is just a brother among brothers. He must never forget that he is only a member of the family. Third, he mustn't acquire the accoutrements of leadership such as horses (i.e., impressive military equipment) and wives and wealth (a dig at Solomon here). And he is to make himself a copy of this Torah and to keep reading it.

FOR REFLECTION AND DISCUSSION

1. How does your church appoint leaders?
2. How have you seen leadership go astray in your church or community?
3. Have you seen trouble arising for lack of leadership?
4. How does your church seek to support and protect its leaders?
5. "If today you'll be a servant to this people": can you think of examples of leaders being servants?

PART FOUR

TEXTS

All the way through this book, I am wanting my readers to pay more attention to the Old Testament text than to what I write. Reading books about the Bible easily becomes a replacement for reading the Bible. It may seem easier. I come across a lot of conviction that the Bible is too difficult for people to understand unless they have been to seminary. I want to demystify it a bit. So there's a lot of the actual biblical text in this book. Quite often it comes at you in big chunks, partly to safeguard against taking individual verses in isolation from their contexts. In part four we look at some whole chapters of the Old Testament that carry particular ethical freight, and even at a couple of entire (but short) books.

29

GENESIS 1

In the Beginning

Fifty years ago, a professor at UCLA argued that the spoiling of the earth that had come about in the modern age was the fault of Christian faith and the teaching of Genesis. One reason why his claim was implausible is that two or three millennia had elapsed since the composition of Genesis and since the beginnings of Christian faith; the time lag seems a bit long. More likely the fault lies with modernity itself. If there is a link with Christian faith, it lies in the abandonment of Christian faith in the context of modernity.

But Genesis does raise some significant questions in connection with our relationship with the created world.

At the beginning of God's creating the heavens and the earth, when the earth was an empty void, with darkness over the face of the deep, and God's breath sweeping over the face of the water, God said, "Light!" and light came into being. . . . God said, "The earth is to put forth vegetation: plants generating seed, fruit trees producing fruit by its species, with its seed in it, on the earth!" So it came to be. The earth brought forth vegetation, plants generating seed by its species, and trees producing fruit with its seed in it by its species. God saw that it was good. . . . God said, "The water is to teem with living creatures, and birds are to fly over the earth, over the face of the dome of the heavens!" God created the big sea monsters and every living creature that moves, with which the water teems, by their species, and every winged bird by its species. God saw that it was good. God blessed them: "Be fruitful, be numerous, fill the water in the seas; birds are to be numerous on the earth." And there was evening and there was morning, a fifth day. God said, "The earth is to bring forth living creatures by their species—animals, moving things, and the living things of the earth, by their species!" So it came to be. God made the living things of the earth by their species, animals by their species, and all the things that move on the ground by their species. God saw that it was good. (Gen 1:1-3, 11-12, 20-25)

First, Genesis sees the created world as one whole. What we call the animate and the inanimate are part of that whole, with a shared relationship with God. It exists in its own right before God, and God thinks it's rather good. It's thus not open for appropriation by us and for being used as if it belongs to us. The Old Testament is more explicit about this matter with regard to the land that God gives Israel to live on. He emphasizes that it belongs to him, and they are only granted the right to live on it as tenants. They can't sell it to one another, and he can throw them out if they offend him—which they do, and he does. But Genesis implies that this principle applies to the entirety of the earth—the areas where Israel (or other peoples) live and the areas that are just there. Its resources of iron and copper (for instance) might be available to us, but not for us to treat as if we have rights over them.

The plant world is created for its own sake, or for God's sake, though it's in this connection that it is then given over to the animal and human world as food. Likewise the animal world is created for its own sake, or for God's sake, and not for humanity's. If anything, the relationship is the other way around. Genesis's view of the world does not see the world as centered on humanity, as I noted in chapter sixteen. Humanity is created to rule it on God's behalf.

God said, "Let's make human beings in our image, as our likeness, so they can hold sway over the fish in the sea, over the birds in the heavens, over the animals, over all the earth, and over all the things that move on the earth." So God created human beings in his image. He created them in the image of God. He created them male and female. God blessed them, and said to them, "Be fruitful, be numerous, fill the earth and subjugate it, hold sway over the fish in the sea, over the birds in the heavens, and over every creature that moves on the earth." God said, "Here, I give you all the plants that generate seed that are on the face of all the earth, and every tree with fruit that generates seed. These will be food for you, for all the creatures of the earth, for all the birds in the heavens, and for all the things that move on the earth that have living breath in them, all the green plants as food." So it came to be. God saw all that he had made, and there—it was very good. (Gen 1:26-31)

It's in connection with humanity's role in the world that Genesis speaks about our being made in God's image and our being male and female, and it's in this connection that he speaks of us multiplying so as to fill the earth. In Christian theology the fact that we are made in God's image has gained a life of its own, and it has become a key to understanding what it means to be human, which is fine. But we need not to lose the original context and significance of the phrase. In Genesis the idea is that we were made in God's image because that fact meant we could represent God in the world as the people who rule it on his behalf—one piece of background is the way a Middle Eastern ruler might erect statues (images) of himself in different parts of his realm to remind people of his rule. The ethical challenge here would be that our ruling the world on God's behalf needs to be undertaken in a way that truly does represent God. The God whom we are called to image is classically characterized as exercising authority with faithfulness, and those would be the qualities to expect of us in our relationship with the world.

Likewise there is a link between our being made in God's image to rule the world and our being made male and female. The point is that we could consequently multiply so that there would be enough of us to run the earth on God's behalf. And if it seems that we have multiplied enough to that end (and indeed are in danger of overrunning the world), we might well infer that it is time for us to stop multiplying.

The language that God uses in connection with our ruling the world is admittedly surprising. God says we were created to subjugate it. God uses the word that Joshua uses about subjugating the Canaanites, the word you would use for taming a lion. For all the fact that the world is good, this goodness doesn't mean it has realized its destiny or realized God's purpose for it. It needs taming so that the different parts of it work together instead of working against each other. Humanity's vocation is to oversee that process.

Our being put in charge of the animal world doesn't imply we can eat it. What about the problem that, while human beings can live as vegetarians, lions apparently can't, and they too are given only plants to eat? One should perhaps simply allow for the metaphorical nature of the language here. When Genesis says that God spent a week creating the world, it's a picture. He could obviously have done it in a flash, and it looks as if actually it took rather longer. But picturing God systematically dividing the work up so that he can take a week over it makes it possible to portray God's week's work as analogous to ours. In a parallel way, implying that we were supposed to be vegetarian may be a metaphor for that idea that we exist for the sake of the animal world; it doesn't exist for our sake. And however we interpret Genesis, it has implications for the way we treat meat simply as a commodity and treat animals as just beings we can subordinate to our desires and manufacture as if they were just things.

There's a link between Genesis 1 and what may seem some odd rules in the Torah.

> You will not sow your vineyard with two species, so the full harvest doesn't become sacred (the seed that you sow and the vineyard's yield). You will not plow with ox and with donkey together. You will not wear a mixture of wool and linen together. (Deut 22:9-11)

> You will not mate two kinds of animals; you will not sow your field with two kinds; you will not put cloth woven of two kinds onto yourself. (Lev 19:19)

Genesis 1 portrays God making an ordered world in which everything has its place, and it portrays creation as a finished work (notwithstanding that need for subjugation). So some of the rules in the Torah say, don't mix things that God made separate. Live and work in accordance with the way God created the world. Be wary of trying to improve on it.

FOR REFLECTION AND DISCUSSION

1. What do you think of the UCLA professor's argument?

2. Are there ways in which you fail to treat the inanimate world as God's?

3. What could you do to reflect God's image in the world?

4. Do you think you should become vegetarian? If not, are there other ways in which you should rethink your attitude to animals?

5. Do you think humanity has multiplied enough?

30

GENESIS 2

To Put It Another Way

When Yahweh God made the earth and the heavens, and no bush of the wild was on the earth yet and no plant of the wild had grown yet . . . Yahweh God shaped a human person with dirt from the ground and blew into its nostrils living breath, and the human person became a living being. Yahweh God planted a garden in Eden, in the east, and put there the human being he had shaped. Yahweh God made to grow up from the ground every tree that's desirable to look at and good for food, with the life tree in the middle of the garden, and the good-and-bad-knowledge tree. . . . Yahweh God took the human being and set him down in Eden Garden to serve it and keep it. Yahweh God ordered the human being: "From every tree in the garden you may definitely eat. But from the good-and-bad-knowledge tree you will not eat, because on the day you eat from it, you will definitely die." (Gen 2:4-5, 7-9, 15-17)

The two creation stories are both about things that really happened; this second story is about how God really created the world, really made humanity to look after it, really made the world an attractive and tasty place, really created men and women as complements to each other, really gave them vast choice in the world but also with a constraint or two. The story of the Garden of Eden is not a story like Jesus' parable about the prodigal son, who as far as we know didn't exist. Yet it is like a parable in the sense that it's not a literal historical story. If God had inspired a literal story about creation, no one would have understood it, and it wouldn't have helped them to understand the world and themselves. This is a story about the real event of creation that's told to help people see who they were created as and what they were created for.

So who are we? We are made from physical stuff. It's often been tempting to think that the real human being isn't the material body but the soul. The Scriptures don't think that way. At the beginning, the first human being started off as a body (and at the end, our bodies will be resurrected). The body is essential to the real me. It *is* the real me. The person is embodied in the body. No body, no person. So the body is to be honored and looked after. As Paul will note, it's the temple of the Holy Spirit. That idea goes back to the beginning. The person is the body with God's living breath breathed into it, with the result that it's then not just a thing lying there unable to move but a living thing, a living person. So we aren't to misuse our bodies or neglect them. And we aren't to misuse other people's bodies or neglect them.

As the body is good so is the world. Genesis doesn't say whether Adam or Eve were good-looking, though I imagine they were. It does comment on how good-looking was the vast variety of trees in the orchard (Israelites would think of grapes, figs, olives, pomegranates, dates, and apricots; we now know about apples, oranges, bananas, and kumquats)—not to say tasting good. The world was made to be a morally good place; it was made to look good and taste good, and ethics involves letting it stay that way and enjoying it that way.

God created humanity with a vast amount of free choice and one limitation. He gave no reason for the strange prohibition regarding the good-and-bad-knowledge tree. In ethics, the question can be asked whether things are good because God says so or whether they are good in themselves and God simply affirms that they are. The Old Testament speaks both ways—sometimes it tells us why things are commanded or forbidden, but here at the beginning it simply asserts what people could do and what they couldn't do, and gives no reasons. Ethics can simply mean doing what God says because God says it, not because you understand it.

> Yahweh God said, "It's not good for the human being to be on his own. I'll make him a helper suitable for him." Yahweh God shaped from the ground every creature of the wild and every bird in the heavens, and brought them to the human being to see what he'd call it. Whatever the human being called a living being, that became its name. The human being gave names to all the animals, to the birds in the heavens, and to all the creatures of the wild. But for a human being he didn't find a helper suitable for him. So Yahweh God made a coma fall on the

human being so he slept, took one of his ribs, and closed up its place with flesh. Yahweh God built the rib that he'd taken from the human being into a woman and brought her to the human being. The human being said, "This, now, is bone from my bones and flesh from my flesh! This one will be called woman, because from a man this one was taken." That's why a man abandons his father and his mother and attaches himself to his woman, and they become one flesh. The two of them were naked, the man and his woman, but they felt no shame. (Gen 2:18-25)

Whereas Genesis 1 tells of God first creating the world, then creating humanity to look after it, in this second story God first creates the creature who is to look after the world, then creates the world. But the aim is the same. The world is not there for us. We are there for the world. The same consideration is the background to the creation of another creature to be alongside the first one. In Western understandings, marriage is about a personal relationship, about being soul mates. The Song of Songs fits with assumptions along those lines, but the Old Testament's first statement about the origin of marriage has its focus somewhere else. The problem about the first human being isn't that he's lonely. It's that he is alone, he has been given a huge job, and he can't do it on his own.

Maybe another form of animate life can help? And it can. Oxen will be useful on the farm. Sheep will provide wool. Donkeys will be useful until someone has invented the pickup truck. Animal hides will fulfill all sorts of functions. The human being is given the privilege of naming all the creatures that God parades before him; it is a sign that he is in charge of them, in authority over them.

But the human being needs a partner; it will help if this partner is capable with him of then generating more people. While marriage was designed to be a personal relationship, it was also designed to be a work relationship. When an Israelite couple work their farm together in a fashion that honors both the wife's role and the husband's, they are fulfilling the aim of their creation. The second human being is made by starting from a part of the first, which establishes that they really are of the same stuff. And it's neat that she is made from his side. A rabbinic tradition that also appears in Christian writers such as Augustine notes that Eve was not created from Adam's head so she could rule him, nor from his foot so she could just be his servant, but from his side so she could stand alongside him. The creation vision soon goes wrong, but that idea was the creation vision. So the first man doesn't name the first woman, as if he had authority over her as he has over the animals. Rather he recognizes her. This is it!

The relationship means the man abandons his father and mother. In a way he doesn't do that physically in Israel, because his wife comes to join him as a subunit within the extended family of which his father is still the head—though maybe when the couple have children they will live in a separate adjacent house. Maybe the point is that precisely because it's his wife who will physically leave her parents to join him (though they will likely live in the same village), it's also important he abandons his parents in the more subtle sense that his primary obligation now is this new commitment.

Associated with that leaving is their cleaving to each other, attaching themselves to each other, forming one flesh. That expression doesn't merely mean they unite sexually—it may not refer to that at all. The expression *one flesh* is related to the idea of the same flesh and blood. It means they do become a new family unit that is semi-separate from either of their previous family units. Yes, this new unit now becomes their first obligation, a relationship of first importance.

Then there is the fact that Adam and Eve were naked but not ashamed. Again that probably doesn't refer to sex, though the Song of Songs would once more support the idea that people can be confident and open with each other sexually. Usually, when the Old Testament refers to nakedness and shame, however, it's referring to the opposite of having resources and honor. The first couple have nothing, but they don't feel ashamed of the fact. They can trust God for everything.

FOR REFLECTION AND DISCUSSION

1. Are there ways in which we fail to take our bodies seriously enough?

2. Are there ways in which we take our bodies too seriously?

3. Are there ways in which your relationship with the animal world is askew?

4. Can men and women stand alongside each other in your community or congregation?

5. In your culture, are there ways in which people don't really leave their parents and form a new unit?

31

LEVITICUS 25

Sabbaths for the Land and the Jubilee

Leviticus 25 is a densely packed set of instructions concerning the land. We don't know that any of the instructions were implemented in Old Testament times—not because Israel was disobedient but because even though they may look like a program, they are really more like a vision. That fact makes them more significant for us. They are not a set of injunctions essentially bound to the life of a largely agricultural society which might thus be of little use outside that context. They are the embodiment of a vision, and we may be able to do something with the vision.

> When you come into the country I'm giving you, the country is to make a Sabbath stop for Yahweh. For six years you may sow your field and for six years you may prune your vineyard and gather its yield, but in the seventh year there's to be a complete stop for the country, a Sabbath for Yahweh. You will not sow your field, you will not prune your vineyard, you will not reap your harvest's afterrowth, you will not cut the grapes of your free vines. It's to be a year of stopping for the country. The country's Sabbath will be food for you, for you yourself, for your servant and for your handmaid, for your employee and for your resident alien living with you, for your animals, and for the creatures that are in your country: all its yield will be for eating. (Lev 25:2-7)

Farming is to stop one year in every seven, and people are to trust that the things that grow without being tended will be enough for them for that year. It's not because it will be good for the land (though perhaps it will). It's to happen for Yahweh's sake. It's similar to the Sabbath day, which is first of all designed to honor Yahweh, though it's also good for people. So a first principle is: our use of the land and our growing must recognize that the land belongs to God and must treat it accordingly.

Then, once every fifty years there is to be a kind of Sabbath year of Sabbath years. It's to be heralded by the sounding of a horn, which in Hebrew is *yobel* or *jobel*, which is thus the origin of the word *jubilee*. The jubilee year also benefits humanity, though it too is equally if not more fundamentally concerned with God. (Maybe the implication is that if we do things in a way that glorifies God, they will work out well for us, but if we put our needs first, they probably won't.)

> You're to count seven Sabbaths of years for yourselves, seven times seven years, so that the time period of your seven Sabbaths of years will be forty nine years. You're to make a blasting horn pass through in the seventh month, on the tenth of the month; on the Day of Atonement you're to make the horn pass through your entire country. You're to make the fiftieth year sacred and call for a release in the country for all the people living in it. It's to be a ram's horn year for you. You're to go back, each individual, to his holding, and to go back, each individual, to his kin-group. The year, that fiftieth year, is to be a ram's horn year for you: you will not sow, you will not reap its after-growth, and you will not cut its free vines, because it's a ram's horn year. It's to be sacred for you. You will eat the yield from the field. (Lev 25:8-12)

In 1994, Pope John Paul II wrote, "As the Third Millennium draws near, in the spirit of the Book of Leviticus (25:8-12), Christians will have to raise their voice on behalf of all the poor of the world, proposing the jubilee as an appropriate time to give thought, among other things, to reducing substantially, if not canceling outright, the international debt." There were some great results from the idea that 2000 should be a jubilee year in which the countries in the developed world should cancel the debts owed them by the majority world. Uganda had $1 billion (£715 million) worth of debt relief and used it to double primary school enrolment. Mozambique was able to reduce its annual payments from $127 million a year to $52 million, and thus spend more on hospitals and housing. The jubilee movement also unlocked $50 billion in government funding for global health, mainly for HIV/AIDS treatment in Africa. But a review of the jubilee movement in 2010 had to

acknowledge that it wasn't clear that there had been as much progress in debt
relief as people hoped.

> In this ram's horn year you're to go back, each individual, to his holding. When
> you sell something to your fellow, or buy from your fellow's hand, you're not
> to wrong one another. It's by the count of the years since the ram's horn year
> that you're to buy from your fellow; it's by the count of the years of yield that
> he's to sell to you. On the basis of the large number of the years you'll pay a
> high price to him; on the basis of the low number of the years you'll pay a low
> price to him, because it's the count of the yields that he's selling to you. You will
> not wrong one another but live in awe of your God, because I am Yahweh your
> God. (Lev 25:13-17)

The prospect of the ram's horn year coming needs to be taken into account
when people are making loans and taking over land, because the land is only
"worth" the number of years to elapse before the jubilee year. The arrival of
that year would be terrific for the families that had lost their land, though any
individual farmer would be unlikely to live long enough to benefit from the
redistribution. Which again indicates that the rule has a bigger framework
than what's good for an individual.

> The land will not be sold permanently, because the land belongs to me, because
> you're resident aliens, settlers, living with me. In the entire land that's your
> holding, you're to grant restoration for the land. When your brother does
> poorly and sells part of his holding, his restorer who is near him is to come to
> him and restore what his brother has sold. When an individual doesn't have a
> restorer, but his means stretch and provide enough for its restoration, he's to
> think over the years since his sale and give the surplus back to the individual
> to whom he sold it, and go back to his holding. (Lev 25:23-28)

Jean-Jacques Rousseau suggested that the introduction of the idea of
private property was the original sin. He meant the idea of staking off a piece
of land and claiming it as exclusively one's own. Leviticus knows that the land
of Israel belongs to God, but he leased it out to Israel and commissioned its
allocation to the twelve clans, and then within each clan to its extended families. The practical fact that lies behind this rule in Leviticus is that over time
some families are unsuccessful and have to give up their land and let it be
taken over by someone else. Maybe it's simply their fault for being lazy or
inefficient, or maybe they are unlucky. Maybe they take out loans (which

mostly means food and seed corn, not money, which hasn't been invented) and they can't pay them back, and have to forfeit their land to their creditor.

If they are lucky, people for whom things have gone badly may have within their extended family a "restorer" or "redeemer." It's what Boaz is for Naomi and Ruth. A restorer is a relative who has done better than you have and has the resources to settle your debt and thus "restore" you to your land. If you don't have someone who can act in that way, maybe over the years your family will do better and you will be in a position to pay off the debt and get your land back. The point about the jubilee rule is to benefit people who have no restorer and whose circumstances don't improve. Once every half-century all the land allocations go back to what they were.

> If an individual sells a dwelling house in a walled town, its restoration may happen up to the completion of a year from its sale. . . . If it's not restored up to the fulfilling of a whole year for it, the house . . . will transfer permanently to the person who bought it, through his generations. It will not go out in the ram's horn year. (Lev 25:29-30)

No human beings created land, even if they did clear it of rocks and irrigate it and help it grow things. Such is the logic behind the principle that people can't own land, only have it on loan from the person who created it. But human beings do build houses, even if the raw material again comes from God. What, then, if someone has to give up their house in a town (as opposed to their homestead or their home in a village where everybody was a farmer)? They might be people who live in the town but go out each day to farm, and the problem might again be laziness or inefficiency, or they might be people who work at a trade, such as bakers or potters, whose business fails. They have just a year to claim their house back, but after that time the sale is final. The jubilee year doesn't help. Here as at other points the jubilee rule has to balance the interests of the debtor and the creditor and try to be fair to both.

> When your brother does poorly and his means fall to you, you're to take firm hold of him as a resident alien, a settler, so he can stay alive with you. You're not to take interest or profit from him; you're to live in awe of your God, so your brother can stay alive with you. You will not give your money to him at interest and you will not give him your food for profit. I am Yahweh your God who got you out of the country of Egypt to give you the country of Canaan, to be God for you. When your brother does badly with you, and he sells himself

to you, you will not make him serve with servile service. He's to be with you as an employee, as a settler. Until the ram's horn year he's to serve with you, then he's to go out from you, he and his children with him, and go back to his kin-group, to his ancestors' holding. Because they're my servants, whom I got out of the country of Egypt, they will not sell themselves as a servant is sold. You're not to hold sway over him with harshness. You're to live in awe of your God. (Lev 25:35-43)

Suppose you're the creditor: that is, you've been hard-working or lucky and you've been able to grow enough for your family and a bit to spare. You can therefore make a loan to someone else in the village, to a "brother." When the Old Testament talks about a brother, it commonly means a fellow Israelite; the people of God is a family, and you're to treat someone as a brother whether or not he's a close relative. You may then have the chance to take over this brother's land. And if your success issued from your efficiency or hard work, you may be able to make a go of this bigger farm. You may then be tempted to treat making a loan to your brother as a way of making a profit. But you're not to treat your brother as some kind of slave. He's not selling himself to you. He's more like a resident alien.

Your servant and your handmaid who belong to you from the nations that are around you—from them you may buy a servant or a handmaid, and also from the children of the settlers who are resident aliens with you. You may buy from them and from their kin-groups that are with you, that give birth in your country, and they will be your holding. You may have them as a domain for your children after you, to possess as a permanent holding. By means of them you may get service. But over your brothers, the Israelites, over one another you will not hold sway with harshness. (Lev 25:44-46)

The situation with foreigners is different. They aren't part of the total community that was commissioned to look after the land. They're people who've just come here looking for a job. They can be bought and sold, though it doesn't mean they can be treated the way African American slaves were treated. We will note in considering the story of Joseph (chap. 39) that in the West we are inclined to have only one way of defining "freedom" and "slavery/servitude," and the Old Testament opens up the possibility of a more nuanced understanding of them and of different ways of defining them.

FOR REFLECTION AND DISCUSSION

1. How far do people in your church know about how one another are
   doing economically: for example, whether they have problems
   with debt?

2. Could there be a system in your church for helping one another
   when people get into debt?

3. Are there other ways in which members of your church can help
   one another get back on their feet in the way this vision suggests?

4. In your town, are there ways in which workers get treated in servile
   fashion? What could you and your church do about it?

32

DEUTERONOMY 15

When a Family's Life Falls Apart

I've just been reading an article about inequality. Apparently countries go through cycles of greater or lesser economic inequality. Paradoxically, an event such as a war is inclined to issue in more equality. When the political situation is stable, it issues in more inequality. Part of the reason is that people with power are then able to use their power in order to benefit themselves. So inequality is likely to grow until there is either a war or a revolution. Sometimes one can see overlapping dynamics at work in ancient Israel. A time of stability like that of Solomon issued in more inequality. The demands of imperial taxes in the time of Nehemiah put pressure on the community, but Nehemiah browbeat people into starting to work with a sense that we are all in this together. And the Torah tries to regulate the way things work in this connection.

There is some overlap between the prescription in Deuteronomy 15 and the one in Leviticus 25. They are two different visionary proposals for dealing with the same sort of problem. I assume that the background of both ultimately lies in Jerusalem in the century or two leading up to the city's fall in 587 BC. The difference might then be that Deuteronomy is closer to being a definite practical proposal—it's a kind of reworking of rulings in Exodus, and Jeremiah berates people in Jerusalem just before 587 for not abiding by these rulings. Leviticus is then more of a vision, yet perhaps one that takes into account the fact that the Deuteronomy ruling turned out to be too demanding.

At the end of seven years you're to effect a release. This is the thing about the release: anyone in a position to make a loan from his hand who makes a loan to his neighbor is not to exact it of his neighbor, his brother, when the release for Yahweh has been called. You may exact it of a foreigner, but whatever of yours is with your brother, your hand is to release. (Deut 15:1-3)

If debts are cancelled after six years, one can imagine the temptation to try to avoid making loans in year five ("I'm sorry, I've got hardly enough for my family for next year"). That moment is when you have to remember that the person in need is your brother. In the narrow sense (to our way of thinking), he's not your brother. He's not your own flesh and blood, and blood is thicker than water. But we note again that the Torah likes reminding Israelites that they all belong to one family—they are all descendants of Jacob-Israel, the father of the twelve sons who gave their names to the clans to which all Israelites belonged. Yes, your neighbor in the village is your brother. Treat him as such.

When there's a needy person among you, one of your brothers, inside one of your communities in the country that Yahweh your God is giving you, you will not firm up your mind and you will not close your hand against your needy brother, because you're to open your hand wide to him and generously lend enough for the lack that he has. Keep watch on yourself so a thing doesn't come into your scoundrelous mind, "The seventh year, the release year, is drawing near," so your eye works badly toward your needy brother and you don't give anything to him, and he calls to Yahweh about you and it becomes a wrong done by you. Give generously to him. Your mind must not work badly when you give to him, because the needy person won't leave off from within the country. That's why I'm ordering you, "Open your hand wide to your weak and your needy brother in your country." (Deut 15:7-11)

The extended family is thus key to the Old Testament's approach to dealing with situations where people get into economic difficulty. The vast majority of Israelites lived in villages or on homesteads and farmed the land around. We have noted that some families would be luckier or smarter than others, or would work harder, and the end of the year would come and some families would have harvested enough to last them through the next year, and other families would not, and the haves were then expected to lend grain and oil and so on to the have-nots, on the assumption that next year, or the year after, they would pay back the loan. But every seven years, loans were cancelled and everyone started again.

There's another rule that nuances the point about lending.

> If you lend silver to my people, to a humble person who is with you, you will not be like a lender to him. You will not make him pay interest. If you take your neighbor's coat as a pledge, before sundown you will give it back to him, because it alone is his covering, his wrapping for his skin. What is he to sleep in? When he cries out to me, I shall listen, because I am gracious. (Ex 22:25-27)

Generosity is a key virtue in the Torah, but it's a generosity in lending as opposed to giving. Lending treats someone with more honor than giving. It's not "charity." It honors the person by assuming that they will work to pay you back, and you will be equal. Indeed, next year, you may need to borrow from them. But the rule in Exodus 22 knows that things may not work out in that way. To start with, you have to resist the temptation to charge him interest, as we noted in chapter eight. Lending is not an arrangement whereby you can make a profit. If he gives you his coat as collateral, give it back to him to sleep in, because it's also his blanket. (Deuteronomy 24 adds that you mustn't take a widow's coat as collateral at all.)

> When your brother, a Hebrew man or a Hebrew woman, sells himself to you, he may serve you for six years, and in the seventh year you're to send him off from you as a free person. When you send him off from you as a free person, you will not send him off empty-handed. You're to supply him liberally from your flock, from your threshing floor, and from your winepress. With what Yahweh your God has blessed you, you're to give to him. Be mindful that you were a serf in the country of Egypt and Yahweh your God redeemed you. That's why I'm ordering this thing today. (Deut 15:12-15)

Suppose a family gets chronically into an economic mess. Israelites aren't expected to bail one another out forever. As an alternative to making an outright loan, you could take a family and its land under your wing for a spell to try to get things back on even keel for it. The farmer who is in trouble might get you to take on his son(s) or daughter(s) as servants, and then might get you to take him on in the same way, and take control of his land to see if you could do a better job of farming it than he has. Modern translations refer to people becoming slaves in this way, but this modern translation is misleading because it suggests the kind of slavery we are familiar with from British and

American history. The Israelite arrangement didn't mean that the master owned the servants and could do as he wished with them. Specifically, Exodus 21 says, if you strike your servant with a club and he dies, you are to submit to redress—it doesn't make explicit what that means (does it count as murder?), but it does indicate that you can't do what you like or treat your servant as a thing. (If the servant recovers, there's no redress, on the grounds that there is a sense in which the servant is the owner's silver—that is, he has wasted his own resources in making his servant incapable of work while he is sick.)

Nor did people have to become servants for life. They were more like employees who got fed in return for working on the farm, and they gained their freedom after six years. The master was then under obligation to send them back onto their land with animals and produce that will give them a fair chance of starting again. The next bit of the rule shows how different this bond-servanthood must be from slavery.

> When he says to you, "I won't go out from you," because he's loyal to you and your household, because things have been good for him with you, you're to get an awl and put it through his ear and through the door, and he'll be your servant permanently. You're also to do this for your handmaid. When you send him off from you as a free person, it shouldn't be tough in your eyes, because he's served you for six years for the equivalent of the wages of an employee. And Yahweh your God will bless you in all that you do. (Deut 15:16-18)

The treatment of their servants that is expected of masters is so fair and generous that Deuteronomy can imagine a servant family declining the chance to have their freedom and saying that they would like to stay as servants! Exodus 21 provides the small print. For instance, if you're a single man and you become a servant, and your master gives you a wife with whom you start a family, at the end of the six years you have to choose between staying with them and leaving on your own. If you're a single girl and your father sells you as a servant with a view to your marrying the master or one of his sons, either you do become a wife or your master lets you be redeemed. The rules again work for compromises with the different parties so as to protect people without being so unrealistic that no one would take any notice of them.

As a halfway stage between being free and being a servant, you might become an employee in a more literal sense. The idea of employment seems natural in the West, but it's seen as odd in the Old Testament. The ideal is not that you sell your labor to someone but that you are part of the family business. But circumstances might drive you into "taking a job." So the rules offer you a bit of protection. Your employer is not to defraud you (whether you are an Israelite or a resident alien), and he is bound to pay you at the end of the day's work, because you need your pay in order to live (Deut 24:14-15).

FOR REFLECTION AND DISCUSSION

1. Are there ways in which it's possible for your community to work more on the basis of being a family?

2. Are there ways in which your congregation could work more on the basis of being a family?

3. What are the key characteristics of the kind of employer whom people want to stay with (maybe even if they could earn a bit more elsewhere)?

4. Are there ways in which people who need loans are taken advantage of in your culture?

5. Can you think of ways in which we can help people gain a new start without simply falling into the same old traps?

33

DEUTERONOMY 20

How (Not) to Make War

The theory called just war starts from the assumption that war is a terrible thing, but that sometimes it's the right thing; sometimes not to go to war would be worse. So just war theory asks about the circumstances in which it might be the least bad thing, and about the least bad ways to go about making war. For instance, you should make war if it's a way of preventing worse atrocities, but you can't make war just to gain territory, and you can only make war as a last resort, and you shouldn't attack civilians. Just war theory doesn't have its background in Christian thinking, and there's no indication that its framework affects the thinking of Old or New Testament, but it's been adopted into Christian thinking, and the actual phrase "just war" apparently comes from Augustine.

The Old Testament implicitly assumes that there were no wars before there was sin in the world, and it assumes that eventually God will abolish wars, but in the meantime, like just war theory, it simply recognizes that war is a reality and it shrugs its shoulders, as Jesus says there will be wars and rumors of wars (Mt 24:6). You could say the Old Testament has its own "just war" theory, of which Deuteronomy 20 is a spectacular expression. And then you could say that its "rules" for just war would be the despair of any commander-in-chief.

> When you go out for battle against your enemies and you see horse and char-
> iotry, a company bigger than you, you will not be afraid of them, because
> Yahweh your God, who got you out of the country of Egypt, will be with you.

When you're drawing near for battle, the priest is to come up and speak to the company, and say to them: "Listen, Israel. You're drawing near for battle against your enemies today. Your heart is not to be soft. Don't be afraid, don't be in haste, don't be frightened before them, because Yahweh your God is going with you to do battle for you with your enemies, to deliver you."

The officials will speak to the company: "Who's the individual who's built a new house and not dedicated it? He's to go and turn back to his house so he doesn't die in battle and another individual dedicate it. Who's the individual who's planted a vineyard and not initiated it? He's to go and turn back to his house so he doesn't die in battle and another individual initiate it. Who's the individual who's betrothed a woman and not taken her? He's to go and turn back to his house so he doesn't die in battle and another individual take her." The officials are to speak further to the people and say, "Who's the individual who's afraid and whose mind is frail? He's to go and turn back to his house so his brothers' mind doesn't melt like his mind." When the officials have finished speaking to the company, they're to appoint army officers at the head of the company. (Deut 20:1-9)

First, the chaplain is in charge of speaking to the troops before battle, but that's okay, because his job is to motivate them by encouraging them to trust in God as they fight. But then some mysterious officials address the army and give the fighters a series of plausible reasons for going home. It turns out that the house you've built, the vine you've planted, and the girl you've courted are more important than the battle you're supposed to fight. Further, if you're afraid, you can also go home—after all, your fear may infect other people.

When you draw near to a town to do battle against it, you're to call for peace to it. If it answers with peace and opens up to you, the entire people that's to be found in it will become yours, as a workforce. They'll serve you. If it doesn't make peace with you and does battle with you, you're to besiege it, and Yahweh your God will give it into your hand. You're to strike down all its males with the mouth of the sword. Only, the women, the little ones, the animals, and everything that's in the town, all its spoil, you may take as plunder for yourself, and devour your enemy's spoil, which Yahweh your God has given you. . . . When you besiege a town for a long time in battling against it to capture it, you will not devastate its trees by thrusting an axe against them, because you're to eat from them. You will not cut them down, because are the trees of the open country human beings, to come before you in a siege work? Only, trees that you know are not trees for food, them you may devastate and cut down so you may build a siege work against the town that's doing battle with you, until its fall. (Deut 20:10-14, 19-20)

So the army is to avoid fighting if it can persuade its foe simply to surrender. They will then become a workforce for you (which is different from being slaves or for that matter dead, or having their eyes poked out as those Ammonites wished to do to the people of Yabesh-in-Gilead in 1 Sam 11). If it won't surrender, you're to fight and kill the men, but not the women and children and the animals, and for that matter you aren't to cut down the fruit trees in building siege works—you can only cut down the non-fruit trees.

These rules look impractical, though we've noted that this consideration applies to many rules in the Torah. It's then maybe not surprising that we don't read of occasions when Israelites implemented them. They are examples of rules that embody the kind of commitments that the nation was supposed to accept. One of these commitments parallels one that appears in the just war tradition—don't make war if you can help it. The rules show an extraordinary concern for the combatants (it's worth keeping in mind that distinguishing between combatants and noncombatants is a recent idea—in a traditional society, all the men were combatants). They don't let war be managed by the military. They show a concern for fruit trees!

A neat story in Numbers 21 offers a variant on the Deuteronomic vision. The Israelites are nearing the edge of the Promised Land and their route requires them to pass through the territory ruled by one Sihon.

> Israel sent envoys to Sihon, king of the Amorites: "I want to pass through your country. We won't turn off into your field or into your vineyard. We won't drink water from your well. We'll go by the King's Road till we pass through your border." But Sihon didn't let Israel pass though his border. Sihon gathered his entire company and went out to meet Israel, into the wilderness. He came to Yahas and battled against Israel. But Israel struck him down with the mouth of the sword and took possession of his country from the Arnon as far as the Yabboq, as far as the Ammonites, because the Ammonites' border was strong. Israel took all these towns. (Num 21:21-25)

The Israelites had no reason to be fighting these particular Amorites. Their land was not land they were destined to take. So they wanted to pass through it peacefully. But Sihon wouldn't have it, and he didn't just refuse Israel passage, like the Edomites in Num 20 (see chap. 25). It was a bad idea on his part.

Amos 1–2 offers another take on proper war making.

> Yahweh has said this:
> For three rebellions by Damascus,
>> for four I shall not turn it back,
> Because of their threshing Gilead with iron sledges. . . .
>
> For three rebellions by Gaza,
>> for four I shall not turn it back,
> Because of their exiling a complete exile community,
>> handing them over to Edom. . . .
>
> For three rebellions by Tyre,
>> for four I shall not turn it back,
> Because of their handing over a complete exile community to Edom;
>> they were not mindful of the brotherhood pact. . . .
>
> For three rebellions by Edom,
>> for four I shall not turn it back,
> Because he pursued his brother with a sword,
>> devastated his compassion.
> His anger tore ceaselessly,
>> his outburst kept watch continually. . . .
>
> For three rebellions by the Ammonites,
>> for four I shall not turn it back,
> Because of their ripping open pregnant women in Gilead,
>> in order to enlarge their territory. . . .
>
> For three rebellions by Mo'ab,
>> for four I shall not turn it back,
> Because of his burning the bones of the king of Edom to lime.
>> (Amos 1:3, 6, 9, 11, 13; 2:1)

Whereas Deuteronomy 20 was concerned with Israel's war making, Amos talks about the war making of neighboring peoples, which are making wars that may not involve Israel. Amos points to series of actions that we might call war crimes. The "three . . . four" expression is a kind of formula for "rebellion after rebellion" and the "turning back" is the revoking of judgment.

The rebellions are rebellions against God's standards. Amos simply assumes that these other people know about right and wrong in connection with war and can be held responsible. You don't need a special revelation to know that atrocities are wrong or that taking a whole people captive and transporting them as slaves is wrong, or that giving up compassion is wrong, or that staying angry and therefore violent forever is wrong, or that ripping open pregnant women (so as to prevent a new generation coming into being) is wrong, or that failing to respect the dead is wrong.

The reference to a brotherhood pact is another reminder that the Old Testament not only sees Israel as a brotherhood: it sees humanity as a brotherhood. That perspective places a tight constraint on what you would do by way of war making. If it were taken seriously, in the end it would stop war altogether.

FOR REFLECTION AND DISCUSSION

1. Are there wars your nation has recently fought that breached scriptural principles?

2. Are there wars your nation has recently fought that breached just war principles?

3. Are there particular actions in war that your nation has recently undertaken that breached scriptural principles or just war principles?

4. Are there wars your nation has recently fought that make it open to the charge of committing war crimes?

34

RUTH

Commitment

A rabbi once asked himself why the book of Ruth was in the Scriptures when it didn't talk about the kind of thing you expect to find in the Scriptures. He knew that one of the most important things that Yahweh wanted of his people was that they should stay distinctive and different in the way they lived, not merely in moral ways but in sacramental ways. For instance, Yahweh told them not to eat certain things, not because there was anything wrong with them but just to mark the fact that they were different. Ruth says nothing about such matters. In fact, it may seem to work against them because it centers on a woman called Ruth who was a Moabite—a people whom Israelites had to be careful about because they'd been known to tempt Israelites into praying to their gods. So why is Ruth's story in the Scriptures?

The story starts with a famine that drives a family to leave Bethlehem to go to live in Moab.

> The man's name was Elimelek, his wife's name was Naomi, and his two sons' names were Mahlon and Kilyon. . . . Elimelek, Naomi's husband, died. She remained, she and her two sons. They took up for themselves Moabite wives; the name of the first was Orpah and the name of the second, Ruth. They lived there some ten years, but the two of them, Mahlon and Kilyon, also died, and the woman was left without her two sons and without her husband. She set off, she and her daughters-in-law, and went back from Moabite country. . . . But Naomi said to her two daughters-in-law, "Go, get back, each one to her mother's

household. May Yahweh act in commitment with you as you've acted with the dead men and with me. May Yahweh grant to you that you find a place to settle down, each one in the household of her husband." She kissed them and they lifted up their voice and cried. They said to her, "But we should go back with you to your people." . . .

They lifted up their voice and cried again and Orpah kissed her mother-in-law, but Ruth attached herself to her. So she said, "There, your sister-in-law has gone back to her people and to her gods. Go back after your sister-in-law." Ruth said, "Don't press me to abandon you by turning back from following you, because where you go I shall go, and where you stay the night I shall stay the night. Your people will be my people, and your God will be my God. Where you die I'll die, and there I'll be buried. So may Yahweh do to me, and so may he do more, if death divides between me and you." (Ruth 1:2-6, 8-10, 14-17)

What the rabbi said to himself in reply to his own question was that the reason the story of Ruth was in the Scriptures was because it was all about *hesed*. Translations have always puzzled about how to translate that word. The King James Version has "mercy." More recent versions have "kindness" or "steadfast love" or just plain "goodness." I think the best English word is "commitment." It denotes the extraordinary kind of self-giving to someone that a person shows when they were under no obligation to show any commitment at all, when there was no particular relationship between the two parties. It also denotes an extraordinary commitment that someone shows when there is an existent relationship, but one of the parties has let the other one down and has thereby forfeited any right to expect faithfulness. If the person who has been let down continues to show faithfulness to the relationship, they are showing *hesed*. "You could say that *hesed* is the opposite of an-eye-for-an-eye," says Kathleen Scott Goldingay.

In chapter one we noted that *hesed* is a defining characteristic of Yahweh. This prayer of Jacob's illustrates the point.

Jacob said, "God of my father Abraham, God of my father Isaac, Yahweh, you who said to me, 'Go back to your country, to your homeland, and I shall do good things with you,' I'm too small for all the acts of *hesed* and all the truthfulness with which you've acted toward your servant. With my cane I crossed this Jordan and now I've become two camps. Save me from the hand of my brother, please, from the hand of Esau, because I'm frightened of him, in case he comes and strikes me down, mother with children. (Gen 32:9-11)

Jacob was on the receiving end of Yahweh's *hesed* in both its senses. First, Yahweh made a commitment that Jacob would be the one through whom his purpose to bless the nations would be put into effect, even though he was the younger of his parents' two sons. And second, Yahweh kept that commitment going even though Jacob consistently showed himself unworthy of it. The prayer in Genesis 32 presupposes the fact, because the reason he is scared to meet Esau is that he long ago cheated Esau of his rights as the firstborn. It was ironic because God intended to give him that blessing anyway, but he cheated his way to it. It made Esau want to kill him, which in turn caused Jacob to make a run for it. Way back in the area where their extended family lived, Jacob has done really well—as he says, Yahweh has shown him great *hesed*. Now when he is about to meet Esau, he needs some more *hesed*. And he gets it. Esau has forgotten about what happened and throws his arms around him.

A story about Rahab and some Israelite spies presupposes a mutuality of *hesed*. Rahab says,

> "Please swear to me by Yahweh, because I've acted in *hesed* with you, that you'll also act in *hesed* with my father's household. Give me a truthful sign that you'll let my father and my mother live, and my brothers and my sisters, and everyone who belongs to them, and that you'll save our lives from death." The men said to her, "Our lives in place of you, to the death, if you don't tell about our business here. When Yahweh gives us the country, we'll act in *hesed* and truthfulness with you." (Josh 2:12-14)

Rahab is taking a risk that may preserve her life or may cost her life. She has hidden the spies from her own people in Jericho and sent the FBI off on a false trail. She has shown *hesed* in that first sense to the spies and to Israel, because on the basis of what she has heard she has had the faith to recognize that Yahweh is indeed God. She needs the spies to show *hesed* to her in return—to spare her and her family when the Israelites execute the rest of the people in Jericho.

There are two ways in which the story of Ruth is about *hesed*. The actual word comes three times, which is a lot for a book of four chapters. And the people in the story keep giving us illustrations of *hesed* even when the word isn't used. It fits with the place of the story in Jewish life. Ruth is read at Pentecost. Pentecost marks the barley harvest, and the key scenes in the story happen at that festival time. But in addition, Pentecost celebrates the giving of the Torah at Sinai, and the Ruth story embodies some key concerns of the Torah.

Orpah and Ruth have shown *hesed* to their husbands and to the father-in-law they had never met. When their husbands died, you couldn't have blamed them if they had then parted from Naomi and gone back to the families they came from. It would likely be the normal thing to do. But they have shown *hesed* to the three men. It's noteworthy that Naomi doesn't speak of it as *hesed* to her. They have shown *hesed* to her in showing *hesed* to the three men by sticking with the person who had been wife to one of them and mother of the other two. We can't know if they had had chance to tell the three men that they would look after Naomi, but one can imagine how guilty and fearful the three men might feel about leaving Naomi alone. Orpah and Ruth have ministered to such sense of guilt and fear.

Naomi therefore prays that Yahweh may show a similar *hesed* to Orpah and Ruth. She's heard that the famine that took the family on that tragic move to Moab is over. She's going back to Bethlehem, and she's assuming that the two young-ish women will now go back to their families in Moab. She asks for Yahweh to show *hesed* to them by enabling them to find new husbands and households. It's quite a prayer because (we will soon learn) Naomi is pretty bitter about the way Yahweh has treated her. One could hardly complain if Naomi has lost faith in Yahweh's *hesed*. Actually, she has lost faith in it for herself, but not for Orpah and Ruth.

In due course Orpah agrees to go, and one should not criticize her. Ruth insists on accompanying Naomi to Bethlehem and makes an extraordinary commitment to Naomi and to Yahweh that doesn't involve the word *hesed* but embodies what it means in spectacular fashion. Without conditions and without qualifications she commits herself "to love and to cherish, till death us do part"—in fact, even then she intends to stay with Naomi.

They get to Bethlehem, it's harvest time, and Naomi sends Ruth off to collect the leavings from the harvest, as needy people were welcome to do. In chapter 26 we noted one passage from the Torah that makes this point. Here is another:

> When you reap the harvest of your land, each of you will not finish off harvesting the side of your field, and you will not gather the gleanings of your harvest or scour your vineyard or glean your vineyard's windfall. You're to leave them for the humble and for the resident alien. I am Yahweh your God. (Lev 19:9-10)

Ruth finds herself in the field of a distant relative of Naomi who makes sure she can be out in the fields safely and makes it possible for her to collect far more than leavings.

> Her mother-in-law said to her, "Where did you glean today? Where did you work? Blessed be the man who recognized you." She told her mother-in-law who she had worked with and said, "The name of the man that I worked with today was Boaz." Naomi said to her daughter-in-law, "May he be blessed by Yahweh, who hasn't abandoned his *hesed* with the living and with the dead." Naomi said to her, "The man is a close relative of ours. He's one of our restorers." (Ruth 2:19-20)

Yes, Yahweh is keeping his commitment with the living (Naomi and Ruth) and with the dead (the three men that these women have lost). The three men do not need to toss and turn with worry in Sheol, the home of the dead. They can just sleep there.

Naomi cooks up a plan for Ruth to beguile Boaz into accepting a proposal of marriage. As is usually the case even in the West, proposing would be the man's business, but these are not women bound by social convention. The plan involves a risky stratagem, but they know the kind of man Boaz is.

> In the middle of the night the man gave a start and twisted around: there, a woman lying at his feet! He said, "Who are you?" She said, "I'm Ruth, your handmaid. You should spread your skirt over your handmaid, because you're a restorer." He said, "May you be blessed of Yahweh, daughter. You've made your last act of *hesed* better than your first in not following the young men, whether a poor one or a wealthy one. So now, my daughter, don't be afraid, all that you say I will do for you." (Ruth 3:8-11)

The proposal involves another risky act of *hesed* on Ruth's part. As far as Boaz can see, he wasn't Ruth's only option, and evidently he's older than many of the men on the village, but she reaches out to him because he's a member of their extended family (and, I might add, because we know what kind of man he is). He's a potential restorer or redeemer (see chap. 31), and he is indeed himself a man of *hesed*.

FOR REFLECTION AND DISCUSSION

1. Have you known God to show *hesed* to you in some way?

2. Has anyone ever shown you *hesed*?

3. Have you ever shown someone *hesed*?

4. Can you think of some act of *hesed* you could show someone now?

5. Is there something in respect of which you wish someone would show you *hesed*?

35

PSALM 72

The Exercise of Authority with Faithfulness

We recently had a presidential election in the United States (I say "we," though I'm still a Brit), and then there was a surprise general election in Britain (I don't get to vote there either; I have taxation without representation in both countries). If you were wondering which candidate to support, what criteria would you bear in mind?

Of course, the Israelites didn't elect their kings, so the question didn't arise, but it didn't stop them having an ethical vision of what the king was for, and expressing it in their prayers. I like to picture them praying the prayer in Psalm 72 in the temple with the king there, with their prayer being addressed to God but the king overhearing so that it was as if they were digging him in the ribs as they prayed it. Special irony attaches to the fact that this prayer is "Solomon's," which doesn't imply that he wrote it, but does imply that it's for him. He should have taken from it his understanding of what it meant to be king. Fat chance!

Solomon's

God, give the king your rulings,
    the royal son your faithfulness.
May he give judgment for your people with faithfulness,
    your humble ones with authority. (Ps 72:1-2)

As well as being a prayer, Psalm 72 is a poem, like any psalm, and the way it works is by expressing its prayers in pairs, so that it takes two thoughts to make a verse. One of the results is that you can never assume you've got the point just on the basis of the first phrase you read in a verse. You have to wait till you can put the second thought alongside it, which can make a big difference.

So to begin with, the king's job is of course to rule, to make decisions, to exercise authority; but the other half of the opening verse immediately adds that this ruling needs to be characterized by faithfulness (*sedaqah*). The second verse repeats the same double idea, in case God and king haven't got it. The king is to be faithful in the exercise of authority (*mishpat*). The words *sedaqah* and *mishpat* often appear together and often come out in translations as "righteousness" and "justice," but both halves of that translation are misleading. In English righteousness is inclined to suggest an individual living a holy life, but *sedaqah* is about how we relate to other people. And justice suggests something inherently ethical, whereas *mishpat* is a power word. So the essence of the Hebrew idea of righteousness is that you do the right thing by the people in your community, the people you're in relationship with—you are fair, generous, honest, and caring toward them, and the first duty of kings, presidents, or mayors is to exercise authority in a way that expresses faithfulness to their people and to exercise authority in a way that facilitates faithfulness among their people.

The words *sedaqah* and *mishpat*, faithfulness and the exercise of authority, often come together. We have noted some passages where they do so; here are some more.

> Yahweh, your commitment is in the heavens,
>> your truthfulness reaches as far as the skies.
> Your faithfulness is like supernatural mountains,
>> your authority is like the great deep. (Ps 36:5-6)

> The blessings of people who keep watch over the exercise of authority,
>> of the person who does what is faithful at all times! (Ps 106:3)

> Exercising authority in a faithful way
>> is to be chosen for Yahweh over a sacrifice. (Prov 21:3)

> He hoped for the exercise of authority, but there—blood pouring out;
>> for faithfulness, but there—a cry. (Is 5:7)

> Exercise authority with faithfulness,
>> rescue the person who's been robbed from the hand of the oppressor,

Don't wrong alien, orphan, and widow,
> don't be violent, don't shed the blood of someone free of guilt in this
> > place. (Jer 22:3)

When an individual is faithful and exercises authority with faithfulness, . . .
> he will definitely live. (Ezek 18:5, 9)

The exercise of authority is to roll like water,
> faithfulness like a perennial wadi. (Amos 5:24)

The two words are often called the Hebrew equivalent to the expression "social justice" in English. But what we mean by *social justice* is ill-defined— it's another of those words like *community* and *relationship*. So it's worth noting what the Old Testament might mean by it. On one hand, it's referring to the idea that within the community we have obligations to one another, we ought to be doing the right thing by one another, we should be being faithful, fair, and generous to one another (in modern Hebrew the word *sedaqah* is the word for "charity"). On the other hand, it's viewing people with power as having responsibility to use their authority to see that the community operates in that kind of way.

May the mountains bear well-being for the people,
> and the hills, in faithfulness.

May he exercise authority for the humble among the people,
> deliver the needy, crush the fraud.

May they live in awe of you while the sun shines,
> and before the moon, generation after generation.

May he come down like rain on mowed grass,
> like downpours, an overflowing on the earth.

May the faithful person flourish in his days,
> and abundance of well-being, until the moon is no more. . . .

May all kings bow low to him,
> all nations serve him.

Because he rescues the needy person crying for deliverance,
> and the humble person who has no helper.

May he have pity on poor and needy,
> so that he delivers the lives of needy people.

From repression and from violence may he restore their life,
> and may their blood be valuable in his eyes. (Ps 72:3-7, 11-14)

Psalm 72 is a prayer and a challenge, but also a promise that there is a link between prosperity and faithfulness. The word for well-being is the word *shalom* (see chap. 12), which suggests things going well in every part of the community's life—here, specifically, the harvest will go well. Faithfulness is the key to a good harvest. God makes things work that way. It doesn't imply prosperity in the sense of the prosperity gospel. It doesn't imply a Cadillac or a private jet. It does imply that you will have enough to feel that you are not just barely surviving but doing okay. When Jesus urges his disciples to put his kingdom and his righteousness first (Mt 6:33), it's almost another way of saying that they are to make *sedaqah* and *mishpat* their priority. He goes on to promise that they'll then have enough to eat and clothes to wear, and so on. He is confirming promises that Psalm 72 makes.

Exercising authority or ruling comes again in the line about the humble and the needy; it's another expression of what faithfulness involves, though it doesn't use the word. The humble are the ordinary people, the people who don't have power. The needy are the people who lack resources. These groups are the people to whom kings, presidents, and mayors have their first obligation. As the psalm puts it later, their job is to rescue the needy person who is crying for deliverance and the humble person who has no helper. It's to have pity on the poor and needy. That line is another one where you mustn't stop until you've read the second thought that goes with it. It's to have pity on them so as to deliver them; pity, like love, is an action, not a mere feeling. It's easy to have pity for people when they are in a mess. The question is whether you do something to get them out of their mess.

To put it another way, the authorities' job is to help people get their lives back together when they have been the victims of repression and violence. In a vivid and intriguing phrase, their commitment is to let the blood of the poor and needy be valuable in their eyes as people in power. In other words, they care about their lives, their safety, and their security.

The other side of the coin is that they have the correlative obligation to crush the fraudulent. Often it's fraud, swindling, or deception that turns people into being powerless and resourceless. Maybe they take out a loan on their land because they've got into difficulty, and *pow*, soon they've lost their land altogether. The authorities' job is to stop that kind of thing. There's no scope for being nice and gentle here. There needs to be a heavy exercise of authority. Frauds need to be crushed. Of course, in practice the authorities can be the biggest frauds. . . .

But if the authorities do work the way the psalm prays for them to, they'll have an effect like rain in encouraging people to grow (or, if you live in the United Kingdom, they'll have an effect like sunshine).

FOR REFLECTION AND DISCUSSION

1. In your country or community, are there ways in which the authorities govern with faithfulness?

2. Are there ways in which they don't?

3. The psalm assumes that things will go well for the country and the government when it rules with faithfulness. Can you see any evidence of that dynamic in your country?

4. How could your church pray more faithfully for the governing authorities?

36

THE SONG OF SONGS

Sex

A Christian discussion site recently posted a question from an anxious grandparent. She had invited her son and his wife to ask her teenage grandson whether he would like to come to stay with her for a week or two during the summer vacation. He could bring a friend, and it would give them something to do during the long summer break as well as enabling her to see him for longer than usual. But then she discovered that it would be a girlfriend that he would want to bring, and she suspected that she would be party to creating opportunities for them to have sex. What was she to do?

Assumptions about such questions have changed monumentally over the past fifty years, which at least reminds us that our assumptions and our questions are culture relative—assumptions and question will be different again in another fifty years, and they are different (for instance) in much of Africa from Europe and the United States. It's not surprising, then, that the assumptions and questions in the Song of Songs are different again. At the beginning, the woman speaks:

> May he kiss me with some of the kisses of his mouth!—
>> because your love is better than wine.
> The fragrance—your oils are good,
>> your name is oil poured out.
> Therefore girls love you;
>> pull me after you, let's run.

The king has brought me into his rooms;
> let's celebrate and rejoice in you.

Let's make mention of your love more than wine;
> rightly they love you.

I am dark but lovely,
> Jerusalem daughters,

Like the tents of Qedar,
> like Solomon's curtains.

Don't look at me because I'm dark-skinned,
> because the sun has stared at me.

My mother's sons were enraged with me,
> they made me someone who guards the vineyards.

My vineyard, the one I had,
> I didn't guard.

Tell me, you whom my entire being loves,
> where do you pasture,
> where do you rest them at midday?

Why should I be like someone covering herself
> by the flocks of your companions? (Song 1:2-7)

The Song of Songs is a collection of love poems. It's not about relationships between God and us, though there are ways in which it can give us insight on that relationship. It's comparable to other love poetry from the ancient world and from the modern world. The poems in the Song portray relationships between two people. I shall speak as if the Song is about one couple all the way through, but we shouldn't make that assumption a key to understanding it, as if it simply is the story of one relationship. It's a work of imagination, comprising a collection of separate poems. The poems are about two people who are in love and who are totally committed to each other, but who are not living together. Right there is a feature that contrasts with the context in which we in the West look at sex, where people are often living together but aren't totally committed. The couple in the Song are apparently not married in a Western sense, but they may be "betrothed" and thus effectively wed according to the customs of their society. They resemble Mary and Joseph, who aren't married in a Western sense, but whose relationship is so formalized that Joseph has to contemplate divorcing Mary—not just breaking off an engagement. Here is a section where the man speaks:

You've captured my heart, my sister,
  my bride, you've captured my heart,
With one of your eyes,
  with one strand of your necklace.
How beautiful is your love,
  my sister, my bride!
How much better is your love than wine,
  the fragrance of your oils than all perfumes!
Your lips drop honey, my bride;
  syrup and milk are under your tongue.
The fragrance of your robes
  is like the fragrance of Lebanon.
A locked garden, my sister, my bride,
  a locked fountain, a sealed fountain:
Your shoots are an orchard of pomegranates,
  with choice fruit,
Henna with much spikenard,
  spikenard and saffron,
Cane and cinnamon,
  with all the incense woods,
Myrrh and aloes,
  with all the top perfumes:
A garden spring,
  a well of living water,
  flowing from Lebanon. (Song 4:9-15)

I don't think the couple in the Song are having sex, but it's not absolutely clear. Certainly they're looking forward to the consummation of the marriage with some enthusiasm, and it would be surprising if the way they speak didn't mean they were getting pretty familiar with each other's bodies. One implication of this picture is that they are growing together in the various aspects of their relationship. The sexual aspect wasn't ahead of the rest, but neither was it behind it. The all-consuming nature of their relationship indicates that they are not two people having a great time sexually without being committed to each other long term. This couple have or are on their way to a lifelong exclusive relationship. Only that assumption makes sense of the passion of their mutual self-giving.

The poems' enthusiasm about the physical aspect to their relationship contrasts with the inhibiting constraint on enthusiasm for sex that has sometimes characterized Christian attitudes. There's no reference to God in the Song of Songs, but that omission doesn't mean the poems belong in a context where God was not part of the picture. The inclusion of the Song in the Scriptures presupposes that the relationship between two lovers is God's business. It's not just God's business because God is especially concerned about ethics; there's no ethics in the narrow sense in the Song. There is hardly any reference to marriage, even though it will be assumed that marriage is where a relationship of this kind is going. The Song is more about life in its fullness as God created it, with its wonder and its joy. The woman, again:

> Make me like a seal on your heart,
>> like a seal on your arm.
> Because love is as fierce as death,
>> passion as tough as Sheol.
> Its darts are darts of fire,
>> a supernatural flame.
> Much water could not quench love,
>> nor rivers overflow it.
> If someone gave all his household's resources for love,
>> people would totally despise him. (Song 8:6-7)

A remarkable feature of the Song is that the woman's voice is so prominent. There is no hierarchy in this relationship. In this respect the two of them are back in the Garden of Eden, back to that time before the relationship between a man and a woman was spoiled and patriarchy came in. Other aspects of the couple's relationship and their experience make clear that they do indeed live outside the Garden. There are fears and anxieties, and puzzling conflicts between the girl on one hand and her brothers and other people in the community on the other. "The course of true love never did run smooth" (*A Midsummer Night's Dream*).

In a seminary class I was once seeking to say something about the Song's implications, and a student asked whether I was really trying too hard to get something deeper from these poems than was appropriate to such expressions of teenage love. This comment does usefully remind us that in a traditional society people marry younger than they do in the West and don't go through a series of relationships before they find "the right one." In such a society, your first (teenage) love may well be your only one. It's one consideration that adds to the ethical complications of sex for us, along with the fact that we live longer. I imagine that couples in Israel were lucky if they celebrated their twenty-fifth anniversary, let alone their fiftieth or sixtieth.

But someone in the same discussion group as that student later told me that the student had subsequently reflected further on his caustic comment. He and his wife could have spoken in the manner of the Song when they were first in love, he said, but they had now been married for a few years and were bringing up a couple of small children, and the spark of which the Song speaks was no longer a reality. The Song made him feel sad.

Relationships change, and it isn't necessarily a bad sign if one no longer has that teenage wooziness. On the other hand, when people have affairs, the teenage enthusiasm is one of the things they seek. So keeping it alive in one's marriage can be of ethical significance. (In light of the Song, another young couple had felt pressured to wait until they got married before having sex, with the encouragement then to expect it to be a lovefest. They discovered that this expectation was unrealistic, and they felt that quite a few people they knew married too young because of this pressure.)

The point emerges in some verses from Proverbs.

> Drink water from your cistern,
>> running water from within your well.
> Should your fountains gush outside,
>> your streams of water in the squares?
> They should be for you alone,
>> so that there's none for strangers with you.
> May your spring be blessed,
>> may you rejoice in the wife of your youth,
> She's a doe to love,
>> a graceful deer.
> Her breasts should drench you all the time;
>> be crazy on her love continually.
> Why be crazy on a stranger, son,
>> and embrace the arms of a foreigner? (Prov 5:15-20)

Unlike the Song, Proverbs is directly concerned about questions of right and wrong, though typically it is inclined to reframe them as questions about being smart or stupid. Here, Proverbs first issues an exhortation to men to marital faithfulness, but it's poetic, like the Song, and it goes on to a poetic description of the wife that also recalls the Song. In effect it draws out an ethical implication from the thinking expressed in the Song which the Song itself doesn't draw out. If a married man has the kind of sexual enthusiasm for his wife that the Song describes, it's the best protection against going astray.

FOR REFLECTION AND DISCUSSION

1. What are the most important things for us to learn from the Song of Songs?

2. What are the differences between attitudes expressed in the Song and in Proverbs and attitudes that prevail in your church?

3. What are the differences between attitudes expressed in the Song and in Proverbs and attitudes that prevail in your culture?

4. Are relationships in your culture or church as egalitarian as the one in the Song?

5. What would you say to the grandmother whom I mentioned at the beginning?

PART FIVE

PEOPLE

A traditional approach to biblical stories takes them as providing positive or negative examples for behavior. One complication with this assumption is that they don't often comment on whether their subjects are doing the right thing or the wrong thing, and thus interpreters who draw moral lessons from them can differ in the moral lessons they draw. A more (post)modern approach to them sees them simply as stories about things that people did or things that happened or things that people might have done or that might have happened, and thus as invitations (to go back to the beginning of this book), as stories to set against the stories of our own lives to enable us to ask once more what sort of people those people were and what sort of people are we, how do they and we think about life, what sort of thing do they do, and what sort of thing do they not do.

37

ABRAHAM

Enoch and Noah lived their lives with God (Gen 5:22; 6:9)—more literally, they walked about with God. Walking with God would place some ethical demands on you, the kind implied by chapter one in this book. God himself lays a slightly different ethical expectation before Abraham, urging "live your life before me and be a person of integrity" (Gen 17:1). More literally, God says "walk about before me." Living your life *before* God implies a transparency that has nothing to hide. It therefore goes along with or is expressed in being "a person of integrity." Translations have Abraham expected to be "blameless," but the word (*tamim*) doesn't indicate the absence of something bad but the presence of something good. It means "whole"—not in a psychological sense but in a moral sense. Abraham was challenged to be a man of moral wholeness.

To say that he was God's "friend" (Is 41:8) covers much of the same ground—it implies walking with God (God as your friend and you as God's friend) and walking before God. The word for "friend" (*ʾoheb*) is the participle of the word for "love." Yahweh's friend is someone who loves Yahweh in the first great commandment sense, someone who is committed, loyal, faithful, and obedient to Yahweh with their entire mind, their entire being, their entire might (Deut 6:5).

Abraham didn't start off as such a person.

A famine came in the country, and Abram went down to Egypt to reside there, because the famine was heavy in the country. When he was near coming into Egypt, he said to Sarai his wife, "Here, please: I know that you're a woman who's attractive in appearance. When the Egyptians see you and say, 'She's his wife,' they may kill me and let you live. Please say that you're my sister in order that things may be good for me on account of you and I myself may live on by means of you." (Gen 12:10-13)

At best, Abraham is being economical with the truth in the sense that he is speaking the truth but not the whole truth; Sarah is his half-sister—at least, Abraham and Sarah say she is, but for all we know, economy with the truth may have given way to downright falsehood. (They are Abram and Sarai at this stage, but throughout this chapter and the next I will use the names familiar from later in the story.) But anyway, hasn't Abraham thought about the implications of his wife being taken into Pharaoh's harem? He is too scared to take account of that possibility. Fear is a serious ethical issue. Further, the result of Pharaoh's appropriating Sarah is that God sends an epidemic to his household to protect her. Maybe Abraham couldn't foresee that result of his deceit, but he carries some responsibility for it.

All ends well, though it's not the last story of this kind that Genesis tells. Abraham repeats his action (Gen 20) and Isaac copies it (Gen 26:1-11). Why might Genesis tell three similar stories? It's said that men are ambivalent about their wives' attractiveness and sexuality. It makes a man feel good to have other men fancy his wife, but it also feels a bit dangerous. So that's one possible reason for including several versions of a story of this kind. Another possibility is that husbands may seek to use their wives in connection with politics or business or church. Women are often pawns, not least in the context of migration.

Abraham's next moral challenge comes as a result of things going well rather than being difficult.

Lot, who went with Abram, also had flock and herd and tents, and the region couldn't support them living together, because their property was great. So they couldn't live together. There was argument between the herdsmen of Abram's livestock and the herdsmen of Lot's livestock (and the Canaanite and the Perizzite were then living in the country). So Abram said to Lot, "Please, there mustn't be arguing between me and you and between my herdsmen and your herdsmen, because we're brothers. The entire country is before you, isn't it? Part from me, please: if you go north, I'll go south, but if you go south, I'll go north." Lot lifted his eyes and looked at the entire plain of the Jordan, that it was well-watered, all of it, before Yahweh devastated Sodom and Gomorrah, like Yahweh's garden, like the country of Egypt as you come to Soar; and Lot chose for himself the entire Jordan plain. So Lot moved on east, and they parted, each from his brother. Abram lived in the country of Canaan, and Lot lived in the towns of the plain and put up his tents near Sodom. Now the people of Sodom were bad, wrongdoers in relation to Yahweh, greatly. (Gen 13:5-13)

Is Abraham just trying to solve a practical problem? Even so, he goes about resolving it in a generous way. As the senior member of the family, he is in a position to choose the land he likes and lean on Lot to move elsewhere. Instead he lets Lot have the choice. It turns out to be an unwise choice in more than one sense.

This consequence doesn't mean that Abraham simply leaves Lot to lie in the bed he has made. Lot could hardly have predicted the political crisis that erupted when the towns in the Jordan Valley asserted their independence from their imperial overlords. The latter came to reassert their authority, and when they left they took captives and property with them, including Lot and his.

Abram heard that his brother had been taken captive and he mustered his trained men, people born in his household, 318 of them, and went in pursuit as far as Dan. He and his servants split up against them by night, struck them down, and pursued them as far as Hobah, which is north of Damascus. He took back all the property, and took back both his brother Lot and his property, and also the women and the company. (Gen 14:14-16)

One doesn't think of Abraham as a warrior, and he never made war in order to gain territory, but he was capable of acting as a warrior to rescue members of his family who had been taken captive. And he then didn't mess around. Genesis says nothing about his asking God's guidance or help—he just did it.

And Melkizedeq king of Salem brought out bread and wine (he was priest of God on High) and blessed him, saying,

Blessed be Abram by God on High,
    Lord of the heavens and the earth.
And God on High be blessed,
    who has delivered your attackers into your hand.

He gave him a tenth of everything. The king of Sodom said to Abram, "Give me the people but take the property for yourself." But Abram said to the king of Sodom, "I raise my hand to Yahweh, God on High, Lord of the heavens and the earth: 'From a thread to a boot strap, if I take anything that's yours. . . .' You will not say, 'I'm the one who made Abram wealthy.' Not me. Only what the boys have eaten, and the share of the men who went with me, Aner, Eshkol, and Mamre—they are to have their share." (Gen 14:18-24)

The priest-king of Salem could recognize God's activity when he saw it. When Abraham won his famous victory, it was God who delivered him. Neither did Abraham let himself be profited by his war making. Just let people have their expenses.

Lot's capture by the imperial army is not the last time he needs rescue as a result of going to live in the region of Sodom. In due course Yahweh decides to do something about the fact that "the people of Sodom were bad, wrongdoers in relation to Yahweh, greatly" (Gen 13:13).

Yahweh said, "Am I going to hide from Abraham what I'm doing, when Abraham is indeed to become a big, numerous nation, and all the nations on the earth are to bless themselves by him? Because I've acknowledged him in order that he may order his children and his household after him so they may keep Yahweh's way by showing faithfulness in the exercise of authority, in order that Yahweh may bring about for Abraham what he's spoken concerning him." . . . Abraham came up and said, "Will you really sweep away the faithful with the faithless? Maybe there are fifty faithful people within the town. Will you really sweep it away and not bear with the place for the sake of the fifty faithful people within it? Far be it for you to do a thing like this, putting to death the faithful with the faithless, so the faithful and the faithless are the same. Far be it for you. Isn't the one who exercises authority over the entire earth to exercise authority?" Yahweh said, "If I find in Sodom fifty faithful people within the town, I shall bear with the entire place on account of them." Abraham answered: "There, please: I've resolved to speak to my Lord, when I'm dirt and ash. Maybe the fifty faithful will be five short. Will you devastate the entire town because of five?" He said, "I won't devastate it if I find there forty-five." He spoke yet again to him: "Maybe forty will be found there." He said, "I won't act, on account of the forty." He said, "May it please not enrage my Lord, and I shall speak. Maybe thirty will be found there." He said, "I won't act if I find there thirty." He said, "There, please, I've resolved to speak with my Lord. Maybe twenty will be found there." He said, "I won't devastate it on account of the twenty." He said, "May it please not enrage my Lord, and I shall speak one last time. Maybe ten will be found there." He said, "I won't devastate it on account of the ten." (Gen 18:17-32)

Genesis 19 portrays Sodom as a perverted city, a place where society is sick. It makes clear that its sexual twistedness isn't its only sickness. Its wickedness is the subject of "outcry" to God (Gen 18:20-21; 19:13). This word is the one used of Abel's blood crying out from the ground to God (Gen 4:10) and of the Israelites crying out because of their oppression in Egypt (e.g., Ex 2:23; 3:7, 9; see also Is 5:7; 42:2). Sodom is a place of oppression (cf. Is 1:10; Ezek 16:46-50). Yahweh reveals to Abraham what is to happen to Sodom because Abraham's vocation relates to *sedaqah* and *mishpat* (Gen 18:19), the exercise of power in a way that does right by the people in one's community (see chap. 35). Perhaps the reference is not to the oppression practiced by one citizen on another (otherwise it would not be the entire community that deserved to be judged) but to the relationship between city and surrounding countryside. That relationship can be one of harmony and cooperation: the country provides the city with food, and the city provides the country with specialized services and manufactured goods. But the city easily ends up being parasitic on the country, exacting tribute and taxes, attracting resources and wealth, and enjoying luxury and indulgence, while the countryside lives at a lower standard.

God hears the plaintive, hurt lament of the people around Sodom and Gomorrah, and decides to discover if what they say is true, declaring the intention, if it is true, to act in judgment on their behalf. But first, God listens to another cry, and responds to it. Indeed, he draws Abraham into crying out on behalf of Sodom. He tells Abraham that he's thinking about acting in judgment, and then waits (while two aides go to check things out there) to see if Abraham wants to say anything. There follows the extraordinary dialogue in which Abraham sees how far God would go in order to reprieve the city. Abraham is to be a means of blessing to the world (Gen 18:18); the way he puts that vocation into effect is by praying for the world. Will God let mercy triumph over deserve? There's no implication that God is more inclined to be merciful than Abraham is or that Abraham has to get God to have a change of mind (though many other Old Testament passages indicate that conversations with God can aim at changing God's mind so that he does not act in judgment and can succeed in doing so). There is an implication that God invites Abraham into discussion about the question, a discussion with ethical implications.

The most ethically challenging Abraham story is still to come.

Subsequently, God tested Abraham. He said to him, "Abraham!" He said, "I'm here." He said, "Please take your son, your only one, the one you love, Isaac, get yourself to the Moriah region, and offer him up as a burnt offering there, on one of the mountains that I shall say to you." (Gen 22:1-2)

Without hesitation Abraham goes to the brink of doing as God says, until God stops him. In the name of ethics, Immanuel Kant declared that God could not say such a thing to Abraham. Abraham must have been mistaken. Genesis does not discuss how Abraham knew it was God rather than his deluded mind speaking, but it does provide a context for working with the possibility. Abraham knows who God is. He knows that God wants to bless Abraham and to bless the world. He knows God is committed to him and that he is committed to God. He has experienced God's grace and protection and provision. He does not hear this bidding from God out of the context of God's relationship with him, and with Isaac. The way the story unfolds indicates that he knows that simply slaughtering Isaac cannot be the end of the story:

> You stay here with the donkey, while the boy and I will go over there and bow low, and come back to you. . . . God is the one who will see for himself to the sheep for the burnt offering. (Gen 22:5, 8)

It's hard to see what Abraham means or how he might think that these expectations will be realized, but evidently Abraham knows that somehow God's action will fit in with the principle of the faithful exercise of authority that God and Abraham affirmed in the Sodom story.

The more modern grounds for protest about Genesis 22 is that Abraham's action counts as child abuse and threatens to justify child abuse. One consideration that needs to be taken into account in this connection is that Isaac is hardly a child. He's big enough to carry a load of wood on his back; he is a teenager or a young adult. A related consideration is the way Genesis implies that Isaac is one with his father in what happens. (Jewish interpretation takes him as a model for when the faithful have to face the possibility of martyrdom.) Further, once again we recall that the story belongs in the context of a relationship between God and Abraham and also between God and Isaac and between Abraham and Isaac.

In connection with both protests it is significant that God's demand has a one-time nature. Whether or not the story is designed to provide the rationale for Israel's awareness that God does not ask for human sacrifice, the Torah does outlaw such sacrifice. There is no basis for assuming that this one-time demand put on Abraham is a demand God puts on anyone else at any other time just as there is no basis for assuming that God's command to Israel to slaughter the Canaanites is ever put on anyone else. It is an aspect of the one-time story of God and the working out of his promises and his purpose.

Ironically, Wilfred Owen (in his poem "The Parable of the Old Man and the Young") and Leonard Cohen (in his song "Story of Isaac") have pointed out that European powers in the First World War and the United States in the 1960s did proceed to the end in slaughtering their young men in their teens and twenties. The ethical significance of Genesis 22 is that in the end God does not require Abraham to do so.

FOR REFLECTION AND DISCUSSION

1. What were Abraham's strengths?

2. What were Abraham's weaknesses?

3. What's the most difficult aspect of living before God with integrity?

4. Who are the oppressed people you might talk with God about now?

38

SARAH AND HAGAR

Abraham found it harder to stand up to Sarah than to some other people. Sarah appears from nowhere in Genesis (see Gen 11–23); originally we are told nothing of her family or background. She first appears as the wife Abram took and who perforce accompanies him and his father from Ur to Harran, and then from Harran to Canaan, and from Canaan to Egypt because there's a famine. When she agrees to say she is his sister because her attractiveness will mean the Egyptians will kill him in order to take her, was she right to collude with his economy over the truth? Admittedly, the Old Testament can be not too worried about lies to protect the weak from the strong.

Sarah cannot have children. It's commonly an agonizing experience for a woman, in Sarah's society as in Western society. It can also be an agonizing experience for a man. Sarah no doubt feels she is letting her husband down, as a wife can think in Western society.

> She had an Egyptian maidservant; her name was Hagar. Sarai said to Abram, "Here, Yahweh has held me back from giving birth to children. You have sex with my maidservant; maybe I can be built up through her." Abram listened to Sarai's voice. Sarai, Abram's wife, got Hagar the Egyptian, her maidservant (after Abram had been living in the country of Canaan for ten years), and gave her to Abram her husband as a wife. He had sex with Hagar and she got pregnant. When she saw that she was pregnant, her mistress became of slight worth in her eyes. Sarai said to Abram, "The violence done to me rests on you. I myself put my maidservant in your arms, she's seen that she's pregnant, and I've become of slight worth in her eyes. Yahweh decide between me and you!"

Abram said to Sarai, "Here, your maidservant is in your hand. Do to her what's good in your eyes." Sarai humbled her, and she took flight from her. (Gen 16:1-6)

Hagar, too, appears from nowhere, except that she is an Egyptian—presumably a servant Abraham and Sarah brought from Egypt after the escapade noted earlier. Sarah bids Abraham take her as a second wife and potential surrogate mother, in keeping with practice in the society. There is nothing illegitimate about the relationship Sarah sets up between Abraham and Hagar. She becomes Abraham's legitimate second wife. She is not a concubine in the sense of a mistress, but Genesis will later imply that she is a "secondary wife," a less misleading expression than concubine. A secondary wife has lower status than a "primary wife," and her children likely do not have the inheritance rights of a "primary wife."

Hagar soon gets pregnant (so evidently the problem did lie with Sarah and not with Abraham), and Sarah is offended at the way this success draws attention to her failure. It wouldn't be surprising if the development disturbs the power differential between the primary wife, who is the mistress of the house but who can't conceive, and the secondary wife, who has a functioning womb and can give her husband the son he wants. It wouldn't be surprising if Hagar develops a spot of attitude, but it also wouldn't be surprising if Sarah is projecting onto Hagar her own sense of being of slight worth. Not surprisingly, Hagar's pregnancy makes her look superior and Sarah inferior, and Sarah cannot cope with it. "It's all your fault," she says to Abraham. "You solve it," says Abraham. Sarah treats Hagar the way the Egyptians will later treat the Israelites, and Hagar makes a run for it.

Yahweh's envoy found her by a spring of water in the wilderness, by the spring on the Shur road. He said, "Hagar, maidservant of Sarah, where have you come from and where are you going?" She said, "From Sarai, my mistress—I'm taking flight." Yahweh's envoy said to her, "Go back to your mistress. Let yourself be humbled under her hand." But Yahweh's envoy said to her, "I shall make your offspring very numerous; they won't be able to be counted because of the large number." Yahweh's envoy said to her, "There, you're pregnant and you'll give birth to a son. You're to name him Ishmael because Yahweh has listened [*shama*] to your humbling. And he—he'll be a wild donkey of a man, his hand against everyone and everyone's hand against him, and he'll dwell over against all his brothers." (Gen 16:7-12)

Why does God bid Hagar to go back? Is it better to be abused with the family through which God is going to bless the world than to return to Egypt, the country that will be under God's judgment? It means that her son will receive great blessing. She and he will experience Yahweh as the God who listens to the affliction of someone who is a foreigner, a servant, a woman. Her son will not be a softie like Isaac, the son Sarah will eventually bear. He will be someone who knows how to fight. He will not be someone people can mess with. He will know how to survive. And indeed the Ishmaelites will.

So God gets her to go back, but her return exposes her to a second experience of Sarah wanting to throw her out, a decade later. Supernatural visitors arrive and promise that Sarah will have a child of her own (Gen 17). She is now not only infertile but beyond childbearing age, so she laughs. It's an ambiguous laugh, and it embarrasses her. But if she finds the idea of having a baby unbelievable, this unbelief makes no more difference to God than her nonfunctioning womb does. She has her baby.

> Yahweh did for Sarah as he had spoken, and Sarah got pregnant and gave birth to a son for Abraham in his old age, at the set time of which God had spoken to him. Abraham named his son, who had been born to him, whom Sarah had born to him, Isaac ["He laughs"]. Abraham circumcised Isaac his son when he was eight days old, as God ordered him, Abraham being a man of a hundred years when his son Isaac was born to him. Sarah said, "God has made laughter for me, since everyone who hears will laugh for me," and said, "Who would have uttered to Abraham, 'Sarah has nursed children'? But I've given birth to a son for his old age." (Gen 21:1-7)

While there was some ambiguity about her first laugh, there's no ambiguity about this one. But now the story tells of another laughter that leads into Sarah wanting to get rid of Hagar and Ishmael, who is by now a teenager.

> The child grew and was weaned, and Abraham made a big banquet on the day that Isaac was weaned. But Sarah saw the son of Hagar the Egyptian, to whom she gave birth for Abraham, laughing. She said to Abraham, "Drive this handmaid and her son out, because this handmaid's son is not to come into possession with my son, with Isaac." The thing was very bad in Abraham's eyes, on account of his son. But God said to Abraham, "It isn't to be bad in your eyes about the boy or about your handmaid. Everything that Sarah says to you,

listen to her voice, because it's through Isaac that offspring will be named for you. The son of the handmaid: I shall make him into a nation, too, because he's your offspring." (Gen 21:8-13)

Ishmael is laughing or making people laugh or making baby Isaac laugh, and it arouses in Sarah the barely repressed awareness that Ishmael was supposed to be the means of fulfilling God's promise to Abraham. She had once tried to set things up that way! But now Ishmael is behaving as if he were the laughing boy, as if he were Isaac. It's too much for her. This time it is not only Abraham who lets Sarah have her way. It is God.

Abraham started early in the morning, got bread and a skin of water, and gave them to Hagar. He put them on her shoulder, and the child, and sent her away. She went, and wandered about in the Beer Sheba Wilderness. When the water in the skin was finished, she threw the child under one of the bushes and went and sat herself down at a distance, a bowshot away, because (she said), "I'm not going to watch the child die." So she sat down at a distance and lifted up her voice and cried. But God listened to the boy's voice, and God's envoy called to Hagar from the heavens and said to her, "What's with you, Hagar? Don't be afraid, because God has listened to the voice of the boy where he is. Get up, lift up the boy, take firm hold of him with your hand, because I'm going to make him into a big nation." And God opened her eyes and she saw a well of water. She went and filled the skin with water, and got the boy to drink. God was with the boy. He grew up and lived in the wilderness, and became a bowman. He lived in the Paran Wilderness. His mother got a wife for him from the country of Egypt. (Gen 21:14-21)

What destiny could Hagar and her son have in the wilderness? It's hardly surprising that the skin of water given to Hagar by Abraham is soon exhausted. She cannot just sit and watch her son die. But God looks after the two of them. In terms of his plan and his promises, it doesn't suit God to have Ishmael as the child through whom his commitment will find fulfilment. But in terms of his own being as the God of faithfulness and commitment, it doesn't suit God simply to abandon Hagar and Ishmael, and Ishmael becomes the recipient of his own promise, that he will become a great nation.

FOR REFLECTION AND DISCUSSION

1. What should a couple do when they cannot have children?

2. Was Sarah right to make that suggestion to Abraham?

3. Was Abraham right to let her treat Hagar as she saw fit?

4. Do you know of contexts in which jealousy has been a corrosive factor in family relationships?

39

JOSEPH

Joseph is the most prominent figure in the last quarter of Genesis, though in another sense his story is just one aspect of something bigger. His story begins in Genesis 37, but that chapter itself opens by telling us that we are about to read about the family of *Jacob*. It relates how God's promise works itself out in the interactions and deceptions and reversals and victories of his sons. It begins with a reference to the new name that God gave Jacob, the name Israel, which reminds the readers of Genesis this story is about the man who gave the people of Israel its name.

Jacob had a string of primary and secondary wives (Bilhah and Zilpah are two of them), and he has a dozen sons who will give their names to the twelve Israelite clans or tribes. Having a quiver full of sons is a sign of God's blessing (Ps 127:5). But it also makes for some tensions and problems, especially through Jacob's being fonder of some than of others.

> Joseph, when he was seventeen years of age, was pasturing the flock with his brothers; he was a boy with the sons of Bilhah and Zilpah, his father's wives. Joseph brought bad criticism of them to their father. Now Israel loved Joseph above all his sons, because he was the son of his old age. He made an ornamented coat for him. His brothers saw that their father loved him above all his brothers, and they became hostile to him and couldn't speak peaceably to him. Joseph had a dream and told his brothers, and they were yet more hostile to him. He said to them, "Please listen to this dream that I've had. There—we were binding sheaves in the middle of the fields. There—my sheaf got up, yes, stood. And there—your sheaves were gathering around and bowing low to my sheaf."

His brothers said to him, "Are you really to reign over us? Or are you really to rule over us?" They were yet more hostile to him because of his dreams and because of his words. He had another dream and recounted it to his brothers. "Here—I had another dream. There—the sun and the moon and eleven stars were bowing down to me." He recounted it to his father and to his brothers, and his father reprimanded him and said to him, "What's this dream that you've had? Are we really to come, I and your mother and your brothers, to bow low to the ground to you?" So his brothers were jealous of him, while his father kept the thing in mind. His brothers went to pasture their father's flock at Shechem. Israel said to Joseph, "Your brothers are pasturing at Shechem, aren't they? Come on, I'll send you to them." . . . They saw him from a distance, and before he got near them they plotted to put him to death. . . . Judah said to his brothers, "What's the gain when we kill our brother and cover up his blood? Come on, let's sell him to the Ishmaelites. Our hands—they shouldn't be on him, because he's our brother, our flesh." (Gen 37:2-13, 18, 26-27)

The Joseph story keeps raising questions that don't get answered until much later and describing events whose significance we don't see until much later. It embodies the way we make ethical decisions without knowing their implications and without knowing all about our own motives. Why did Joseph criticize his brothers to his father? Was it the right thing to do or the wise thing to do? Is Jacob himself wise? Do parents always have favorites, and can they help showing who their favorites are? Can one blame the brothers for their jealousy and resentment? Why did Joseph tell his brothers and his father about the dreams? Is it an indication that he is a bit full of himself? It's a question worth bearing in mind as the story unfolds. But we also have to bear in mind that Joseph's dreams broadly come true. The answer to the questions that his brothers and his father ask, about whether they are really going to bow down to him, is yes!

While Joseph is the most prominent figure in Genesis 37–50, alongside Jacob the figure of Judah is important; and Joseph and Judah are the ancestors of the dominant clans in Israel. So the Joseph story is also the Judah story, and Judah has to go through some character development as it unfolds. Here he at least makes a contribution to stopping the brothers doing their worst to Joseph.

So Joseph had been taken down to Egypt and an Egyptian, Potiphar, Pharaoh's courtier, the guards' officer, had acquired him from the hand of the Ishmaelites who had taken him down there. But Yahweh was with Joseph and he became a successful man. He was in the household of his Egyptian lord. . . . Joseph was attractive in shape and attractive in appearance, and subsequently his lord's wife set her eyes on Joseph and said, "Sleep with me." He refused, and said to his lord's wife, "Here, with me, my lord doesn't know about what's in the house. Everything that belongs to him he's put into my hand. There's no one bigger in this household than me. He hasn't held back anything from me except you, because you're his wife. How could I do this massively bad thing, and do wrong in relation to God?" When she spoke to Joseph day after day he didn't listen to her about sleeping beside her or being with her. On such a day he came into the house to do his work. None of the people of the household was there in the house. She caught hold of him by his coat, saying, "Sleep with me." He abandoned his coat in her hand, fled, and went outside. When she saw that he had abandoned his coat in her hand and fled outside, she called the people of the household and said to them, "Look, he brought us a Hebrew man to fool about with us! He came to me in order to sleep with me, and I called out in a loud voice, and when he heard that I raised my voice and called out, he abandoned his coat beside me and fled, and went outside." She set his coat down beside her until his lord came home, and she spoke to him in the same words, "The Hebrew servant that you brought to us came to me in order to fool about with me, and when I raised my voice and called out he abandoned his coat beside me and fled outside." When his lord heard his wife's words that she spoke to him, "These very things your servant did to me," his anger raged. Joseph's lord took him and put him in the jailhouse. (Gen 39:1-2, 6-20)

Yesterday was the anniversary of the traditional date of the execution of William Tyndale in October 1536. It was Tyndale who first translated much of the Bible from Hebrew and Greek into English; his translation lies behind the King James Version. He translated Genesis 39:2: "the Lord was with Joseph and he was a lucky fellow." One might have thought that the story of Joseph's life so far indicates that God is not with him and that he is neither lucky nor successful (and you could say the same of Tyndale), but God is at work behind the scenes of his story.

Israel was not the only people in the Middle East that viewed adultery as a most heinous wrongdoing—perhaps partly because it imperils family life and partly because it threatens to make it unclear who is the father of a child and thus has responsibility for the child. In Western culture, the person with whom a man has an adulterous relationship is quite likely to be someone whose husband he knows—a friend or a relative. There is thus an extra level of betrayal involved. Joseph sees it that way, even though Potiphar is not a friend, not even just an ordinary boss, but the person who owns Joseph. It would add an extra level of temptation to the advances Joseph experiences. But Potiphar trusts him implicitly. Is Joseph to betray that trust? And is he thus to sin against God? Because adultery turns out not to be merely a wrong done to a human being. Maybe the fact that God has been with Joseph and made him "a lucky fellow" adds to the force of this consideration. In light of what then happens, however, does he come to question whether God really is with him and whether he really is a lucky fellow?

And what is Potiphar angry about? He could have had Joseph executed, but he just puts him in jail. Is he angry with himself for neglecting his wife, or does he suspect her of encouraging Joseph? But in jail, Joseph proves to two of Pharaoh's staff that he is not only a dreamer but also a dream interpreter, and eventually Pharaoh learns about it.

> At the end of two years, Pharaoh himself was dreaming, and there, he was standing by the Nile. There, from the Nile seven cows going up, attractive in appearance and sturdy in body, and they pastured among the reeds. And there, seven more cows going up from the Nile after them, bad-looking in appearance and thin in body, and they stood beside the cows on the bank of the Nile. The cows that were bad-looking in appearance and thin in body ate the seven cows that were attractive in appearance and sturdy. . . . Pharaoh sent and called for Joseph. . . . Joseph said to Pharaoh, "Pharaoh's dream is one. God has told Pharaoh what he's going to do. The seven good cows are seven years and the seven good ears are seven years. It's one dream. The seven empty, bad-quality cows that were going up after them are seven years, as are the seven thin ears of grain, scorched by the east wind. There will be seven years of famine. . . . So now, Pharaoh should look for a discerning, smart man and set him over the country of Egypt. Pharaoh should act and set appointees over the country and take a fifth of the country of Egypt in the seven years of abundance. They should collect all food in these good years that are coming and lay up grain in the towns as food, under Pharaoh's care, and keep it. The food will be for appointing for the country for the seven years of famine that are going to happen in the country of Egypt, so the country is not cut off by the famine." The thing was good in the eyes of Pharaoh and in the eyes of all his servants, and Pharaoh said to his servants, "Shall we find a man like this man, in whom is the spirit of God?" (Gen 41:1-4, 14, 25-27, 33-38)

I don't understand economics, but I know that there is a thing called Keynesian economic theory (well, several forms of Keynesian theory) that derives from the work of a Brit called John Maynard Keynes at about the time of the Great Depression, and I think I know that he approved of capitalism and of the market but urged that sometimes the state has to intervene in economic affairs. That is what Joseph urges on the basis of Pharaoh's dreams. If there are going to be great harvests for a while, then people will simply eat well or not work so hard on the farm. It will be wiser for the state to make sure that some grain is set aside for the time of famine that Pharaoh's dreams have announced. So the state should buy up the surplus and save it. And someone needs to be in charge of that arrangement. One wonders whether Joseph knew exactly what he was doing when he made the recommendation to Pharaoh that would issue in his being appointed overseer of supplies and in due course be one of the most powerful people in the kingdom.

The dynamics of famine in Egypt and in Canaan would be different, and it would be a nasty coincidence that both countries experienced famine at the same time. Egypt's harvest depended on the Nile and thus on rain falling hundreds of miles to the south. Canaan's harvest depended on rain that came from the Mediterranean side of the country. Egyptians were inclined to pity peoples who had to rely on rain, which was less predictable than the Nile. In later centuries Rome used to import grain from Egypt, but even the Nile could let Egypt down. On this occasion, at least, Pharaoh's dreams and Joseph's insight enabled them to cope with the situation and even to be a resource for people in Canaan.

> Jacob said to his sons, "Why do you look at one another?" He said, "Here, I've heard that there's grain in Egypt. Go down there and buy us grain from there, so we may live and not die." . . . Joseph recognized his brothers but they didn't recognize him. Joseph brought to mind the dreams that he had about them. He said to them, "You're investigating; you've come to see the country's vulnerability. . . . By this you'll be tested: by the life of Pharaoh, you won't leave here unless your youngest brother comes here. Send one of you so he can get your brother. You, be imprisoned, so your words will be tested, whether there's truthfulness in you. And if not, by the life of Pharaoh, you're investigating." . . . They said to one another, "Well, we're paying the penalty for our brother. We saw the pressure in his spirit when he pleaded for grace with us and we didn't listen. That's why this pressure has come to us." (Gen 42:1-2, 8-9, 15-16, 21)

Was Joseph just playing with his brothers, getting his own back? Once more it's hard to tell at the time what is going on in his mind. It's easier to see the result of his action. His brothers needed to come to some insight about themselves and to face up to the implications of their own action. And they are starting to do so. They go to and fro between Egypt and Canaan, and eventually Judah makes a deeply felt, remorseful speech, and Joseph can keep the secret no longer.

> Joseph said to his brothers, "Please come up to me," and they came up. He said, "I'm Joseph your brother, whom you sold into Egypt. But now: don't be pained, don't let it make you rage at yourselves because you sold me here, because it was to save life that God sent me before you. Because this has been two years of famine within the country, and there will be five more years in which there will be no plowing or reaping. But God sent me before you to put in place for you a group remaining on the earth, to keep it alive for you as a big escape group. So now it was not you who sent me here but God. He's made me a father for Pharaoh and lord of all his household, and ruling over the entire country of Egypt." (Gen 45:4-8)

"It was not you who sent me here but God"? It's a magnificent oversimplification. Is Joseph in danger of taking away their responsibility for their action? It wouldn't matter, because they have now accepted responsibility for it. But looking at events and at people's wrongdoing in light of what God might be able to do through them helps Joseph form or maintain an attitude to his brothers that is not characterized by resentment.

> But bread: there was none in the entire country, because the famine was very heavy. The country of Egypt and the country of Canaan withered because of the famine. Joseph collected all the silver that was to be found in the country of Egypt and in the country of Canaan in payment for the grain that they were buying. Joseph brought the silver into Pharaoh's house. When the silver from the country of Egypt and from the country of Canaan came to an end, all Egypt came to Joseph, saying, "Give us bread: why should we die in front of you because the silver has gone." Joseph said, "Bring your livestock, and I'll give it to you in exchange for your livestock, if the silver's gone." So they brought their livestock to Joseph and Joseph gave them bread in exchange for the horses, for the livestock in the flock, for the livestock in the herd, and for the donkeys. He sustained them with bread in exchange for all their livestock that year. When that year came to an end, they came to him the next year and said to him, "We

won't hide from my lord that the silver has come to an end, and the animal stocks belong to my lord: nothing remains before my lord except our bodies and our land. Why should we die before your eyes, both we and our land? Acquire us and our land in exchange for bread. We ourselves and our land will become serfs to Pharaoh. Give seed, so we may live and not die, and the land not become a waste." So Joseph acquired all the land in Egypt for Pharaoh, because the Egyptians, each of them, sold his fields because the famine was so hard on them, and the country came to belong to Pharaoh. The people: he got them to pass over into the towns from one end of Egypt's border to its other end. He only didn't acquire the priests' land, because the priests had a statutory allotment from Pharaoh and they ate their allotment that Pharaoh gave them. Therefore they didn't sell their land. Joseph said to the people, "Here, today I've acquired you and your land for Pharaoh. Here's seed for you. You are to sow the land, and with the yield you are to give a fifth to Pharaoh, but four-fifths will be yours, as seed for the fields and as food for you and for those in your households, and for eating by your little ones." They said, "You've kept us alive. May we find grace in the eyes of my lord. We will become serfs to Pharaoh." Joseph made it a decree, until this day, for the land in Egypt: a fifth is Pharaoh's. Only the land of the priests on their own didn't become Pharaoh's. (Gen 47:13-26)

In a modern Western context, we are used to a straightforward antithesis between individual freedom on one hand and the kind of slavery that Britain and America invented and profited from for several centuries. It's the only way to think about freedom and bondage. Yet it's just one way to categorize them, as British and American history and realities in the modern world remind us when we reflect on them. As is the case with the way the Torah talks about servitude, the way Genesis describes the serfdom into which the Egyptians are reduced gives us other models for understanding them. Joseph's action turns the Egyptians into Pharaoh's serfs, but they are not slaves in the sense that we use the term, and they know that they are way better off than they would have been had there been no dreams and no Joseph.

So Jacob and Joseph enjoy a long-postponed reunion that maybe neither of them had expected. In due course Jacob dies and Joseph keeps his promise to bury his father in the Promised Land.

But Joseph's brothers saw that their father was dead, and said, "What if Joseph feels hostile to us and really gets back at us for all the bad fate that we dealt to him?" So they gave order to Joseph: "Your father gave order before his death:

'Say this to Joseph: "Oh, please carry your brothers' affront and their wrong-doing, that they dealt a bad fate to you."' So now please carry the affront of the servants of your father's God." Joseph cried when they spoke to him. His brothers also came and fell before him and said, "Here are we as servants to you." Joseph said to them, "Don't be afraid. Am I in the place of God? Whereas you yourselves thought up something bad for me, God thought it up for good, in order to act today to keep alive a numerous people. So now, don't be afraid. I myself will provide for you and your little ones." Thus he consoled them and reassured them. (Gen 50:15-21)

Back in chapter one, we noted that the Hebrew word for "forgive" is the ordinary word for "carry." When you forgive someone, you carry their wrong-doing instead of making them carry its consequences. You decline to let it spoil the relationship. You absorb the force of their wrongdoing, as physically you may absorb the force of someone's punch and not return it. It's not clear whether the brothers are lying about Jacob—the story has not told us that Jacob instructed them to instruct Joseph to forgive them. Either way, Joseph shows that he is the best embodiment in the entire Old and New Testament Scriptures of the kind of priorities that Jesus will eventually lay before his people, not least in embodying what forgiveness means.

FOR REFLECTION AND DISCUSSION

1. If you were not the only child, were you aware of your parents having a favorite child? Or as a parent, do you have a favorite child?

2. What do you think is the attitude to adultery in your culture?

3. If you put yourself in the position of Potiphar's wife, what do you think might have pushed her into making advances on Joseph?

4. What do you think of the strategy whereby Joseph turned all Egypt into Pharaoh's serfs?

5. Have you ever been put into a situation like Joseph's, where you had to forgive someone for something really bad—or where someone had to forgive you?

40

SHIPHRAH AND PUAH, YOKEBED AND MIRYAM

It's only a chapter later, but the situation has totally changed in Egypt, and changed for the descendants of Jacob in Egypt.

> A new king rose up over Egypt who didn't acknowledge Joseph. He said to his people, "Here, the people of the Israelites is vaster and more numerous than us. Come on, let's act smart with it so it doesn't become so vast that when battle comes, it even gathers together with our enemies and does battle against us, and goes up from the country." So they set work-force officials over it in order to humble it by means of its labors. It built supply towns for Pharaoh, Pitom and Raamses. But as they would humble it, so it would become vaster and spread out. People were dismayed about the Israelites. So the Egyptians made the Israelites serve with harshness. They made their lives hard with tough servitude, with mortar, with bricks, and with every form of servitude in the fields. Every form of the servitude that they had them undertake was with harshness. (Ex 1:8-14)

Maybe fear is not ethically wrong, but fear tempts people to do what is ethically wrong. As an Israelite, Joseph had been prime minister of Egypt, practically its savior. But that was a long time ago, and there had been a change of government, and who cared about Joseph and his people now. Yet paradoxically and amusingly, when people in power try to put down people who should be their underlings but seem a threat, it can make the underlings flourish rather than fade away.

> The king of Egypt said to the Hebrew midwives (one of whom was named
> Shiphrah, the second Pu'ah), "When you're delivering the Hebrew women,
> look at the stones. If it's a son, put him to death, but if it's a daughter, she may
> live." But the midwives lived in awe of God and didn't do as the king of Egypt
> had spoken to them. They let the boys live. The king of Egypt called for the
> midwives and said to them, "Why have you done this thing and let the boys
> live?" The midwives said to Pharaoh, "Because the Hebrew women are not like
> the Egyptian women, because they're lively. Before the midwife comes to them,
> they give birth." God was good to the midwives, and the people became vast
> and very numerous. Because the midwives lived in awe of God, he made
> households for them. (Ex 1:15-21)

We don't know the name of the man who was Pharaoh at the time, but we
do know the names of these two midwives (as we do of Moses' mother and
sister, Yokebed and Miryam). Whereas he is afraid, they are fearless. Whereas
he is stupid (if you want to control population growth, don't let the girls live!),
they are smart. Whereas he is in awe of the Israelites, they are in awe of God.
Yes, fear or awe (the same word in Hebrew) has ethical implications, in a bad
way or in a good way. (We don't know what "looking at the stones" means.)

They are not afraid to engage in deception. Your mother told you that it was
important to tell the truth, and she told you that the Ten Commandments say
so, but she wasn't telling the truth, because they don't (it was in her interests
for you to tell the truth). In the Old Testament, truth covers more than merely
the way our statements correspond to facts. Truthfulness is a relationship.
Pharaoh owes truthfulness to the people over whom he exercises authority,
and they owe truthfulness to him—truthfulness in action and truthfulness in
words. Powerful people (parents, professors, police) owe truthfulness to the
people they serve (children, students, citizens). But if they abandon truthfulness, they cannot expect it. Pharaoh has abandoned truthfulness, and the
midwives owe him no truthfulness now, at least on behalf of other people.

Their deception saves many children, though it only postpones a
further crisis.

> Then Pharaoh ordered all his people, "Every son who's born, you're to throw
> into the Nile, but every daughter you can let live." A man from the household
> of Levi went and got a daughter of Levi. The woman got pregnant and gave
> birth to a son, and she saw he was good-looking. She hid him for three months
> but she couldn't hide him any longer. So she got a papyrus container for him,

tarred it with tar and with bitumen, put the child in it, and put it in the reeds by the bank of the Nile. His sister took a stand at a distance so she would know what would be done to him. Pharaoh's daughter went down to bathe in the Nile, while her girls were walking on the bank of the Nile. She saw the container in the middle of the reeds and sent her handmaid, and she got it. She opened it and saw the child: there, a boy crying. She felt pity for him, and said, "This is one of the Hebrews' children." His sister said to Pharaoh's daughter, "Shall I go and call for a woman from the Hebrew women who is nursing for you, so she can nurse the child for you?" Pharaoh's daughter said to her, "Go!" The girl went and called for the child's mother. Pharaoh's daughter said to her, "Take this child and nurse him for me. I myself will give you your wages." So the woman took the child and nursed him, and the child grew up. Then she brought him to Pharaoh's daughter and he became her son. She named him Moses [Mosheh]; she said, "Because I pulled him out [*mashah*] from the water." (Ex 1:22–2:10)

Under oppression, life may go on. People continue to get married. They make love. They have babies. They see their babies as the most beautiful babies in the world. How could they then simply surrender them to infanticide? They engage in crazy experiments of hope. Or perhaps they engage in cunning ventures of scheming and manipulation. A mother, a sister, a daughter, and a handmaid unwittingly work as a team to ensure the survival of a baby who will grow up to be the Israelites' savior and the Egyptians' scourge. And the Egyptian coffers pay the costs.

During that time, Moses grew up, and he went out to his brothers and saw their labors. He saw an Egyptian man striking down a Hebrew man, one of his brothers. He turned his face this way and that, saw that there was no one, and struck down the Egyptian and hid him in the sand. He went out the next day and there, two Hebrew men were fighting. He said to the one in the wrong, "Why do you strike down your neighbor?" He said, "Who made you someone as an official and an authority over us? Are you thinking of killing me as you killed the Egyptian?" Moses was afraid. He said, "Then the thing has become known!" And Pharaoh heard about this thing and sought to kill Moses, but Moses took flight from before Pharaoh and lived in the country of Midyan. (Ex 2:11-15)

The women scheme, and the beneficiary of their scheming kills someone? Is that ethical, too? Actually Exodus leaves that question rather open. It looks as if Moses thought he did the right thing, but it issued in fear on his part (fear again features). Nor was his fear unjustified—indeed there is a sense in which every fear in these opening chapters of Exodus is justified. So should he stay or should he go?

His mother's desperate but trusting action had saved his life and provided him with his Egyptian upbringing, but he did not become overly attached to Egypt. His attack on the Egyptian showed that he had not forgotten who he was identified with. His intervention in the intra-Israelite fight showed that he lived on the basis of some moral principle and not simply of ethnic commitment. Nor was he afraid to intervene in someone else's quarrel, notwithstanding the warning in Proverbs about such deeds. His own desperate but perhaps trusting action in fleeing for his life also saved his life, provided him with a wife and sons, and took him into the location in Sinai where God would meet with him and summon him to his service. Sometimes we don't know how to make an ethical evaluation of our actions either beforehand or afterward. In a letter to Philip Melanchthon, Martin Luther once said that sometimes one has to "sin boldly." Sometimes, when a situation looks ambiguous, you just have to take action anyway.

FOR REFLECTION AND DISCUSSION

1. Do you know anyone who has been put in a position at all like that which the midwives faced?

2. Is it possible to lay down any guidelines for when it's okay to tell lies, as the midwives did?

3. Is it possible to judge whether Moses was right to strike down the Egyptian, and does it matter?

4. Is it possible to judge whether he was then right to run for it, and does it matter?

41

DAVID

David's story begins with the kind of puzzling ambiguity that runs all the way through it. You would never have dreamed that David would end up as king. For one thing, Israel had a king already. For another, he was just the little brother to six older brothers who would look more impressive than him. But when Samuel looks first at David's eldest brother, God says to him:

> Don't look at his appearance or at the loftiness to which he stands, because I've rejected him, because it's not what a human being sees, because a human being sees what appears to the eyes, but Yahweh sees into the mind. (1 Sam 16:7)

(English translations have "the heart," which might be right, but see chapter nine.) In light of this observation, it's a surprise when the story reports David's arrival on the scene and offers this description:

> He was tanned, with lovely eyes, good-looking. Yahweh said, "Get up, anoint him, because this is the one." (1 Sam 16:12)

Further, when one of Saul's servants commends him in the following terms to Saul as someone who might be able to play Spanish guitar in a soothing fashion:

> I've seen a son of Jesse the Bethlehemite who knows how to play. He's a forceful strong man, a man of battle, but smart with words and good-looking, and Yahweh is with him. (1 Sam 16:18)

David commends himself to Saul for his killer instinct:

> Your servant has been shepherding over the flock for his father. A lion or a bear comes and carries off a sheep from the flock, and I go out after it and strike it

down and rescue it from its mouth. It rises up against me, and I get firm hold of it by its beard and strike it down and put it to death. Both lion and bear your servant has struck down. This foreskinned Philistine will be like one of them, because he's reviled the ranks of the living God. Yahweh who rescued me from the hand of the lion and from the hand of the bear: he will rescue me from the hand of this Philistine. (1 Sam 17:34-37)

That last declaration of trust in Yahweh is the key addition to the note about his killer instinct. His trust is one of the instincts that Yahweh sees when he looks inside David. David kills the seven-foot Philistine warrior because he is fearlessly brave, because he is skillful and lucky, and because he trusts in God.

Samuel had told Saul that Yahweh intended to replace Saul with "a man after his own heart/mind" (1 Sam 13:14). Given David's failings, it may seem a puzzling statement. There are two possible ways of resolving the puzzle. One is that we misunderstand the phrase. It doesn't imply that David's heart and mind are one with God's. It simply means he is somebody on whom God has set his heart and mind, someone God has decided on. (The same phrase comes with a meaning of this kind in 2 Samuel 7:21 and Psalm 20:4, though translations use different words.) The other is that for all his faults David was someone who kept up trust in Yahweh and served Yahweh alone, unlike some other kings we could mention.

David is by nature a warrior. In due course Yahweh determines that David can make the plans for building a temple but not implement them because he's killed too many people (1 Chron 22:8); his body count has been estimated at 140,000. The point is not that he is therefore morally guilty. The decision reflects an awareness of the ambiguity of war itself and of causing people's death. The Torah presupposes that contact with death or with sex made it impossible to go into Yahweh's presence. The best guess regarding the rationale for this assumption is that both are incompatible with God's nature. They are in that sense defiling, though not morally wrong. By extension, it would be inappropriate for David the great killer to be the person who built the temple

When David becomes king, his best moment comes at the beginning of his reign, as (I noted in chap. 28) is the case with Saul and Solomon. In David's story the point is made in a brief phrase you could miss: "David reigned over all Israel and David exercised authority in faithfulness for all his people" (2 Sam 8:15).

If a king exercises authority in faithfulness, it's all you could ask for (see chap. 35). A number of the stories about him show that he is also someone who knows how to combine power and authority with mercy and forgiveness. But as happens with Saul and Solomon, the other shoe soon falls.

> At the turn of the year, at the time when the kings go out, David sent Yoab and his servants with him, and all Israel, and they devastated the Ammonites and besieged Rabbah, while David was staying in Jerusalem. (2 Sam 11:1)

Why was the commander-in-chief staying in Jerusalem when the army was fighting across the Jordan? Was he focusing on exercising authority in faithfulness back home? What follows does not suggest such a charitable interpretation.

> During evening time David got up from his bed and walked about on the roof of the king's house, and from on the roof saw a woman bathing. The woman was very good-looking. David sent and inquired about the woman. They said, "She's Bathsheba bat Eliam, the wife of Uriyyah the Hittite, isn't she." David sent envoys, got her, and she came to him. He slept with her, while she was making herself sacred from her taboo, and she went back to her house. The woman got pregnant, and she sent and told David, "I'm pregnant." (2 Sam 11:2-5)

The roof is the most private part of the house, the place you would go to pray. The trouble is that the houses of ordinary people are down the hill from the palace. The palace is a good place from which to keep an eye on the city— from which to concern oneself with exercising authority in faithfulness, in fact. But that commitment is not the priority in David's mind. It's a puzzling story. David has eight primary wives and ten secondary wives, so he has sex with at least this number of women. Why engage in this risky illicit adulterous relationship? I guess that one answer is that he is a sex addict. Another factor is that one of the characteristics of leaders (along with their tending to be addicts of one kind or another) is that they think they can get away with anything (see chap. 28).

David gets Uriyyah back from the front and tries to get him home to sleep with Bathsheba, but Uriyyah won't play. His commitment to the army's work contrasts with David's lack of commitment. So David sends him back to the front with a chilling letter: "Place Uriyyah near the front of the fiercest battle, and pull back from after him so he may be struck down and die" (2 Sam 11:15). The ploy works.

"Uriyyah's wife heard that Uriyyah her husband was dead, and she lamented over her master. The grieving passed, and David sent and gathered her to his house. She became a wife for him, and gave birth to a son for him. But the thing that David did was bad in Yahweh's eyes" (2 Sam 11:26-27). Yahweh therefore declares,

> I'm going to make something bad arise for you from your household. I shall take your wives before your eyes and give them to your neighbor. He'll sleep with your wives before the eyes of this sun. Because you yourself acted in secret, but I myself will do this thing before all Israel and before the sun. (2 Sam 12:11-12)

That shame will not be all. In chapter 22 we noted the story of his son Amnon and his daughter Tamar (2 Sam 13). It's just the beginning of a story of strife within David's household. When David is almost on his deathbed, the narrative makes this comment about another of David's sons:

> Now Adoniyyah ben Haggit was elevating himself, saying "I shall be king," and he prepared himself chariotry and cavalry and fifty men running ahead of him. His father had not pained him in all his years by saying "Why have you acted like this?" (1 Kings 1:5-6)

It's been said that the clue to understanding David is that he was a gifted leader but was clueless about personal relationships and the family. It's not the complete story, but it's an illuminating comment. Just within his family, Bathsheba, Tamar, and Amnon were not the only people he let down. Absalom is another. David is portrayed as having a deep love for Absalom, but it doesn't help David to relate to him. When David does nothing about Amnon's rape of Tamar, Absalom eventually kills his half-brother and runs to escape the consequences. Eventually David gets him to come back, and Absalom responds by attempting a coup. Now it's David who flees. Yet here is when David's trust in Yahweh again manifests itself.

> The king said to Zadoq, "Take God's chest back into the town. If I find grace in Yahweh's eyes, he will let me come back and let me see it and its home. But if he says this, 'I don't want you,' here I am: he can do with me as it is good in his eyes." (2 Sam 15:25-26)

As the story is nearing its end, it gives us David's testimony as he looks back.

Yahweh, my crag,
    my stronghold, the one who enables me to survive,
My God, my crag in which I take shelter,
    my shield, the horn that delivers me, my turret,

My retreat, my deliverer,
>   you deliver me from violence.
As one to be praised, I call on Yahweh,
>   and from my enemies I find deliverance. . . .
He brought me out into a roomy place;
>   he pulled me out because he delighted in me.
Yahweh dealt to me in accordance with my faithfulness;
>   in accordance with the purity of my hands he gave back to me.
Because I have kept Yahweh's ways
>   and not been faithless to my God.
For all his rulings have been before me;
>   his decrees—I haven't departed from them.
I've been a person of integrity with him,
>   and I've kept myself from waywardness I might have done.
>   (2 Sam 22:2-4, 20-24)

One rubs one's eyes in disbelief. Did David really make that claim? Does the storyteller really imagine David making that claim? One weekend in the 1990s, a British newspaper reported "a bizarre political crisis over King David." It was alleged that the Israeli Foreign Minister (Secretary of State, in US terms) had slandered David in a parliamentary debate in Israel. There was some danger that it would issue in a vote of no confidence that could bring the government down. What the Foreign Minister had said was, "Not everything that King David did, on the ground, on the rooftops, is acceptable to a Jew or is something I like." The deputies who were incensed at those words were people who had seen no irony in 2 Samuel 22. David's story indeed illustrates a theme that emerged in chapter 28. Leaders tend to be more holy before they become leaders. Leaders tend to become sinners.

FOR REFLECTION AND DISCUSSION

1. Could anything have been done for David or about David?

2. Can anything be done for power addicts?

3. Can anything be done for sex addicts?

4. Do you know a David?

42

NEHEMIAH

Nehemiah's family was among the people who didn't return to Judah when everyone had the chance to do so after Persia took over from Babylon as the imperial power in 539 BC. Nehemiah must have been born in Persia in the next century, and he was doing well in the Persian administration. But he knew that Jerusalem was where his ancestors had come from, and when he heard about the city's sorry state, he was able to use his position to get the king's support for a project to restore the city's walls.

The city's physical state wasn't its only problem.

There was a great outcry by the people and their wives toward their Judahite brothers. There were some saying, "Our sons and our daughters, we are many. We must get grain so we can eat and live." There were some saying, "Our fields, our vineyards, our homes—we're mortgaging them so we can get grain during a famine." And there were some saying, "We've borrowed silver for the king's tax—our fields and our vineyards. Now, our flesh is the same as our brothers' flesh, our children are the same as their children, but here— we're binding our sons and our daughters as servants. Some of our daughters are bound. There's no power in our hand; our fields and our vineyards belong to other people." It enraged me very much when I heard their outcry and these words. When my mind had counseled me, I argued with the important people and the overseers: "Are you advancing loans, one with his brother?" and I set a big congregation against them. I said to them, "We acquired our Judahite brothers who'd been sold to the Gentiles, as far as it lay in us. Will you indeed sell your brothers so that they may be sold to us? . . . The thing that you're doing isn't good. Will you not walk in awe of God to avoid reviling before our Gentile enemies? Indeed, I, my brothers, and my boys are advancing loans of silver and grain with them. Please let's abandon this advancing of loans. Please give them back this very day their fields, their vineyards, their olive trees, and their houses, and the percentage on the silver, the grain, the new wine, and the fresh oil that you're advancing them." (Neh 5:1-11)

Times of pressure put pressure on people. The Judahites have at least three problems. The city is in that bad state. The harvests have been failing. And they have to pay imperial taxes. The people whose farms or business are doing okay are coping by making loans to their fellows and charging interest on the loans, in breach of what it says in the Torah (see chaps. 31-32). The people whose farms or businesses are in trouble not only have to take out the loans, with their homes and farms as collateral, but also have to put their children to servitude—Nehemiah is likely referring not (or not only) to child labor but to the fate of teenagers or young adults. "But we are all the same flesh and blood," they protest. Yet the people who are doing okay are not treating their fellow Judahites as if that were true. The challenge of tough times is to share the pain rather than take advantage of the situation.

Abel's blood cried out to God, and the oppression of people in Sodom did the same (Gen 4; 19), and Isaiah once commented that the people of Jerusalem are a collection of Sodomites (Is 1:10). They are evidently the same in Nehemiah's day. In that context, Nehemiah, like Saul, shows how anger can be a fruit of the Spirit. He gets pretty confrontational about their desecration of the Sabbath, too (Neh 13:15-22; see chap. 15 of this book).

In a nice observation Nehemiah expresses the awareness that he needs to cool down a bit before he confronts the leaders of the community, who are no doubt better off than the people who are in trouble and are able to work the system to their advantage. The community had been freed from direct servitude to Gentiles, and now Judahites were putting each other into servitude! Nehemiah argues with them that their being members of the same people and their being members of the people of God over against the Gentile world ought to make a difference in the way they behave toward one another. Not only so, but they are ignoring the fact that living in the right way in this respect is a necessary expression of living in awe of God—ethics and spirituality cannot be separated. And they are ignoring the fact that failing to live in the right way earns them opprobrium from those Gentiles—ethics and witness cannot be separated.

Nehemiah also acknowledges that he and his staff are apparently involved in some of the practices that are causing hardship. He is quite a complicated person in quite a complicated position.

> They said, "We'll give them back, and we won't seek anything from them. We'll act in this way, as you're saying." So I called for the priests and swore them to act in accordance with this word. I also shook out my pocket and said, "May God shake out like this anyone who does not implement this word, from his house and from his labor. May he become shaken out like this and empty." The entire congregation said "Yes," and praised Yahweh, and the people acted in accordance with this word. Further, from the day I was ordered to become governor in the country of Judah, from the twentieth year until the thirty-second year of Artaxerxes the king, twelve years, I with my brothers didn't eat the governor's food. The previous governors who were before me made things heavy for the people, and for food and wine for one day took from them forty sheqels of silver (further, their boys had power over the people). I didn't do so, out of awe for God. And further, I strengthened the work on this wall; we didn't acquire fields, and all my boys were collected there for the work. The Judahites and the overseers, 150 individuals, and the people who came to us from the nations that were round us, were at my table. What was being prepared for one day, an ox, six choice sheep, and birds, they were prepared for me with all kinds of wine in quantity at an interval of ten days, but with this I didn't seek the governor's food, because the service was heavy on this people. (Neh 5:12-18)

Although it looks as if Nehemiah and his staff were involved in the practices that were causing hardship, in other respects Nehemiah can defend the way he has exercised his leadership. Nehemiah claims not to have benefited from his position; he would be unwise to claim it if it wasn't true. He reminds one of Samuel, who said

> "I have walked about before you from my youth until this day. Here I am. Vow against me in the presence of Yahweh and in the presence of his anointed. Whose ox have I taken? Whose donkey have I taken? Whom have I defrauded? Whom have I crushed? From whose hand have I taken a ransom so I might

close my eyes to him? I'll give it back to you." They said, "You haven't defrauded us, you haven't crushed us, you haven't taken anything from anyone's hand." (1 Sam 12:2-4)

You have to have a clear and trustworthy conscience to be able to make the claims that Nehemiah and Samuel make to people who are in a position to call your bluff.

There was yet another occasion when Nehemiah got angry.

In those days I also saw the Judahites had got Ashdodite, Ammonite, and Moabite women to come to live. Their children were speaking half in Ashdodite, and none of them knew how to speak Judahite, but in accordance with the tongue of one people or the other. I argued with them and slighted them, and struck some of them down and pulled out their hair, and made them swear by God: "If you give your daughters to their sons or if you get some of their daughters for your sons or for yourselves. . . . It was in these things that Solomon king of Israel did wrong, wasn't it. Among the many nations there was no king like him. He was loved by God, and God made him king over all Israel; foreign women caused even him to do wrong. Are we to listen to you doing this great bad thing, trespassing against our God by getting foreign women to come to live?" One of the sons of Yoyada, the son of Elyashib the big priest, was son-in-law to Sanballat the Horonite. I made him take flight from me. Be mindful with regard to them, my God, because they polluted the priesthood, the pact of the priesthood and the Levites. I purified them of everything foreign and put the watches in place for the priests and for the Levites, each one in his work, and for the wood offering at designated times and for the first fruits. My God, be mindful for me for good. (Neh 13:23-31)

No, you wouldn't want to get the wrong side of Nehemiah. Both Ezra and Nehemiah took tough stances to Judahites "marrying out"—marrying Gentiles. I've heard it said that marrying out is the biggest threat to the Jewish community in Los Angeles. In the twenty-first century we like the attitude to intermarriage in Ruth's story. We don't care for the attitude in Ezra and Nehemiah. Our sympathies lie with the Ashdodite, Ammonite, and Moabite women and their children, especially when Ezra actually makes their Judahite husbands divorce them.

The Ruth story makes things easier by having Ruth making a commitment to Yahweh and to Israel so that she becomes an honorary Israelite. The ethical challenge of her story compares with one that faced churches in Los Angeles in the early part of the twentieth century and churches in Britain in the middle of the twentieth century. In the first context, as part of the migration of African Americans from the South, a minority came to cities such as Los Angeles, and the ones who were Episcopalian (at least) sought to join Episcopal churches here and were asked to sit in the balcony or encouraged to find another congregation. (It is how the congregation to which I have belonged for the last twenty years came into being.) In the second context, people from the Caribbean were encouraged to emigrate to Britain to drive our buses and nurse in our hospitals. They tried to join evangelical churches and were asked to go elsewhere; I have heard someone describe how this happened to her mother and her in a church in Birmingham that I used sometimes to visit as a teenager. It's easy to see now that churches in Los Angeles and Birmingham were failing to learn from the Ruth story that the people of God by its nature is open across ethnic boundaries when God has made them one people of faith. The question is, what are we blind to in the twenty-first century?

And it wouldn't surprise me if the answer is that we have something to learn from Ezra and Nehemiah. They recognize that their communities face a clash between two sets of principles. There is the principle that marriage is lifelong and that husbands have obligations to wives and children. And there is the principle that God has set the people of Israel apart and that it needs not to be swallowed up by the Gentile world (otherwise, we might reflect, there will be no community from which the Messiah can be born). Sometimes principles clash and we have to decide which principle has priority at this moment. We do then also have to see what we can do to safeguard what the other principle stands for. And it is reasonable to wonder what happens to the Ashdodite, Ammonite, and Moabite women and their children. The fact that Ezra and Nehemiah don't tell us need not indicate that their husbands just threw them out heartlessly on the street; if they did so, they ignored other principles in the Torah. The point in Ezra and Nehemiah is that this is a moment when the principle of keeping Israel in being has to have priority. As is the case with Abraham in Genesis 22, ethics doesn't have the final word.

FOR REFLECTION AND DISCUSSION

1. Can you see ways the members of your congregation are failing to treat one another as the same flesh and blood?

2. Can you see ways your local community is failing in this way?

3. Can you see ways you could appropriately both claim to live generously but also acknowledge living selfishly?

4. Can you see ways we need to learn from the stance Nehemiah takes to intermarriage?

43

VASHTI, ESTHER, AND MORDECAI

The story of Esther relates an attempt to cleanse the Persian Empire of the Judahite people. It begins with a joke, not its only joke. (The story takes the Jewish view that if you want to survive, you had better learn to laugh.)

In the days of Xerxes, that Xerxes who reigned from India as far as Sudan over 127 provinces—in those days, when King Xerxes sat on his royal throne which was in the Shushan fortress, in the third year of his reign, he made a banquet for all his officials and his servants. . . . On the seventh day, when the king was in good heart because of the wine, he said to Mehuman, Bizzeta, Harbona, Bigta, Abagta, Zetar, and Karkas, the seven eunuchs who ministered to the presence of King Xerxes, to get Vashti the queen to come before the king in her royal diadem, to let the peoples and the officials see her beauty, because she was good-looking. Queen Vashti refused to come at the king's word by means of the eunuchs. The King was quite furious. . . . Memukan said before the king and the officials, "It's not against the king alone that Vashti the queen has gone astray, but against all the officials and against all the peoples that are in all King Xerxes's provinces. Because the thing about the queen will get out to all the women, so as to make them despise their masters in their eyes, when they say, 'King Xerxes said to get Vashti the queen to come before him, and she didn't come.' This day the leading women of Persia and Media who have heard the thing about the queen will say it to all the king's officials, with quite enough despising and fury. If it seems good to your majesty, a royal word should issue from his presence, and it should be written in the laws of Persia and Media and not pass away, that Vashti will not come before King Xerxes. The king should give her royal position to another woman who is better than her." (Esther 1:1-3, 10-12, 16-19)

So Vashti loses her position, and the king issues such an edict to make sure that men can still rule in their own households. One way the Esther story reads differently in the Western world in the early decades of the twenty-first century from the way it read in the early decades of the twentieth century is that the position of women is very different. I write just after the celebration of the hundredth anniversary of women gaining voting rights in the United States. Vashti is a woman who said no two and a half millennia ago. I imagine she could imagine the consequences, and she was willing to accept them.

Subsequently, when King Xerxes's wrath had subsided, he was mindful of Vashti and what she had done and what had been determined against her. The king's boys ministering to him said, "They should seek for the king young, good-looking girls. The king should appoint people in all the provinces of his realm so they can collect every young, good-looking girl to the Shushan fortress, to the women's household, into the control of Hege, the king's eunuch who keeps watch over the women, and their cleansing treatments should be given them. The girl who seems good in the king's eyes should reign in place of Vashti." . . . The king liked Esther more than all the women and she gained grace and commitment before him more than all the young girls, and he put a royal diadem on her head and made her queen in place of Vashti. The king made a great banquet for all his officials and his servants, "Esther's Banquet." He made a holiday for the provinces and gave gifts in accordance with the capacity of the king. (Esther 2:1-4, 17-18)

So an orphan girl called Esther wins a compulsory beauty contest to find a new queen, though she keeps quiet about being a Judahite. One can imagine that Vashti would be disgusted at Esther's collaboration. (In the *Veggie Tales* version of the story, Esther tries to escape the van collecting young girls, but she fails.) But there are some people who by nature or by calling properly take Vashti's stance, and others who by nature or by calling take Esther's stance. In due course Esther will use her womanly power in a different way.

Subsequently, King Xerxes promoted Haman ben Hammedata the Agagite. He elevated him and put his seat above all the officials who were with him. All the king's servants who were at the king's gateway would kneel and bow low to Haman, because the king had ordered this regarding him. But

Mordecai didn't kneel and didn't bow low. The king's servants who were at
the king's gateway said to Mordecai, "Why are you transgressing the king's
order?" But when they said it to him day by day, he didn't listen to them. They
told Haman to see whether Mordecai's words would stand, because he had
told them that he was a Judahite. Haman saw that Mordecai was not kneeling
or bowing low to him, and Haman filled with wrath, but in his eyes he de-
spised laying hand on Mordecai alone, because they had told him Mordecai's
people, and Haman sought to annihilate all the Judahites who were in
Xerxes's entire kingdom—Mordecai's people. (Esther 3:1-6)

Incensed because Mordecai, Esther's uncle and guardian, will not bow
down to him, Haman gets Xerxes to authorize the annihilation of the Judahite people on the basis of their insistence on behaving differently from
everyone else. Esther agrees to take the risk of unilaterally approaching
Xerxes to ask him to change his mind, and implements a complex plan to
manipulate Xerxes into doing so. In the meantime, Xerxes discovers action
Mordecai had once taken to uncover a plot against the king's life and directs
Haman to honor Mordecai in a way Haman himself would like to be honored.
In Haman's presence, Esther reveals that Haman's scheme implicates her because she is a Judahite. The king storms out, Haman crumples onto Esther,
the king returns, thinks he is raping Esther, and orders him to be executed.
The king revokes his decree and gives the Judahites the right to self-defense,
which they exercise with enthusiasm.

So in the twelfth month (i.e., the month of Adar), on the thirteenth, the day
when the king's word and his law were due to be acted on, on the day when the
Judahites' enemies expected to be in power over them, that was turned around,
so that the Judahites—they were in power over the people hostile to them. The
Judahites in their towns in all King Xerxes's provinces congregated to lay a
hand on people who sought something bad for them, but no one stood up
before them, because dread of them had fallen on all the peoples. All the king's
provincial officials, satraps, governors, and people doing work were elevating
the Judahites, because dread of Mordecai had fallen on them, because Mordecai was big in the king's house and report of him was going through all the
provinces, because the man Mordecai was getting bigger and bigger. So the
Judahites struck down all their adversaries with a stroke of the sword, with
killing and obliteration, and acted against the people hostile to them in accordance with what was acceptable to them. In the Shushan fortress the

Judahites killed and obliterated five hundred people, and killed Parshandata, Dalphon, Aspata, Porata, Adalya, Aridata, Parmashta, Arisay, Ariday, and Vayzata, the ten sons of Haman ben Hammedata, the Judahites' adversary, but didn't lay their hand on the plunder. (Esther 9:1-10)

There are at least two ways of reading the ethical significance of the Judahite people's action. One Jewish reading involves grinning at the latter part of the Esther story and at the irony involved in the fact that the Jewish people turn out to behave the same way as their Gentile oppressors wanted to. (There is further humor in the portrait of thousands of Persian people walking into the trap of attacking Judahites whom the king has commissioned to slaughter them if they do.) Another Jewish reading links with the comment that Esther now reads differently from the way it did a century ago. In the middle of the twentieth century Hitler tried to "solve the Jewish problem" by eliminating the Jewish people. He was a latter-day Haman. The Esther story invites the Jewish people to stand up for themselves rather than walk into gas chambers. An extraordinary aspect of the story is that it never mentions God or faith or prayer, yet paradoxically it gives a vivid portrayal of the way God looks after his people. But God does so by operating behind the scenes through coincidences and through people taking responsibility for their destiny.

FOR REFLECTION AND DISCUSSION

1. Are you more inclined to Vashti's stance or to Esther's? Does one have a choice which stance one takes?

2. Mordecai gets into trouble because he won't bow down to Haman. Why would one refuse to do so?

3. If the end of the story invites Jewish people to ask if they are any better than Gentiles, what is the answer when you ask that question of your congregation?

4. Are there ways in which you should be actively seeking to ensure that some twenty-first-century Haman or Hitler does not succeed?

CONCLUSION

In the course of delivering a charge to one of his aides, Paul issues this exhortation:

> From infancy you have known the Sacred Scriptures, which are able to make you wise for salvation through faith in Christ Jesus. Every Scripture is God-breathed and is useful for teaching, rebuking, correcting, and training in righteousness, so that all God's people may be thoroughly equipped for every good work. (2 Tim 3:15-17)

Although one can apply Paul's words to the New Testament, he himself is talking about the Old Testament; he hasn't finished writing the New Testament yet. In rereading those verses as I complete this book, I am struck by the double focus of his words. Both halves of his statement may seem astonishing.

On one hand, he assumes that the Old Testament can contribute significantly to an understanding of salvation through faith in Christ Jesus. What he writes elsewhere indicates the kind of insight he has in mind. You want to understand God? Read the Old Testament. You want to understand the way God relates to us? Read the Old Testament. You want to understand faith? Understand the Old Testament. You want to understand Jesus? Read the Old Testament.

But this book focuses on the implications of the second half of his statement. The entirety of the Old Testament is significant for "teaching, rebuking, correcting, and training in righteousness, so that all God's people may be thoroughly equipped for every good work." Some translations have not "every Scripture" but "all Scripture," which implies that Paul is continuing to speak of the Scriptures as a whole—it doesn't make much difference. His point is that the entirety of these Old Testament Scriptures is significant for the life that Timothy lives and for the lives lived by the people Timothy is ministering to. It has a role to play in equipping them for good works. The people for whom it is significant are "God's people"—Jews no doubt, but in the context of this letter, Gentiles too.

It's significant for their ethical lives because of the story it tells—because of the way it relates the story of God's working out his salvation purpose and his involvement in people's lives. It's significant for their ethical lives because of the rules it lays down, sometimes because people are simply to do as those rules say, sometimes because the rules embody a vision whose practical implications people need to apply to their context. It's significant for their ethical lives because of the grief and anger and warnings on God's part that it reveals and the promises and hope it expresses. It's significant for their ethical lives because of the insight it formulates about how life works. It's significant for their ethical lives because of the prayers it prays. Maybe the thinking and the lives of people who believe in Jesus have always been shaped as much by the culture in which they live as by the Scriptures. I'm sure it's the case in the world in which I live. So go back to read the Old Testament and see how it confronts you in order to teach, rebuke, correct, and train.

POSTSCRIPT

But What About the Canaanites?

When Western people think about Old Testament ethics, we have noted that one of the first things they think about is the ethics of the Israelites slaughtering all the Canaanites, which seems a contradiction to Jesus' talk of loving your enemies. This book has been looking at the way the Old Testament itself sees ethics and the way we can learn from it, rather than focusing on the way it raises problems for Western readers. But I had better say something about this particular issue or you will feel cheated.

One basis on which I could avoid saying anything about the question is that the Old Testament itself doesn't base any ethics on its account of the Israelites and the Canaanites. It doesn't treat the idea of the Israelites slaughtering the Canaanites as a model for the way Israel was to relate to foreign peoples. Actually, I exaggerate slightly. Attacking the Canaanites required extraordinary trust in Yahweh, because the Canaanites were more numerous and their weaponry was more sophisticated. And trust in Yahweh is a key ethical principle in the Old Testament and a key principle when you are waging war or thinking about waging war (see chap. 5).

A consideration underlying God's acting in judgment on the Canaanites was the unethical nature of their own lives. The specific issue to which the Old Testament often refers is the practice of offering their children as a sacrifice to their gods (see Deut 7). Archaeological evidence confirms that it was an accepted practice. If you really wanted to show that you were committed to the god and you really wanted him to answer your prayer, sacrificing your son or daughter would be a sign of your devotion. Yahweh is appalled at that practice. This aspect of the Canaanites' faith and life is one thing that shows that the Canaanites were not just nice people who were simply unlucky to be in the wrong place at the wrong time because God wanted to give their land to Israel. The point is neatly made in one of God's first promises to Abraham.

Yahweh said to Abram, "You can know for sure that your offspring will be resident aliens in a country not theirs. They will serve them, and they will humble them for four hundred years. But the nation that they serve I'm indeed going to judge. After this they will get out with much property. But you: you will go to your ancestors with things being well. You'll be buried in a good old age. In the fourth generation they'll come back here, because the Amorites' waywardness is not yet complete." (Gen 15:13-16)

Although Yahweh promises that Abraham's descendants will eventually possess the land of Canaan, he declares that they are going to have to wait for four generations, because the Amorites' waywardness isn't complete yet (Amorites is another word for Canaanites). In other words, it wouldn't be fair to throw them out without reason. They have to be given every chance to come to their senses. Then when they have used up their chances, he will throw them out—but he doesn't tell Abraham that his descendants will annihilate them. Nor does he talk in those terms to the Israelites at Sinai.

Here, I'm going to send an envoy before you to keep you on the way and to bring you to the place that I've prepared. Keep watch before him. Listen to his voice. Don't defy him, because he won't carry your rebellions, because my name is within him. But if you do really listen to his voice and do everything I speak, I'll be an enemy to your enemies, an adversary to your adversaries, because my envoy will go before you and bring you to the Amorite, the Hittite, the Perizzite, the Canaanite, the Hivvite, and the Yebusite, and I shall efface them. You will not bow low to their gods, you will not serve them, you will not do as they do, but completely tear them down and completely break up their columns. . . . I shall send off a dread of me before you, and it will throw into turmoil all the people among whom you come. I shall make all your enemies turn their back before you. I shall send a hornet before you, and it will drive out the Hivvites, the Canaanites, and the Hittites from before you. I shall not drive them out from before you in one year, in case the country becomes a desolation and the creatures of the wild multiply against you. Little by little I shall drive them out from before you until you're fruitful and you have the country as a domain. I shall set your border from the Reed Sea to the Philistines' Sea and from the wilderness to the river [Euphrates], because I shall give into your hand the people living in the country, and you will drive them out from before you. You will not solemnize a pact with them or with their gods. They won't live in your country, in case they cause you to do wrong in relation to me because you serve their gods, because it would be a snare to you. (Ex 23:20-24, 27-33)

Drive out the Canaanites, yes, but the question of annihilating them arises only some decades later, when the Israelites are on the edge of the Promised Land. Annihilating them is then Israel's idea, to which Yahweh agrees.

> The Canaanite, the king of Arad, who lived in the Negeb, heard that Israel was coming by the Atarim road, and he battled against Israel and took some of them captive. Israel made a pledge to Yahweh: "If you actually give this people into my hand, I will devote [*haram*] their towns." Yahweh listened to Israel's voice and gave the Canaanites over, and they devoted them and their towns. So they named the place Hormah. (Num 21:1-3)

The word for "devote," the word often translated "annihilate," strictly denotes giving something over to God—hence my use of that English word to translate it. Previously in the Torah, the verb and the related noun that means something devoted (*herem*) have been used in connection with giving something over to God in a way that doesn't involve their death at all (see Lev 27:21-28), though it's also been used for capital punishment in connection with an Israelite worshiping other gods (Ex 22:20; cf. Lev 27:29). So the word doesn't simply mean slaughtering people.

If there's a frightening ethical point in this first use of the verb in connection with slaughtering the Canaanites, it's that sometimes God agrees to our suggestions, as he often does in the Old Testament. So be careful of your bright ideas. God does subsequently affirm with energy the idea of devoting by killing, though he also compromises it by taking the focus off the idea of killing and putting it back onto the idea that Israel needs to avoid living with the Canaanites in a way that would imperil the people's own relationship with God.

> When Yahweh your God brings you into the country where you're coming to take possession of it, and clears away many nations from before you (the Hittite, the Girgashite, the Amorite, the Canaanite, the Perizzite, the Hivvite, and the Yebusite, seven nations bigger and more numerous than you), and Yahweh your God gives them up before you and you strike them down, you're to devote them totally. You will not solemnize a pact with them. You will not grace them. You will not make marriages with them. You will not give your daughter to his son or take his daughter for your son because he'll turn your son aside from following me and they'll serve other gods, and the anger of Yahweh will rage

against you and he'll quickly wipe you out. Rather, you're to do this to them. You're to demolish their altars. You're to break up their columns. You're to cut down their totem poles. You're to burn their statues in fire. (Deut 7:1-5)

The devoting of which Moses speaks wasn't the general principle for the Israelites relating to other peoples. It was a one-time action related to the special offensiveness of the Canaanites and the special thing that God planned to achieve through Israel at that time. There's no basis for making it the excuse for (say) settlers in the Americas killing off Native Americans.

The subsequent story about Rahab (which we noted in chap. 34) may indicate that the dynamic whereby people follow-up their own bright ideas can work well. Yahweh had never told the Israelites that they could exempt from annihilation any friendly whores who came to believe in Yahweh, but some Israelite young men worked it out for themselves.

From Acacias, Joshua ben Nun sent two men to investigate quietly: "Go and look at the country, and at Jericho." They went, and came to the house of a woman who was a whore named Rahab, and they slept there. . . . She said to the men, "I acknowledge that Yahweh has given you the country, that a dread of you has fallen on us, and that all the people living in the country have melted away before you, because we heard how Yahweh dried up the water of the Reed Sea before you when you got out of Egypt and what you did to the two Amorite kings who were across the Jordan, to Sihon and to Og, whom you devoted. We heard, and our mind melted. There was no spirit rising up in anyone in the face of you, because Yahweh your God is God in the heavens above and on the earth below. So now, please swear to me by Yahweh, because I've acted in commitment with you, that you'll also act in commitment with my father's household. Give me a truthful sign that you'll let my father and my mother live, and my brothers and my sisters, and everyone who belongs to them, and that you'll save our lives from death." The men said to her, "Our lives in place of you, to the death, if you don't tell about our business here. When Yahweh gives us the country, we'll act in commitment and truthfulness with you." (Josh 2:1, 9-14)

Maybe the young men worked out that the kind of instruction that Deuteronomy gives was never designed to be taken too literally or too universally. And Rahab was far from being the only Canaanite who escaped annihilation. The story of the Israelites' arriving in the land in Joshua makes clear that the Israelites didn't actually eliminate the Canaanites at all. It was several centuries before the Israelites were in complete possession of the land. Sometimes they failed to take the land because they didn't try. Sometimes they tried and failed. The subsequent Old Testament story makes clear that the worry Yahweh had was quite justified—the Canaanites were still in the land, and the Israelites followed their way of worship, including sacrificing children. The result was that the Israelites paid the same penalty as the Canaanites. The Canaanites got thrown out (eventually) because of the way they had behaved in the land, and the Israelites got thrown out because they behaved the same way.

> Your first ancestor—he did wrong,
>> and your interpreters—they rebelled against me.
> So I treated the sacred officials as ordinary,
>> gave Jacob to being devoted, Israel to taunts. (Is 43:27-28)

To exaggerate somewhat, the Canaanites got annihilated; and to exaggerate somewhat, the Israelites got annihilated too. God gave Israel over to being devoted. What the Canaanites were liable to, the Israelites were liable to.

If we are to understand our problem with the idea of the so-called annihilation of the Canaanites, we may have to separate it into two problems. Part of the background is that the Old Testament does not portray the Canaanites as already the Israelites' enemies, which is why they attacked them. The Canaanites were not the Israelites' enemies. They were God's enemies, and God was using Israel as the means of acting in judgment against them.

The two problems are whether God acts in judgment against people, and whether he used Israel to do so. I suspect we really don't like the first idea (I don't care for it much) but that our dislike for it gets displaced onto our dislike for the second idea (a dislike I also share). We can then see the latter idea as confined to the Old Testament and as an Israelite misapprehension that we can more easily set aside.

But the first idea runs through the words of people such as Jesus and Paul, and the fact of God's acting in judgment is surely the real challenge to our thinking. The idea that on one occasion God used his people in this connection (though the Old Testament more usually speaks of God doing the annihilating) is a less tricky matter. Why did he involve Israel on this occasion? Maybe the reason is hinted in Deuteronomy 7. It will express Israel's commitment to avoiding Canaanite ways. Or maybe we just don't know.

Perhaps awarenesses of this kind underlie the fact that the New Testament never hints that Joshua and the Israelites were in breach of the principle of loving your enemies when they did devote Canaanites. The saintly Stephen, who dies with a prayer for his killers on his lips, is enthusiastic about the way the Israelites got into Canaan (Acts 7). And Hebrews sees people like Joshua as great heroes of faith.

> By faith the walls of Jericho fell, after being marched around for seven days. By faith Rahab the prostitute didn't perish with the people who were disobedient, having received the spies with peace. And what more shall I say? Time fails me to tell about Gideon, Barak, Samson, and Jephthah, and David and Samuel and the prophets, who through faith conquered kingdoms, put into effect what was right, experienced promises, shut the mouths of lions, quenched the fury of fire, escaped the edges of the sword, were given power instead of weakness, became strong in battle, routed armies of foreigners. (Heb 11:30-34)

No, there's no New Testament basis for being unhappy with Joshua's treatment of the Canaanites.

SUBJECT LIST

SCRIPTURE INDEX

ALSO BY JOHN GOLDINGAY

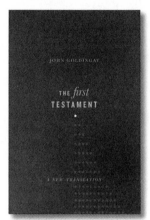

The First Testament
978-0-8308-5199-7

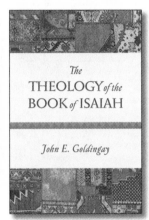

**The Theology
of the Book of Isaiah**
978-0-8308-4039-7

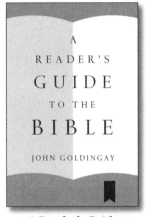

**A Reader's Guide
to the Bible**
978-0-8308-5174-4

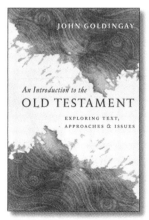

**An Introduction
to the Old Testament**
978-0-8308-4090-8

**Do We Need
the New Testament?**
978-0-8308-2469-4

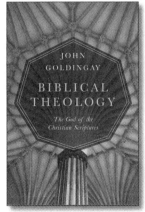

Biblical Theology
978-0-8308-5153-9

Finding the Textbook You Need

The IVP Academic Textbook Selector
is an online tool for instantly finding the IVP books
suitable for over 250 courses across 24 disciplines.

ivpacademic.com